THE UNSCARY ZOMBIE COLORING BOOK

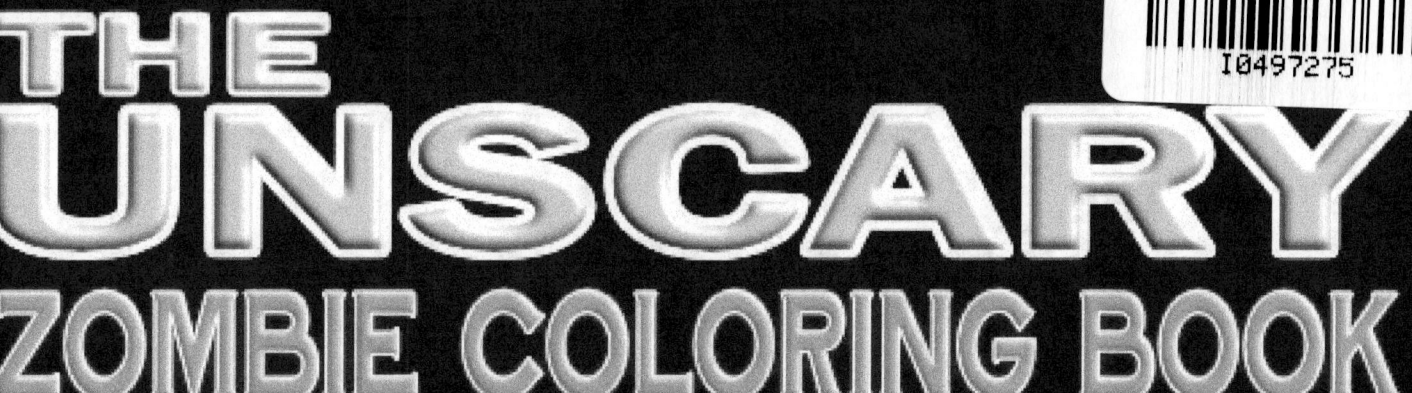
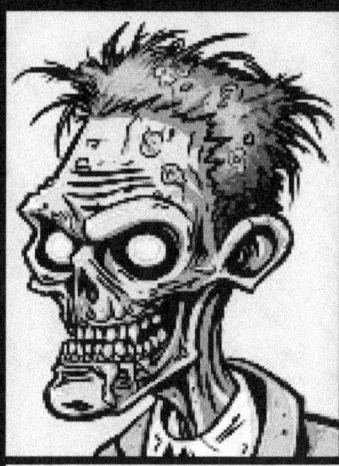
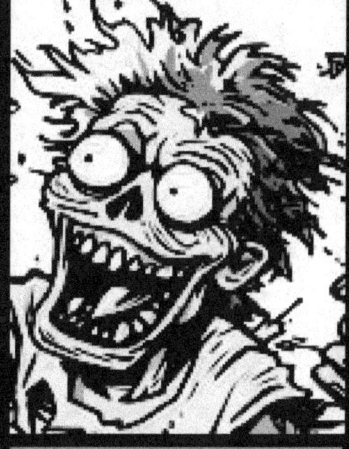
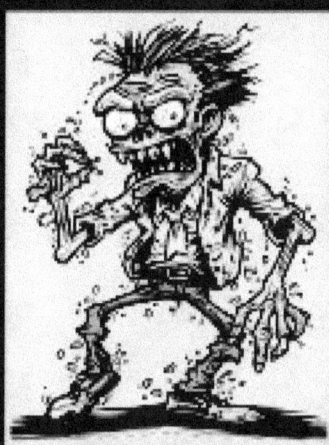

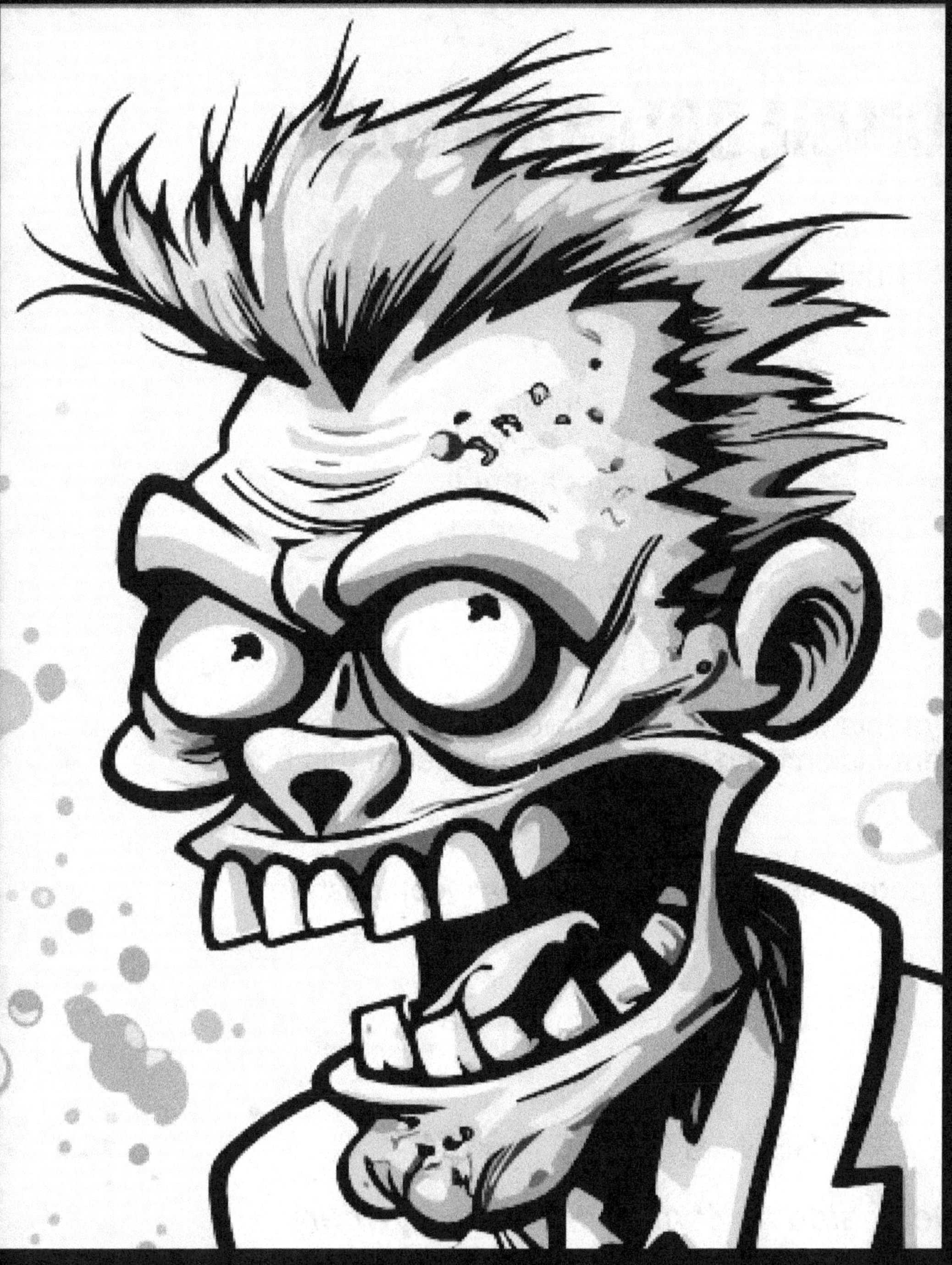

RICHARD SWIKA DESIGNS

THE UNSCARY

ZOMBIE COLORING BOOK

Published by *Richard Swika Designs*

114 Ann Street
Peckville PA 18452
ricswika@comcast.net

Copyright © 2023 Richard Swika

All rights reserved.

No portion of this book may be reproduced in any form without prior permission from the copyright owner of this book.

For permissions contact: ricswika@comcast.net

Cover by Richard Swika

ISBN: 9798850145064

Dedicated to Zombie Fans everywhere

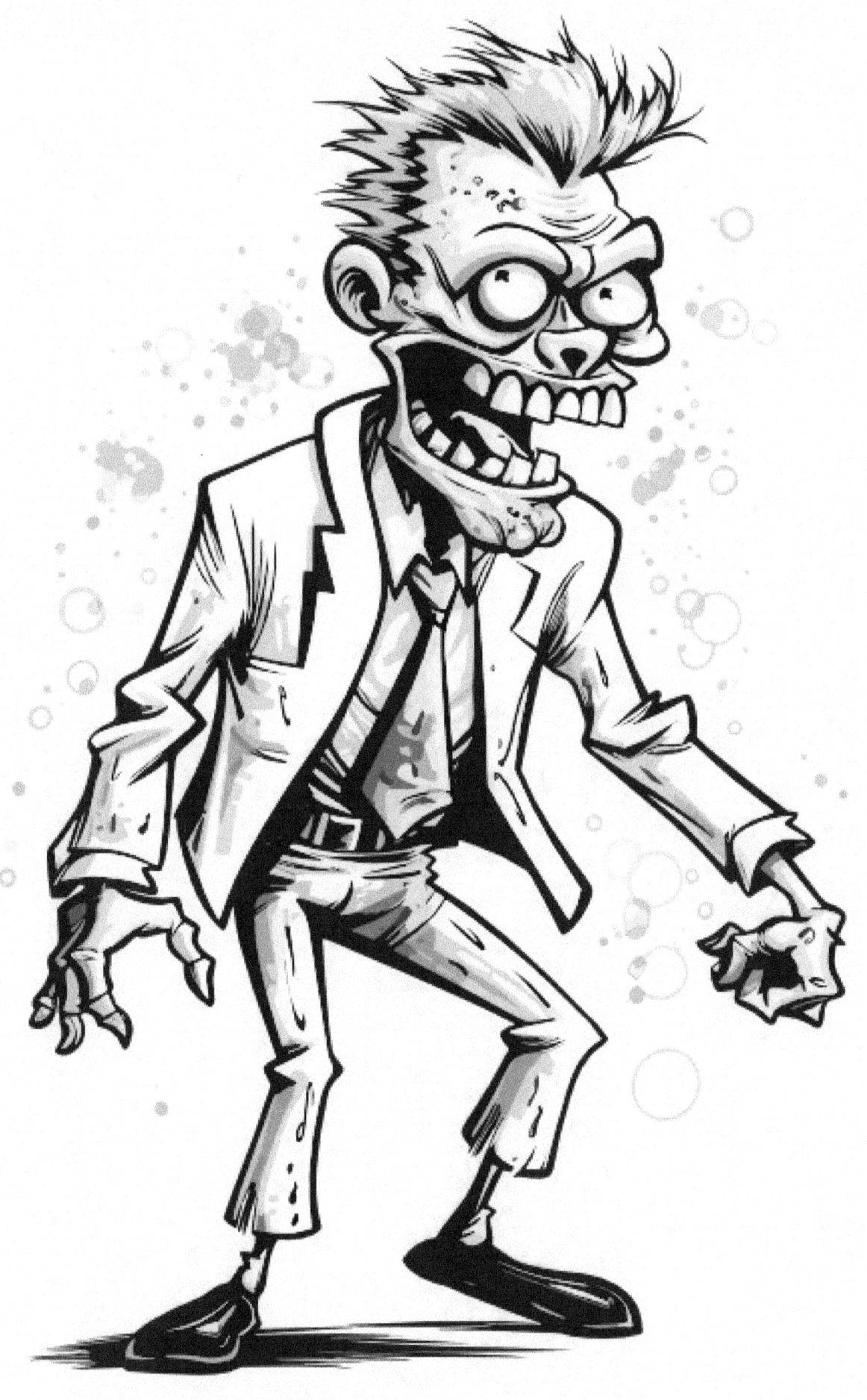

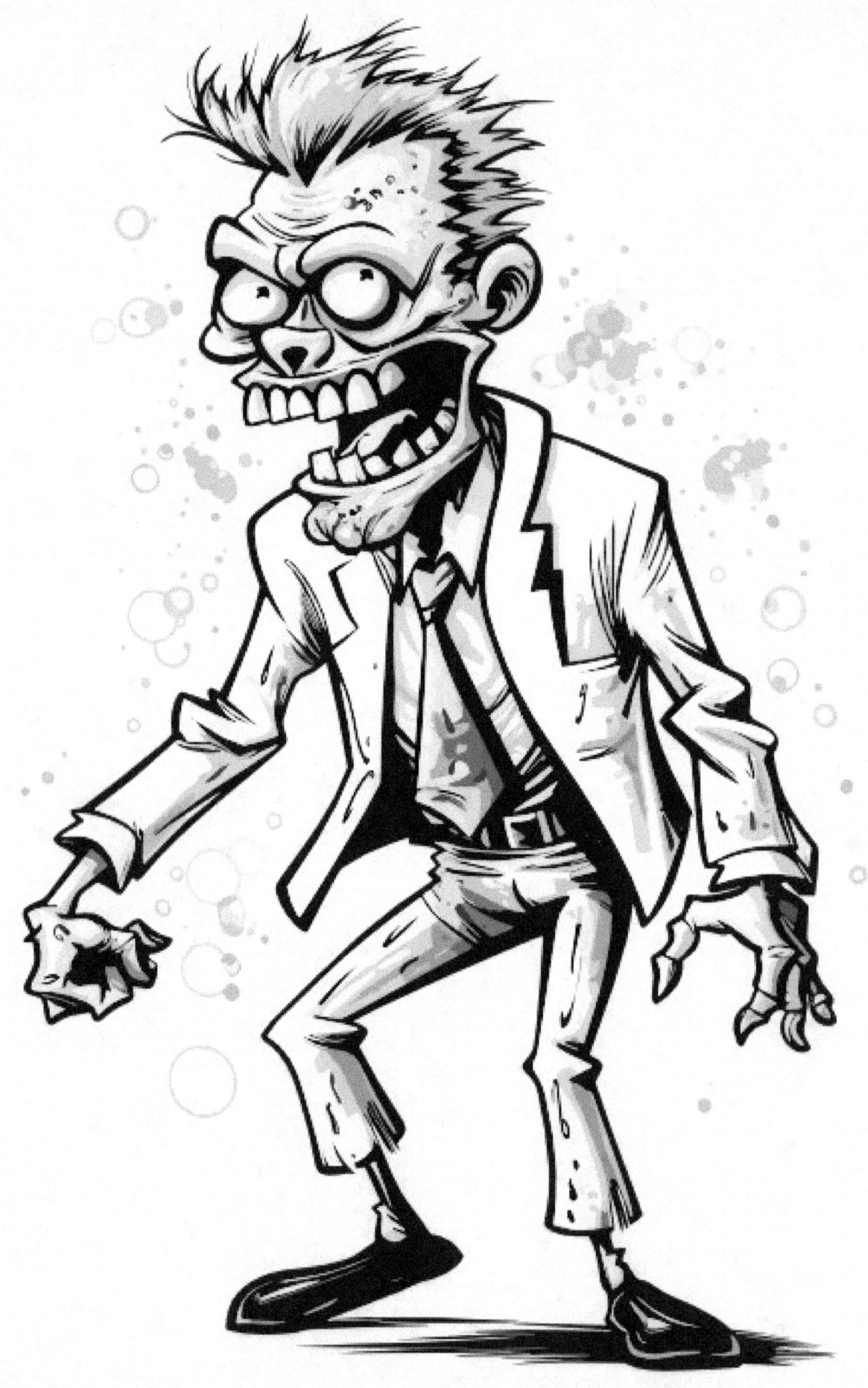

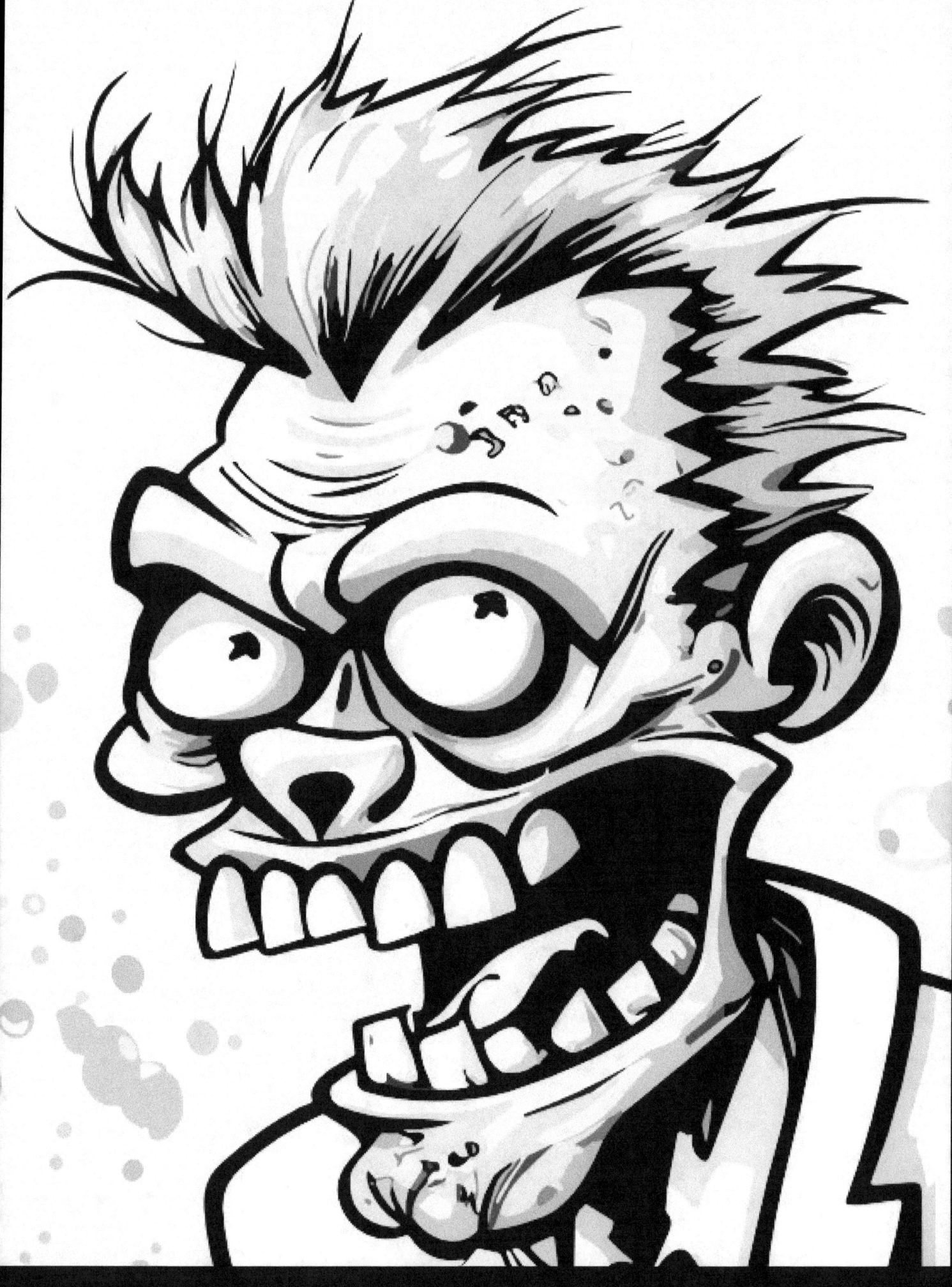

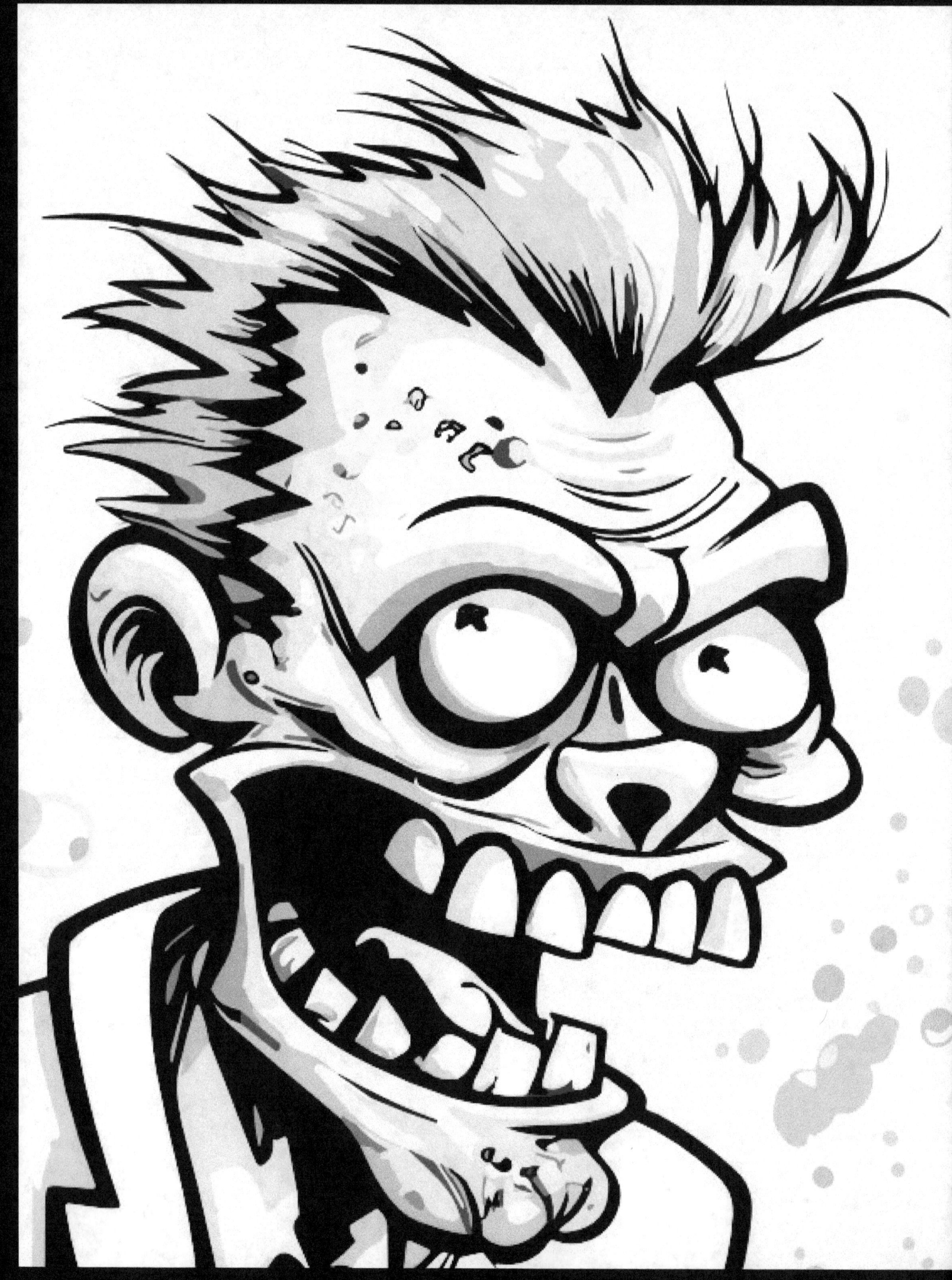

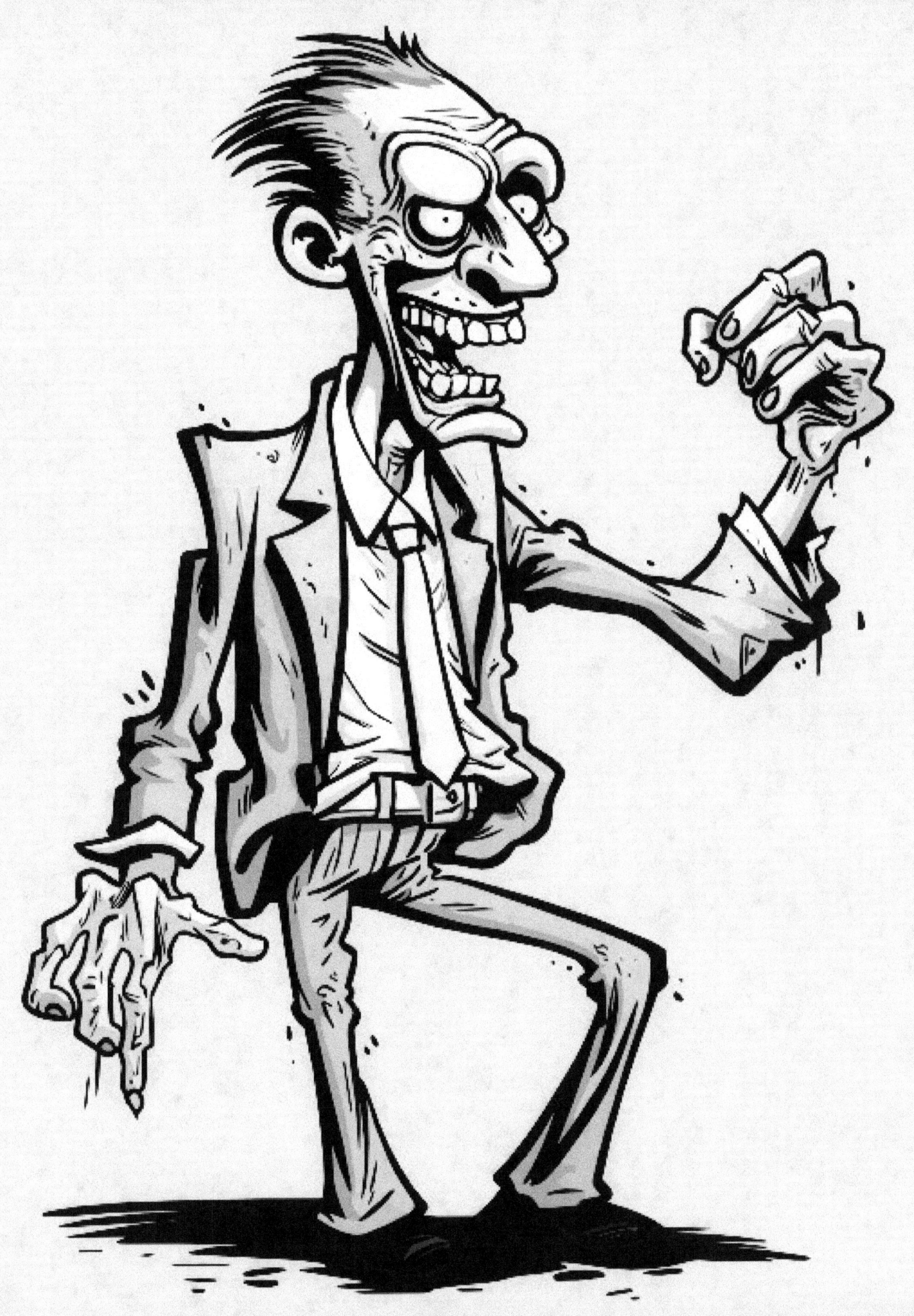

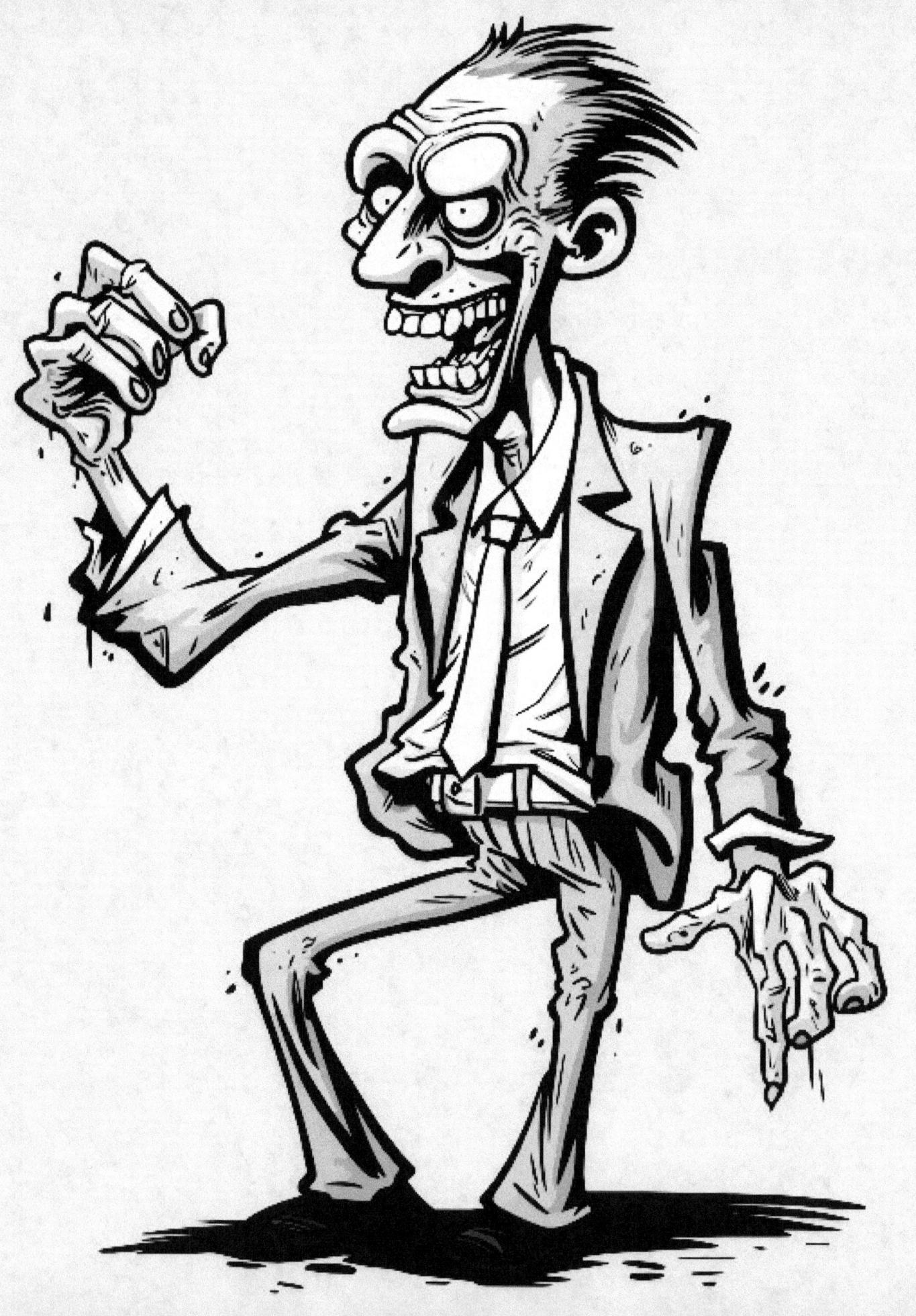

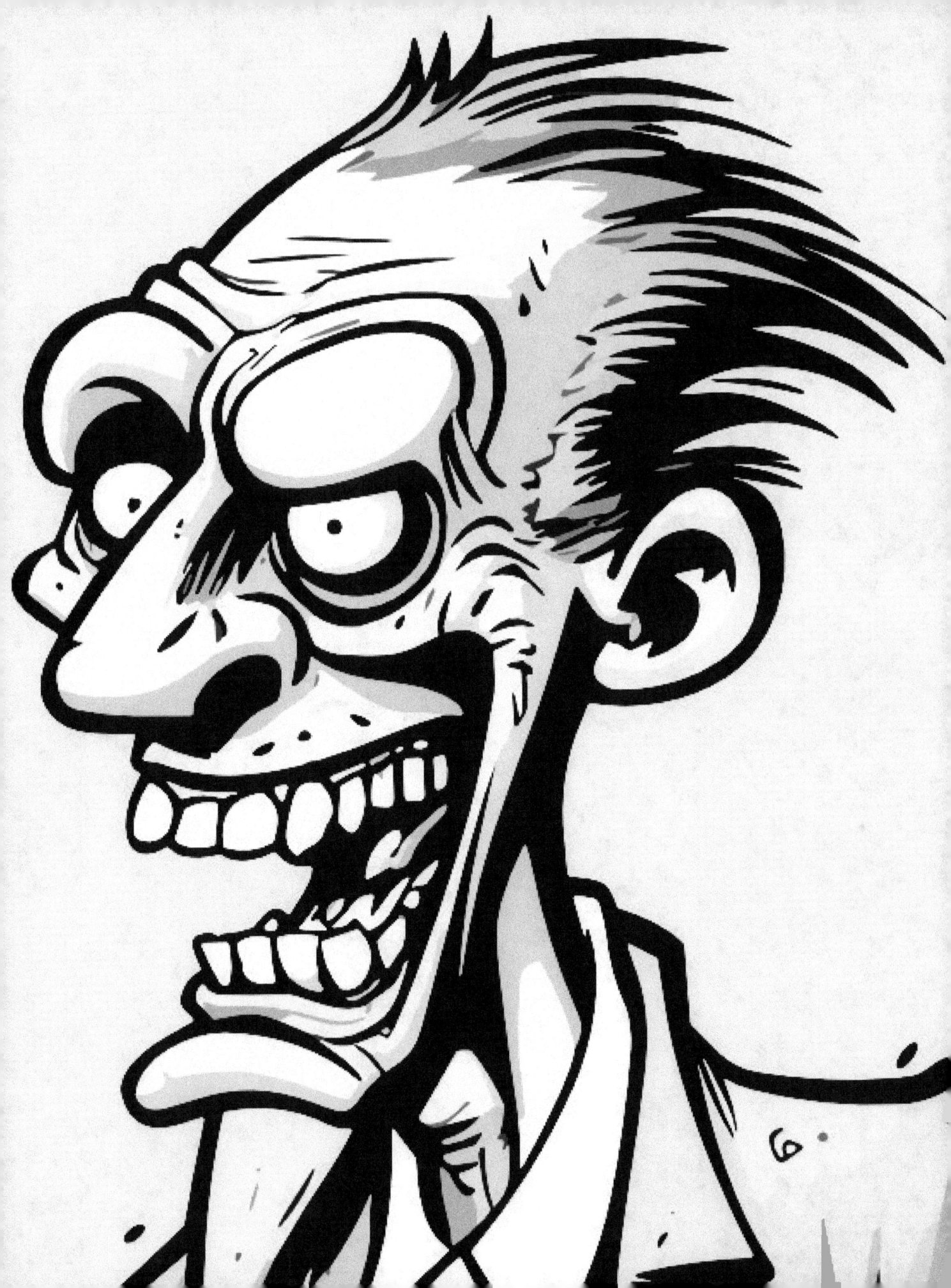

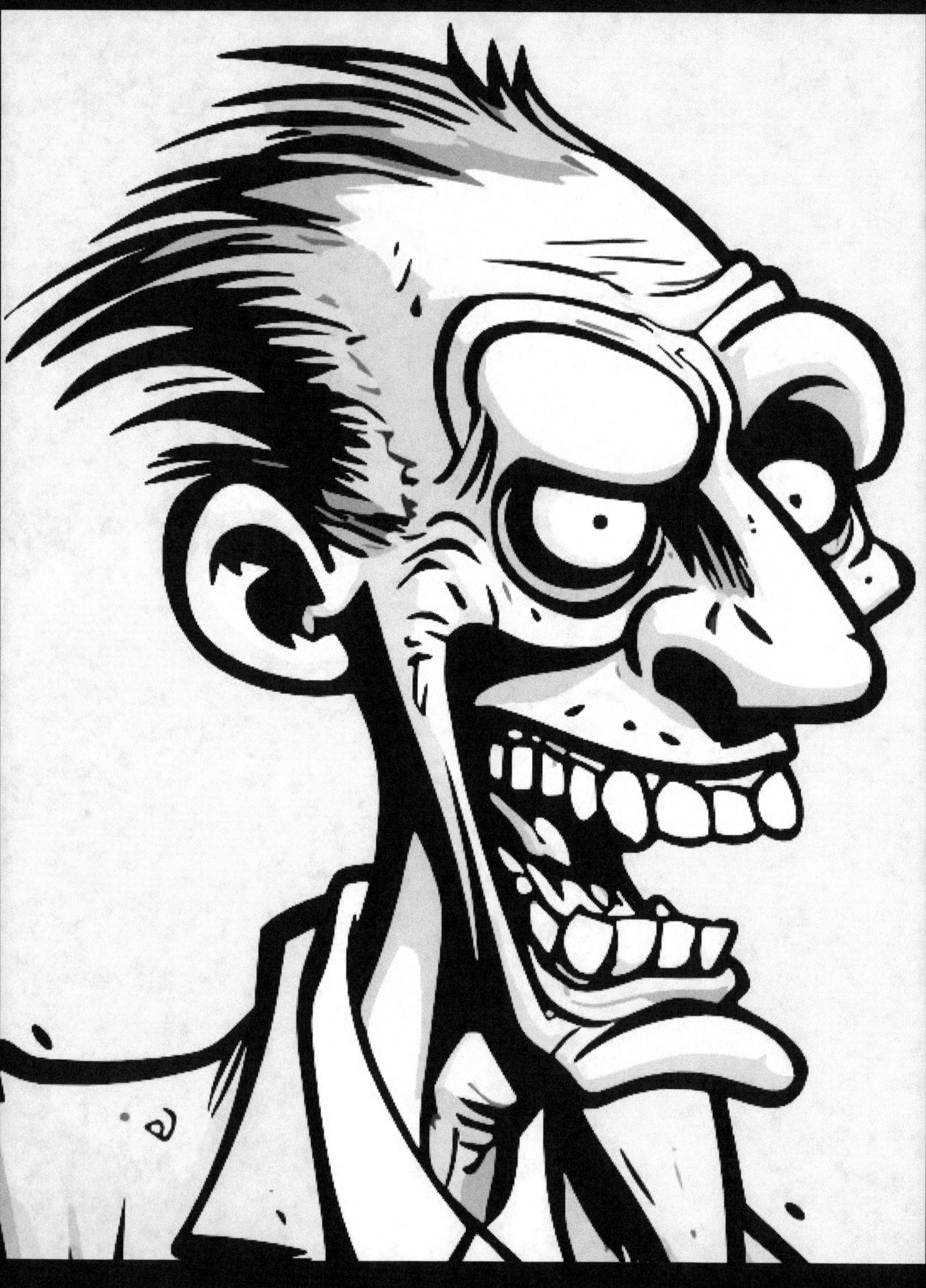

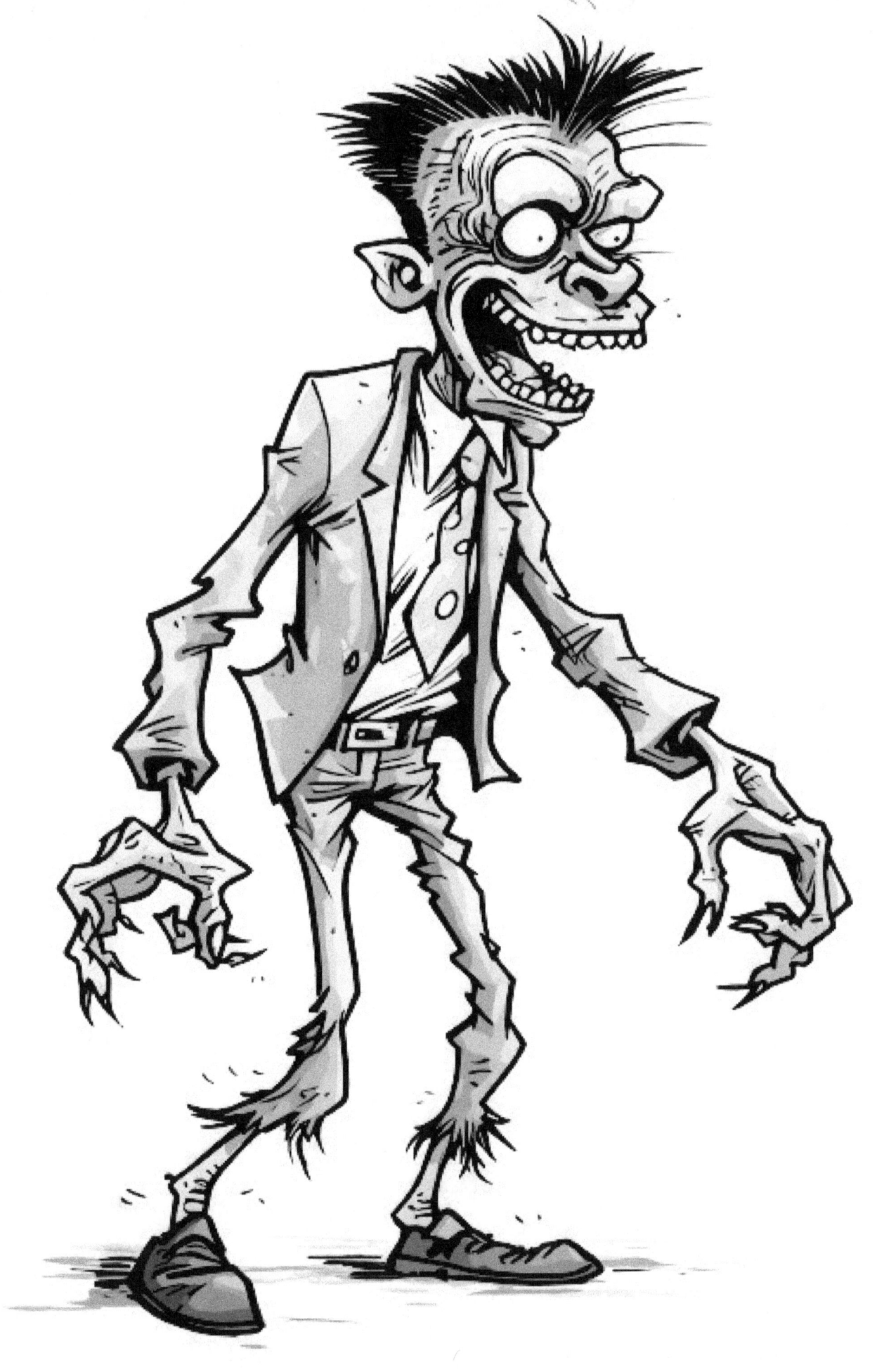

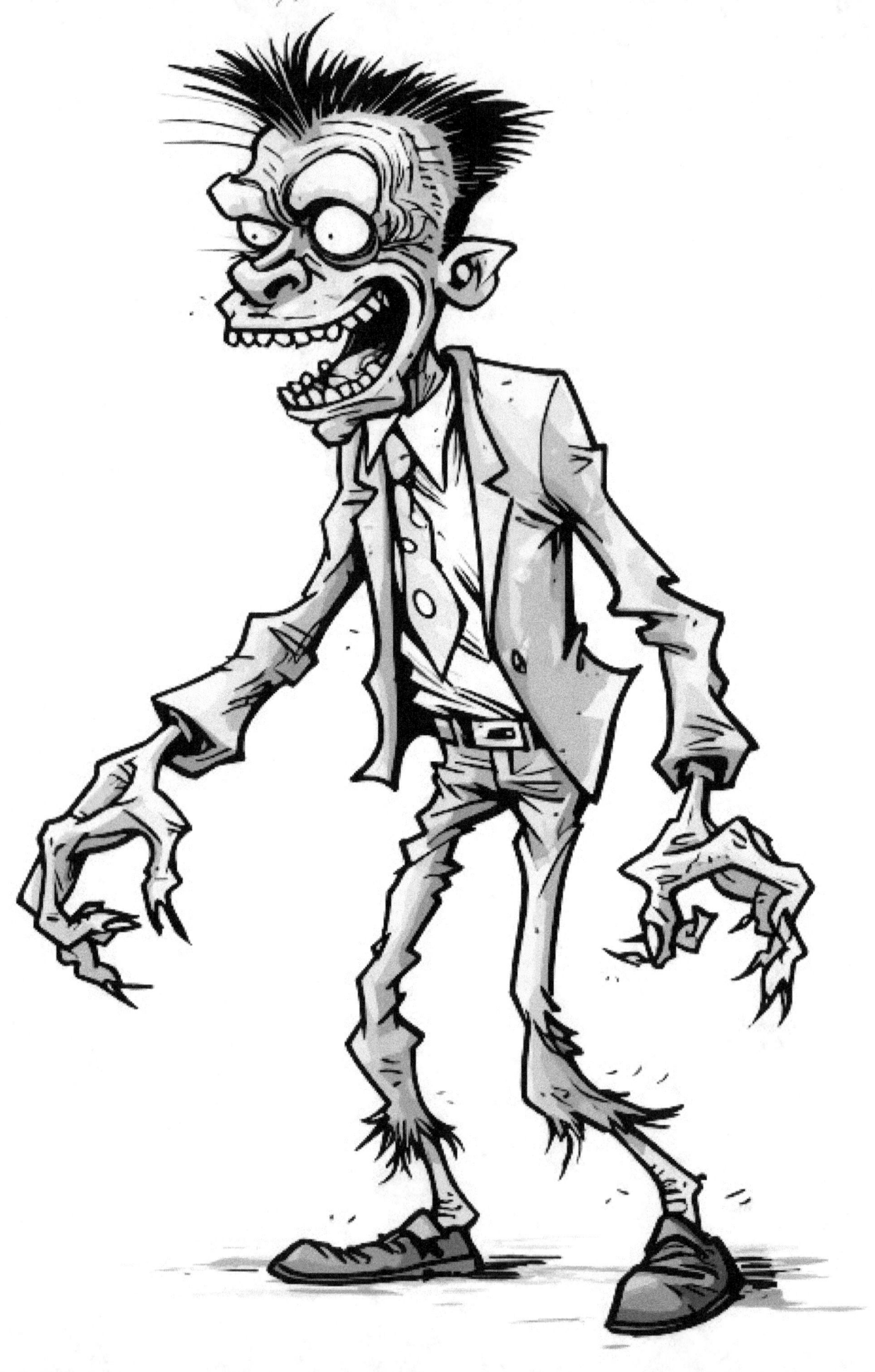

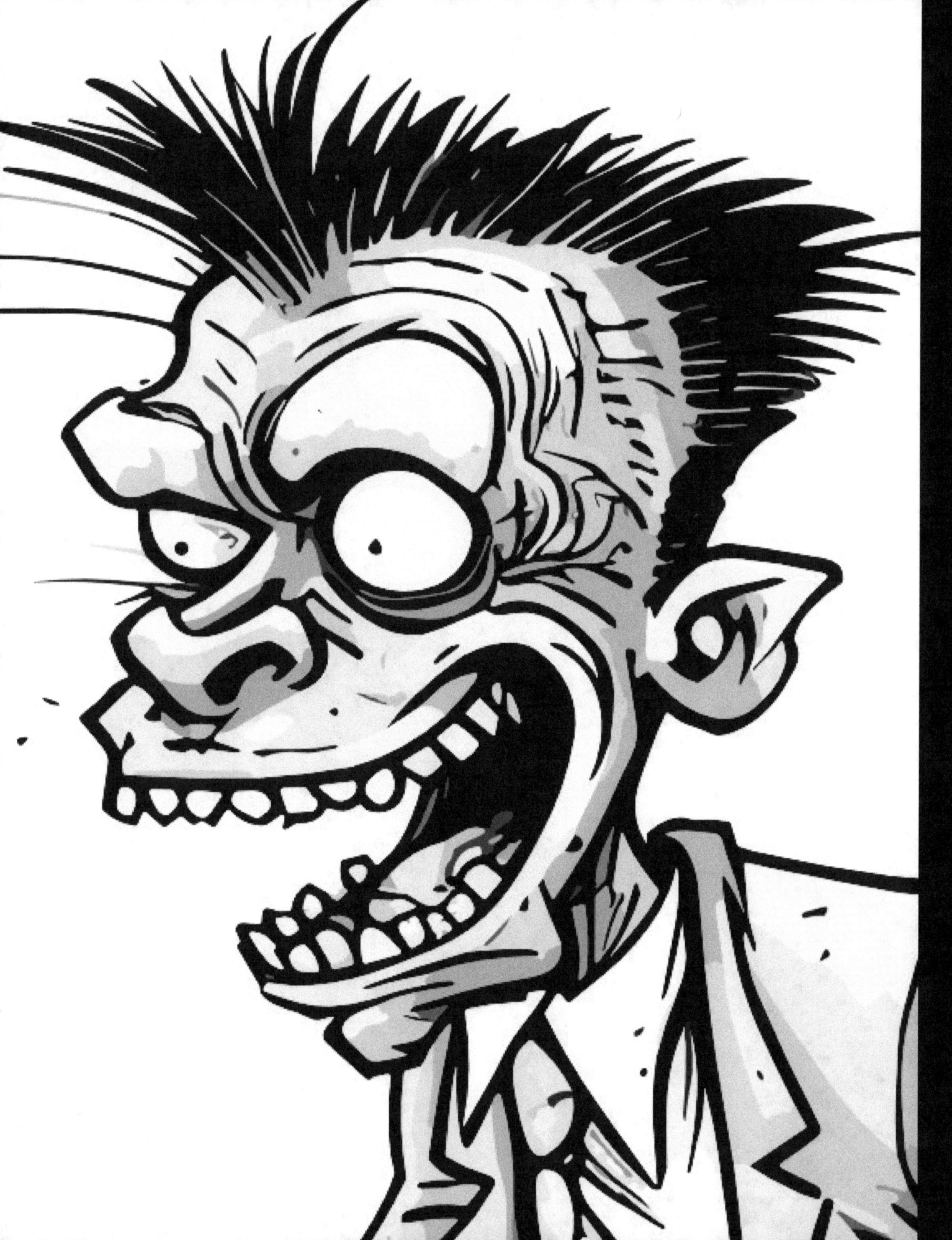

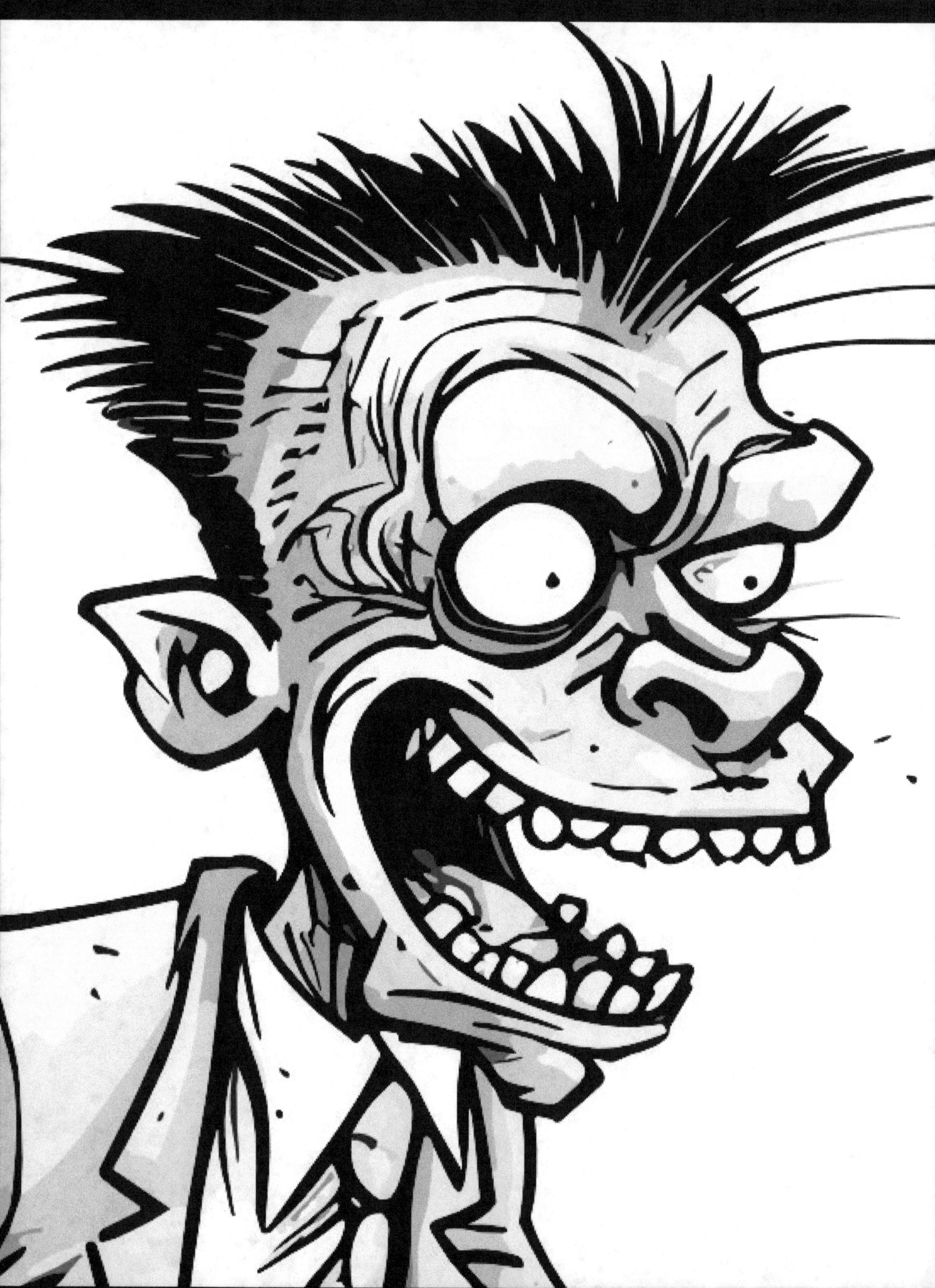

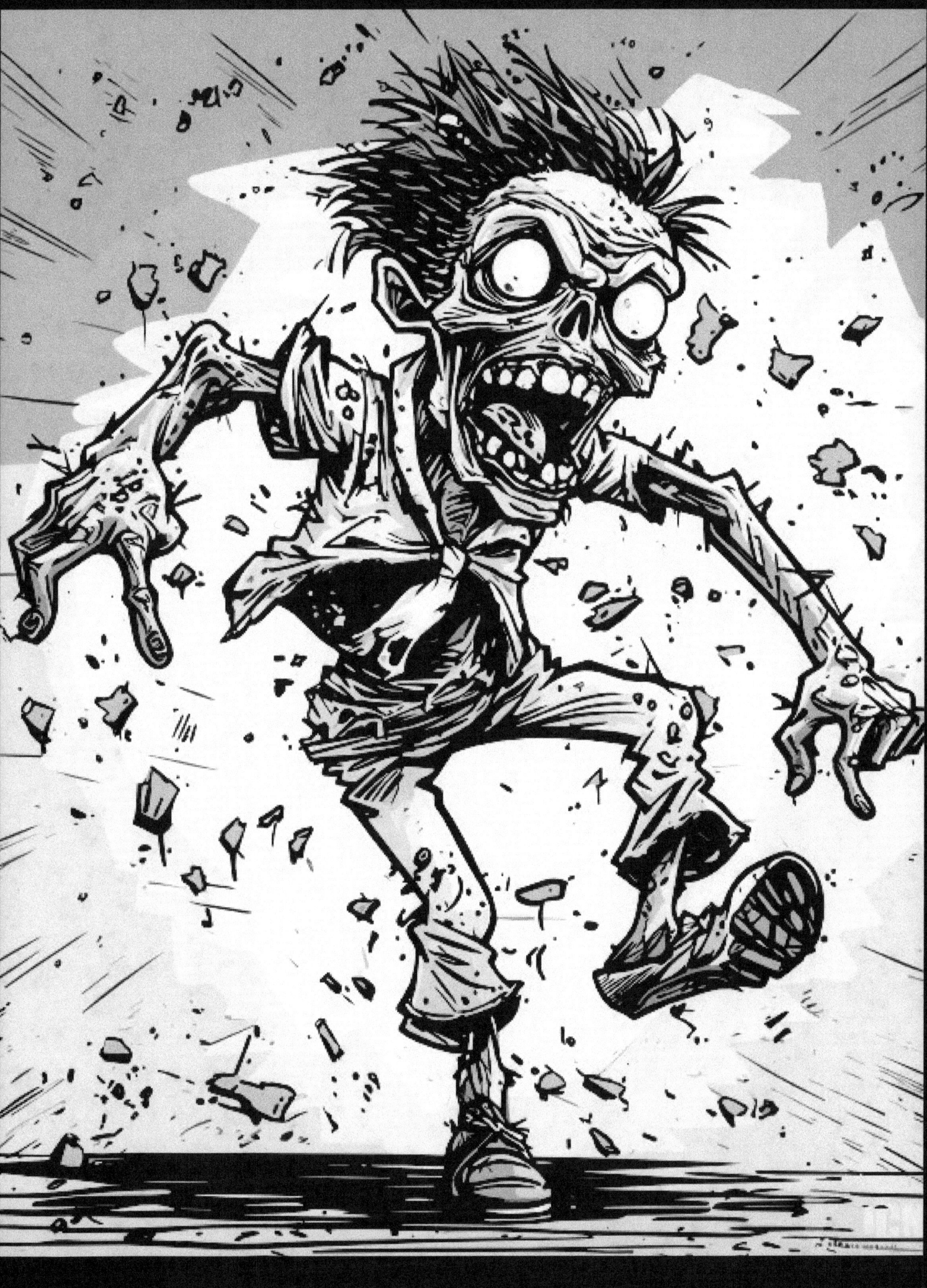

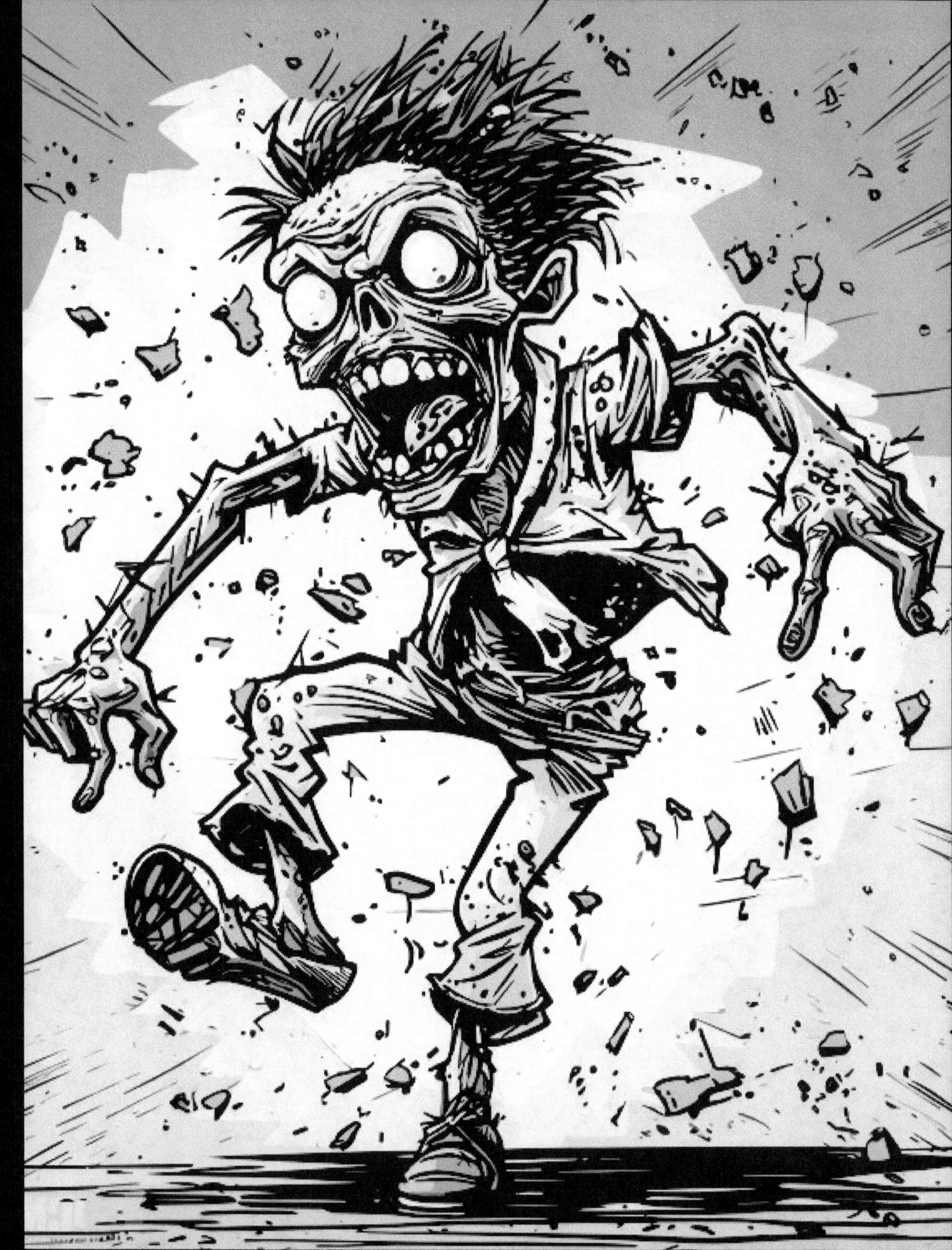

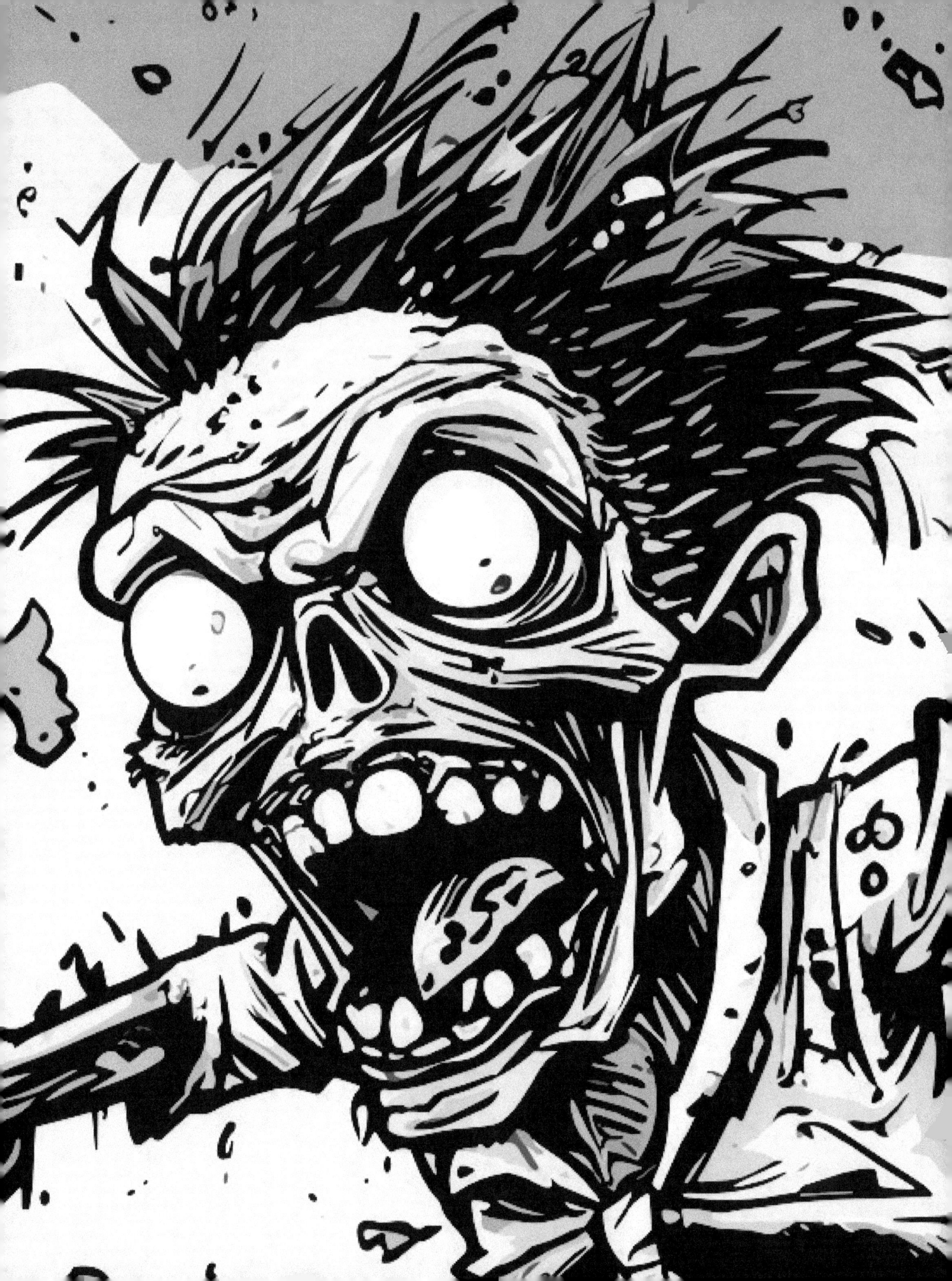

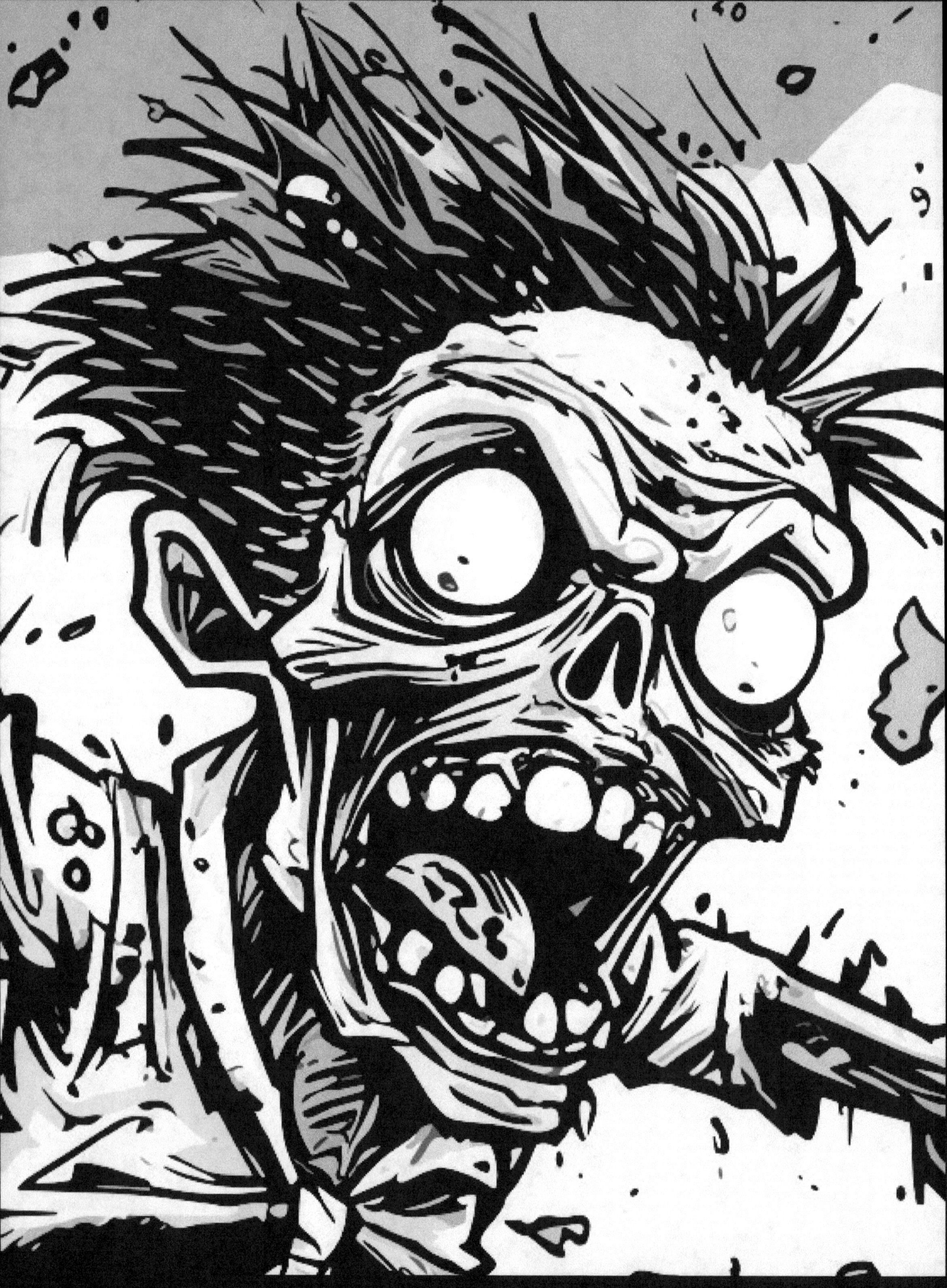

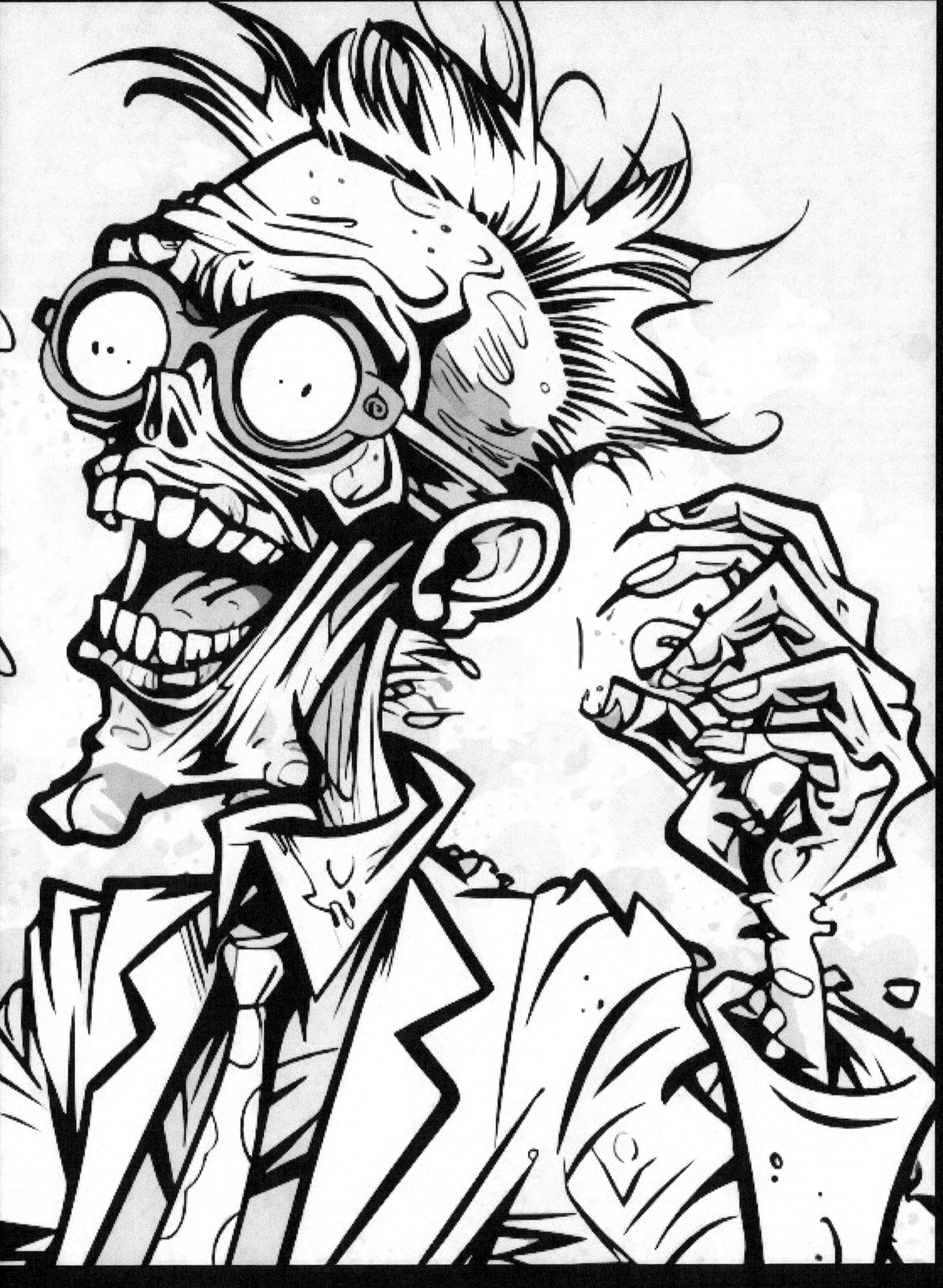

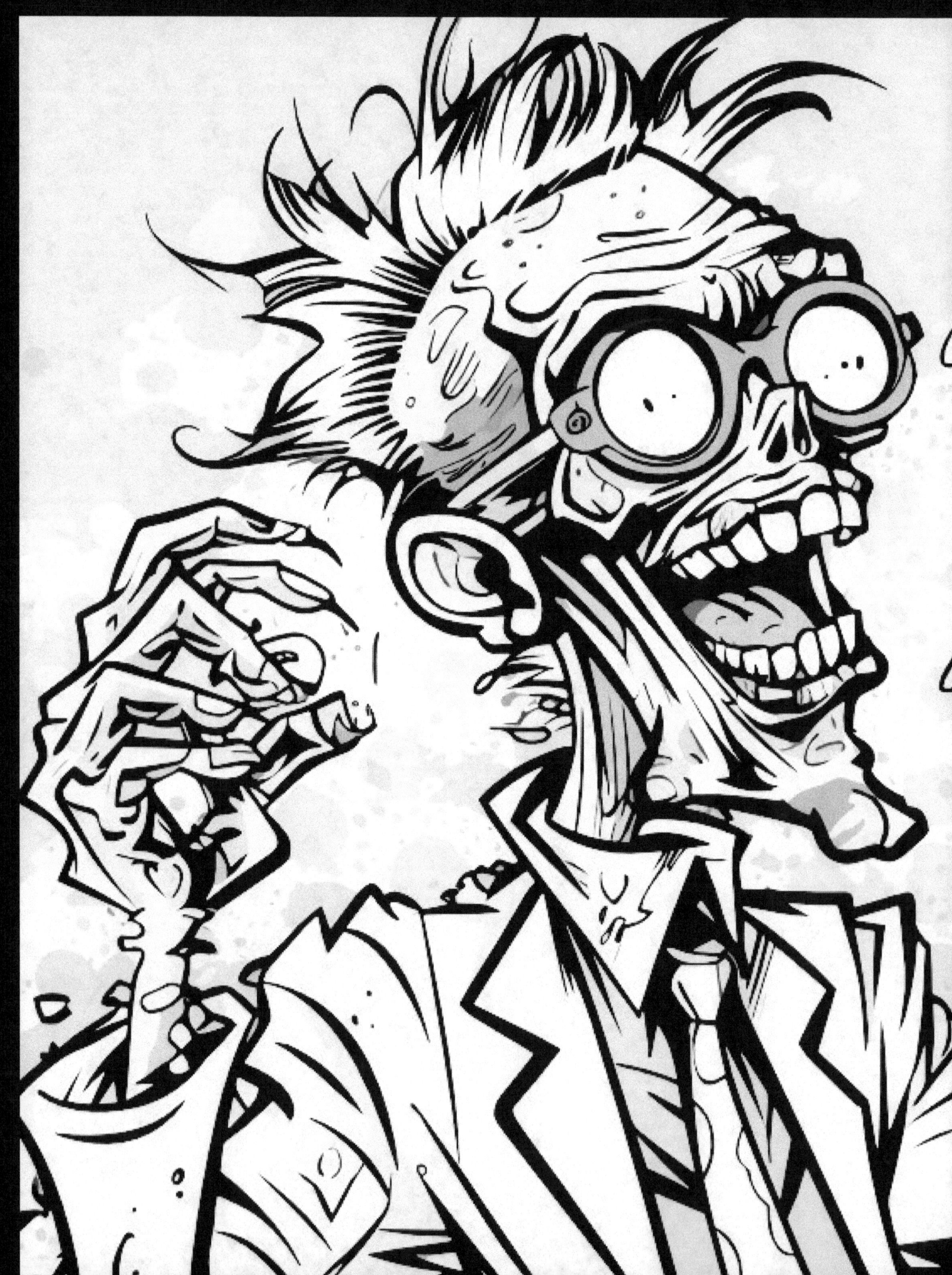

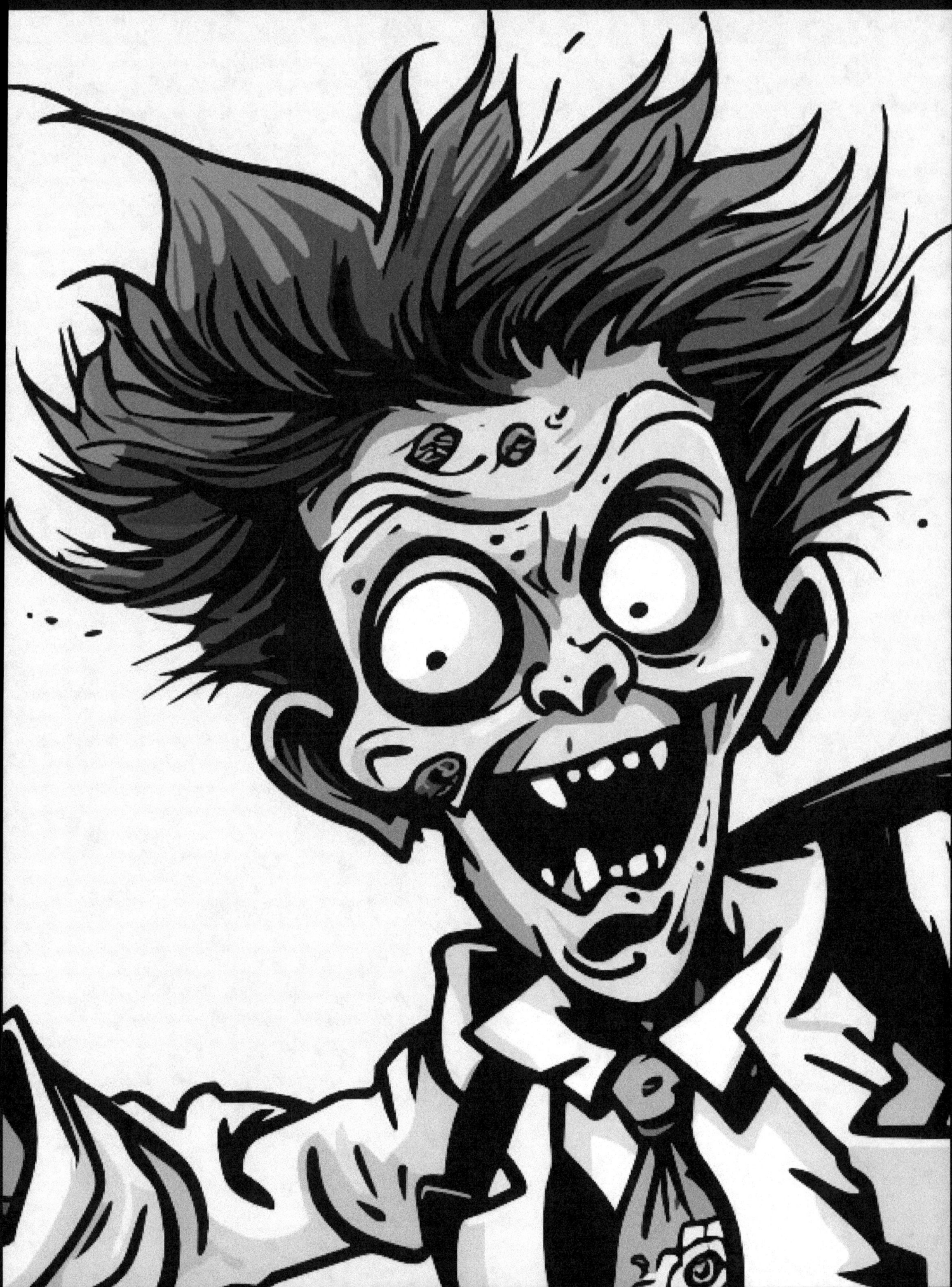

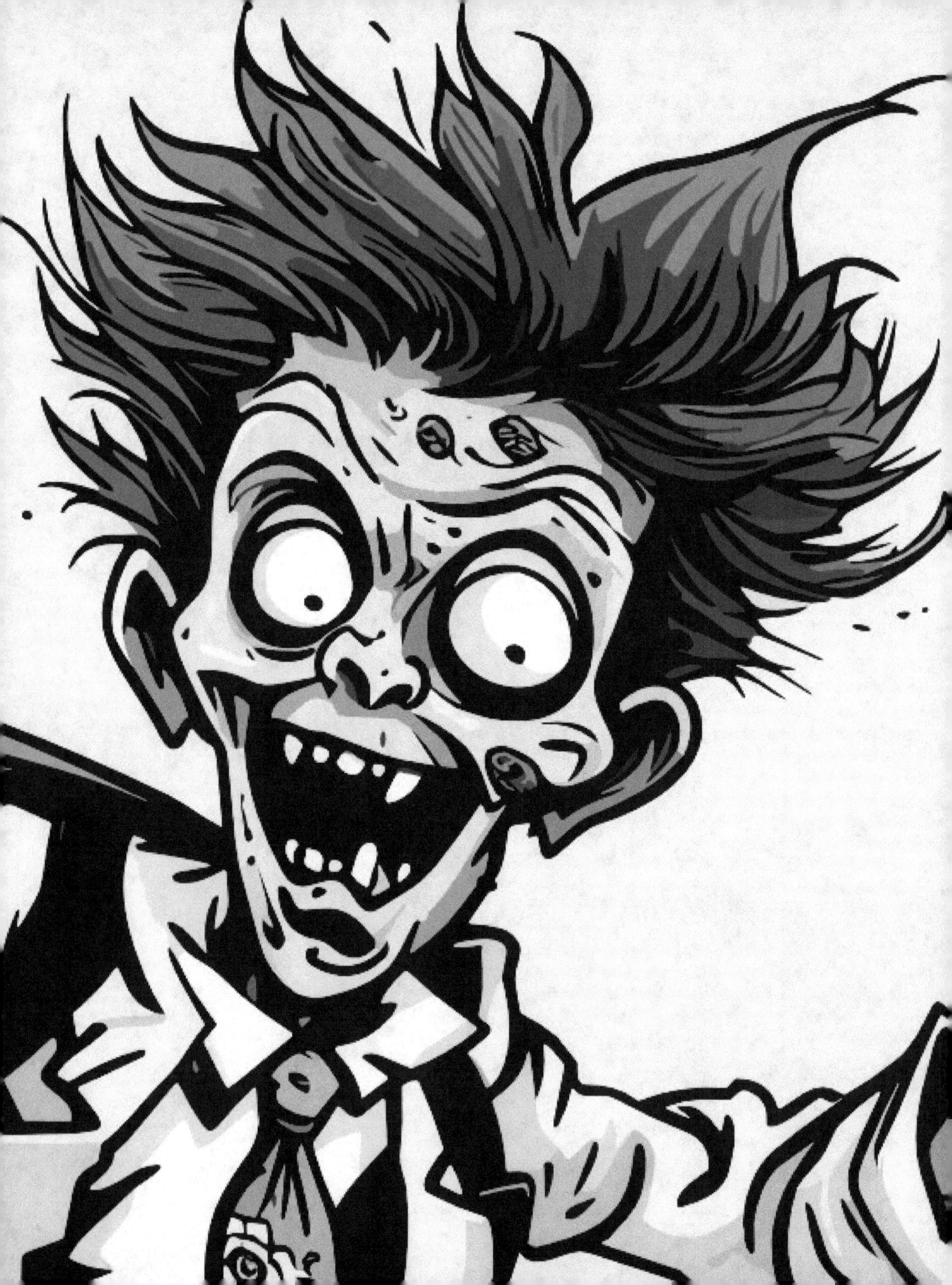

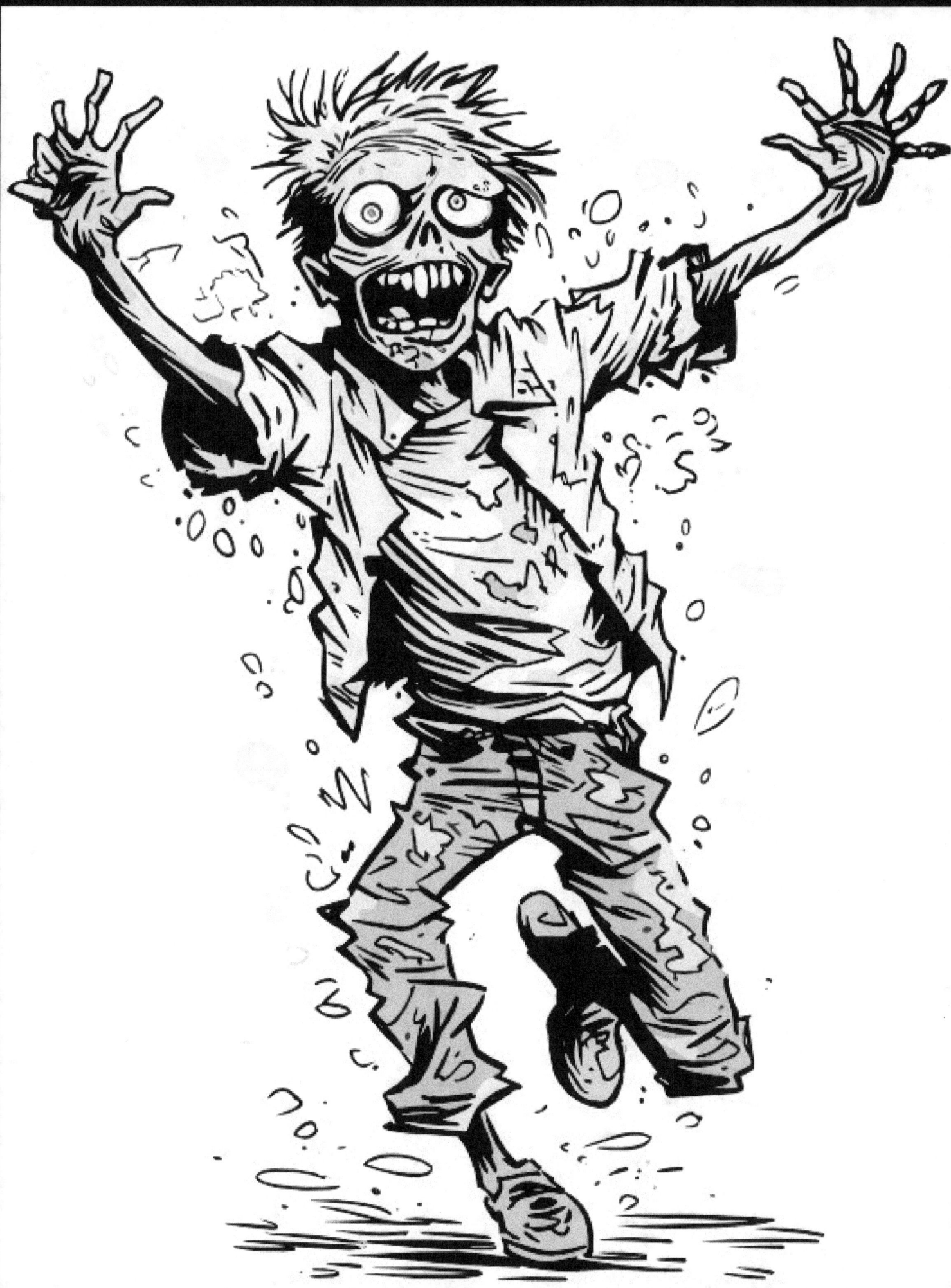

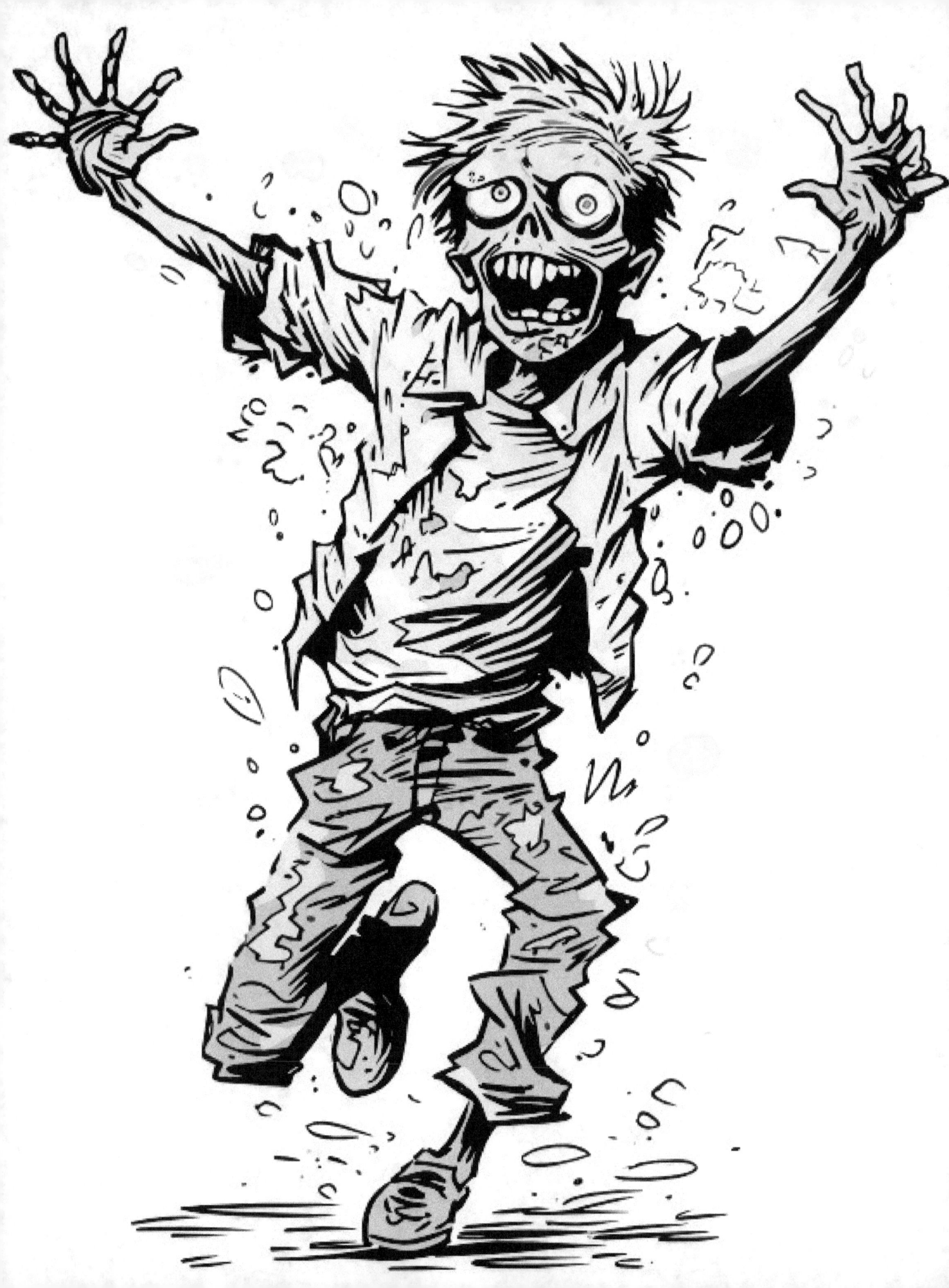

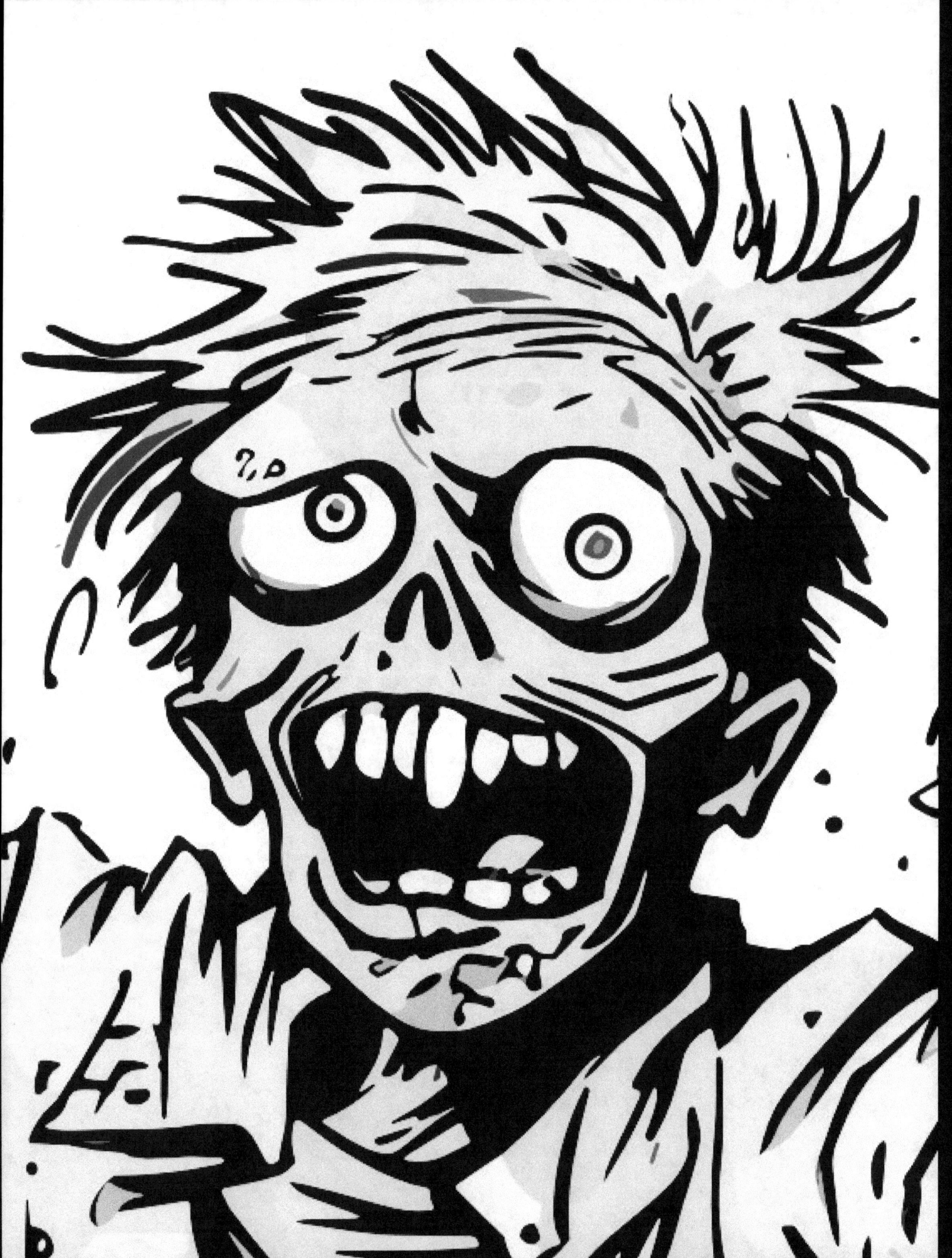

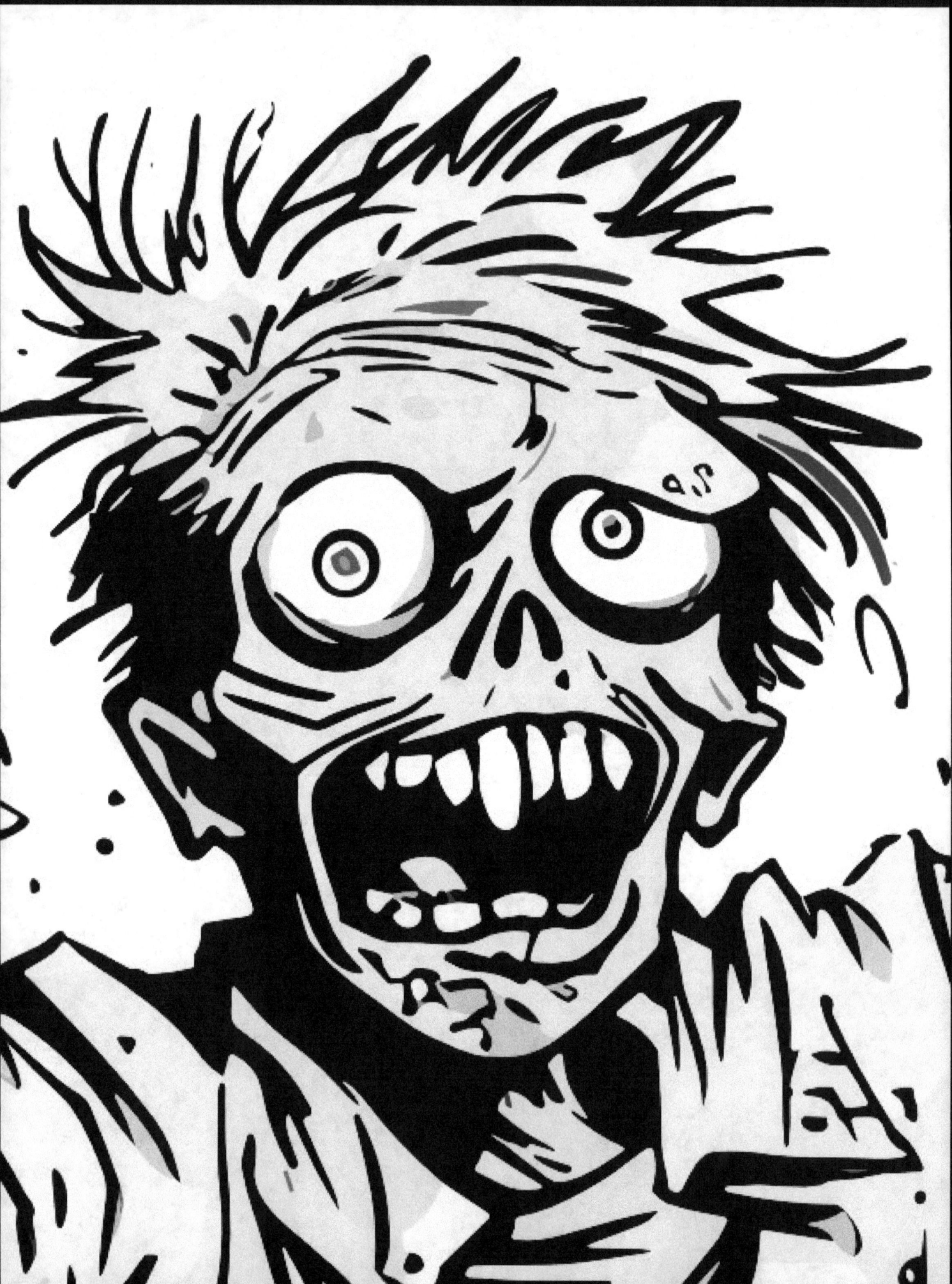

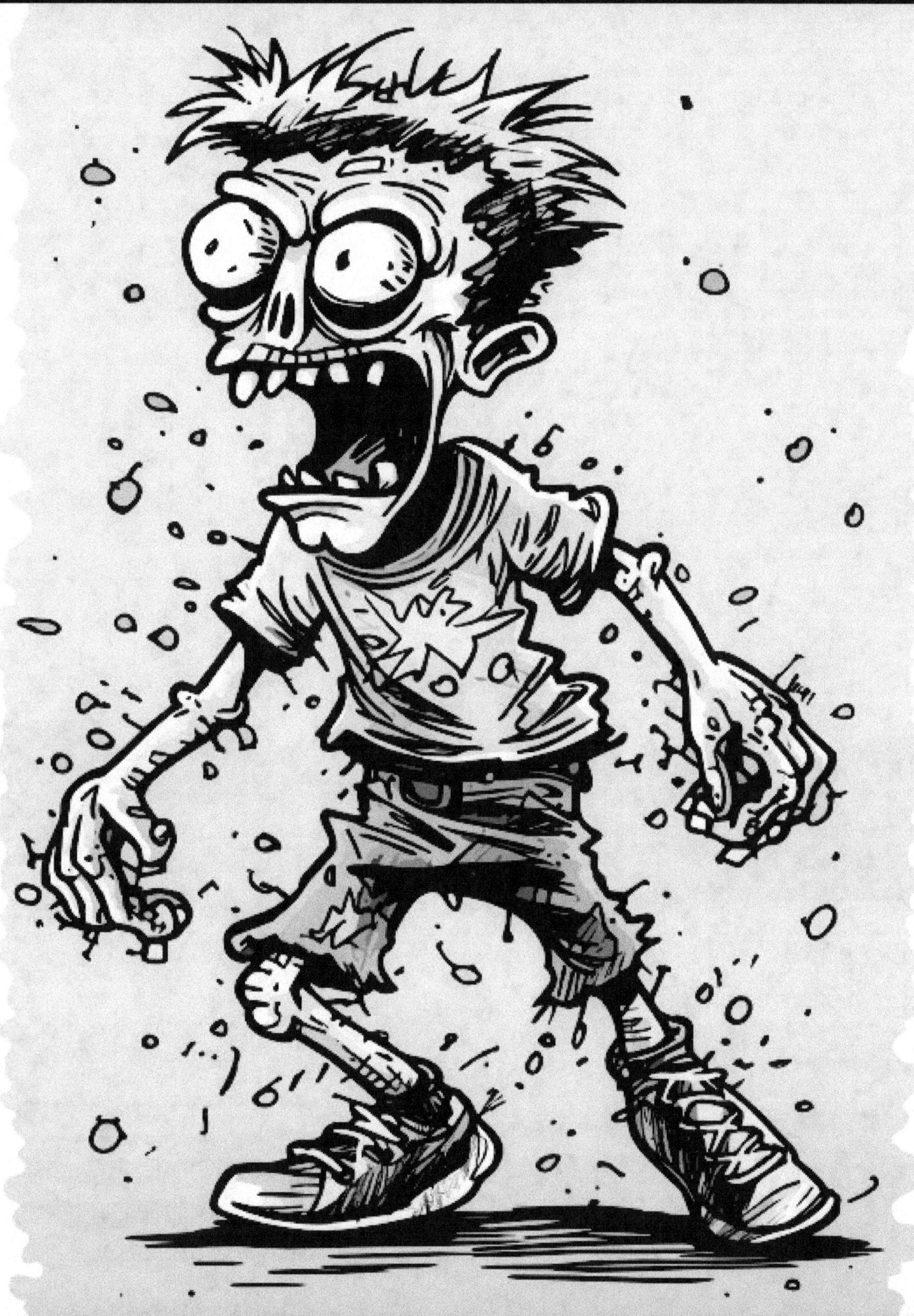

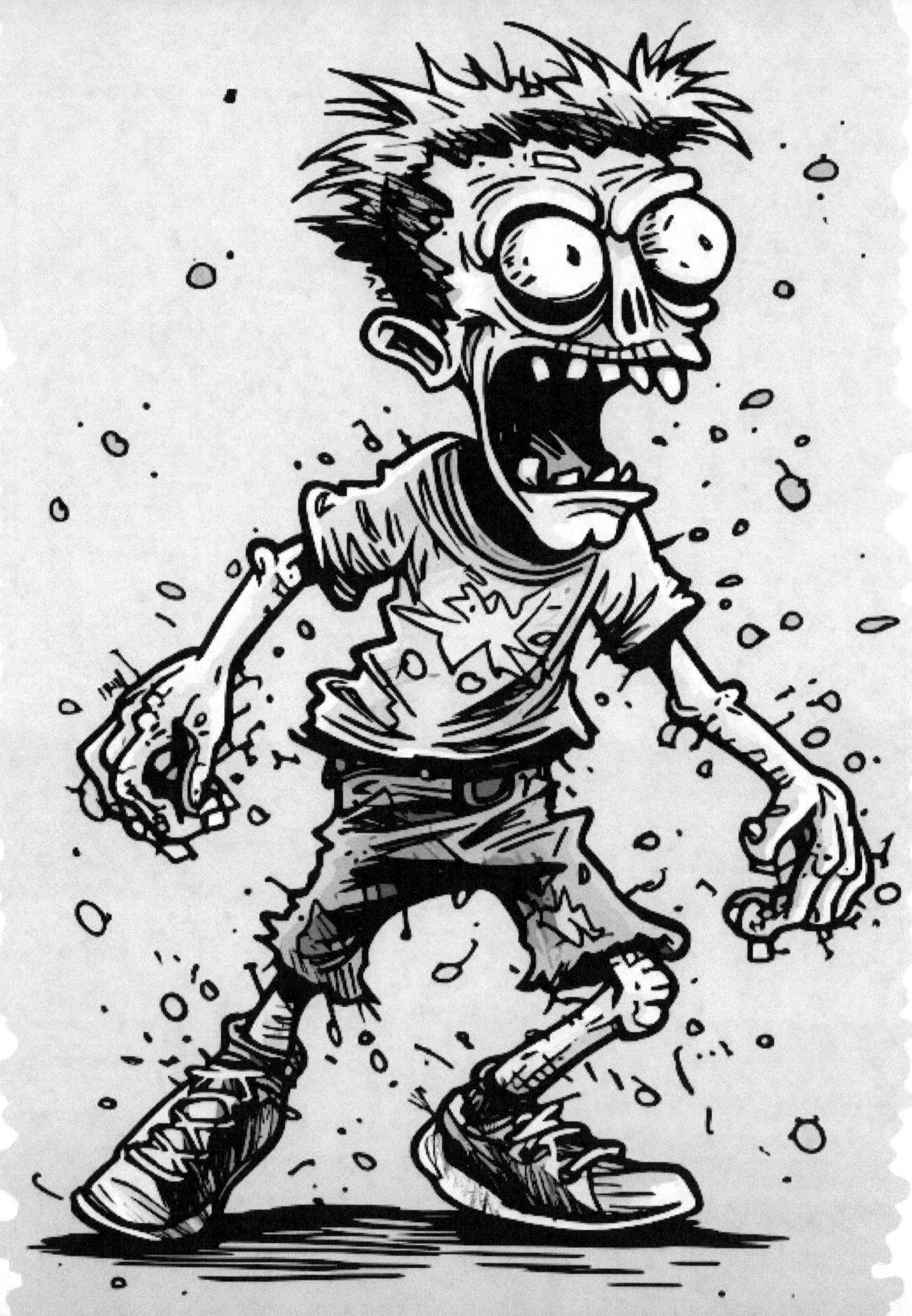

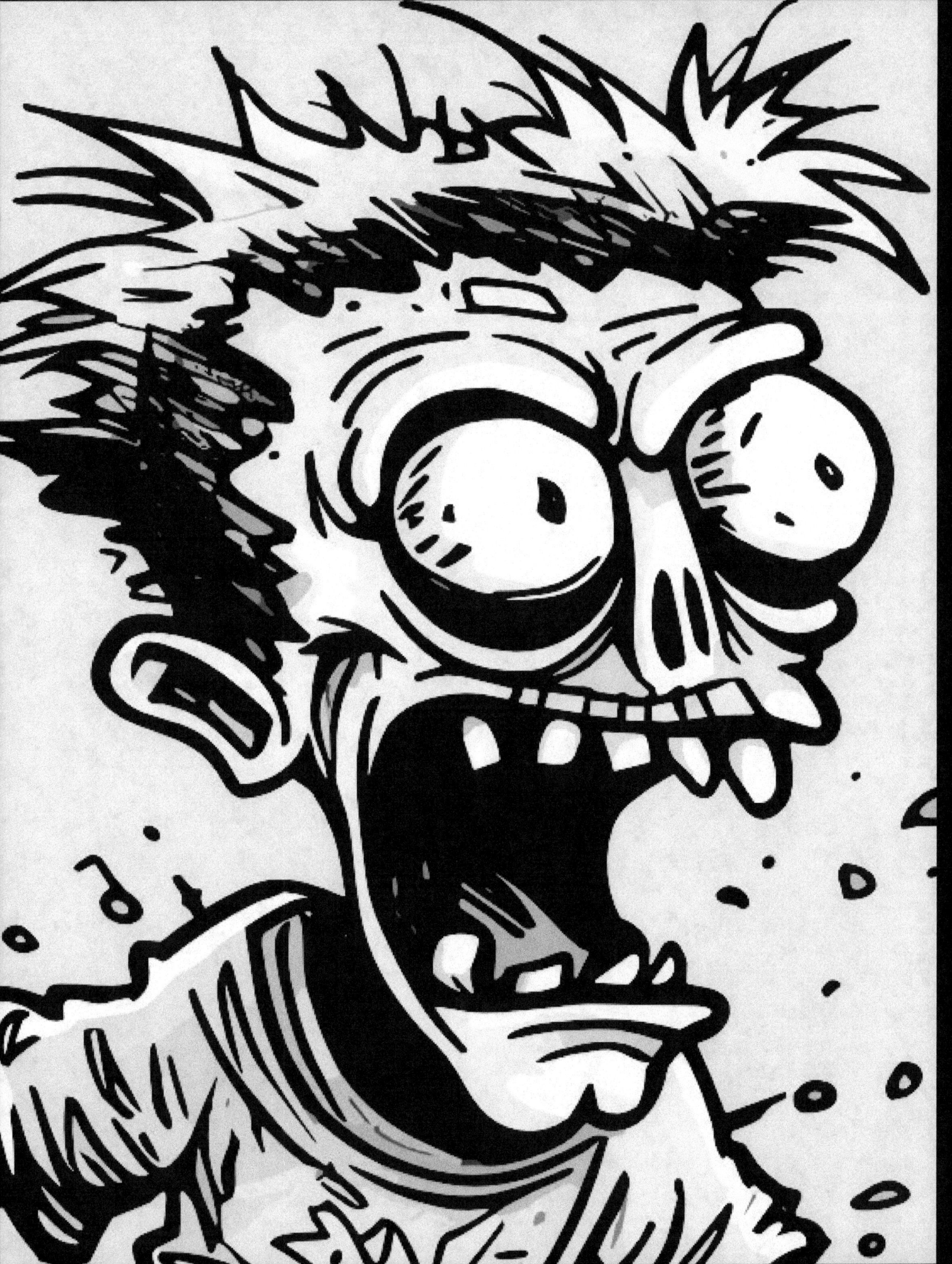

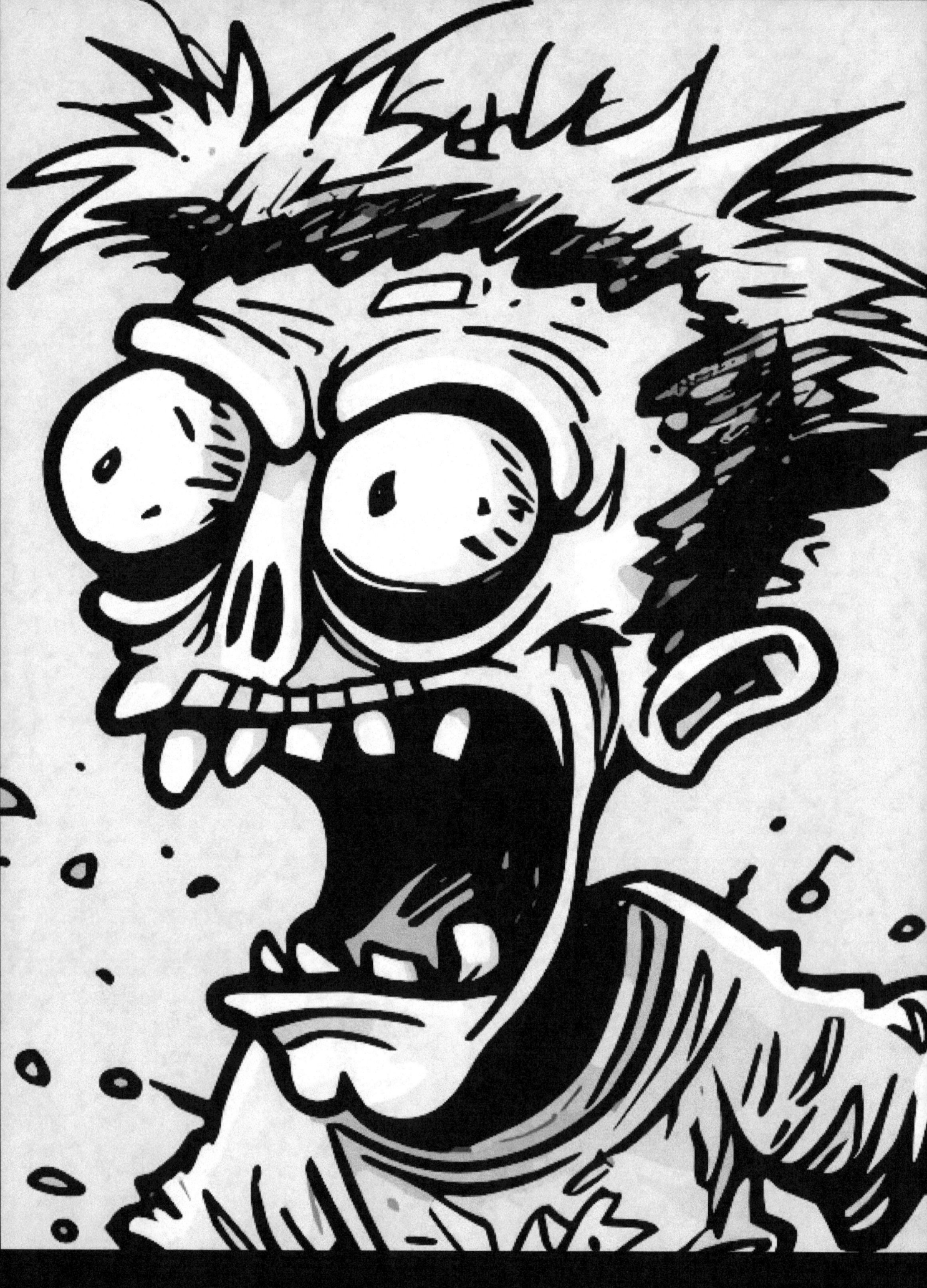

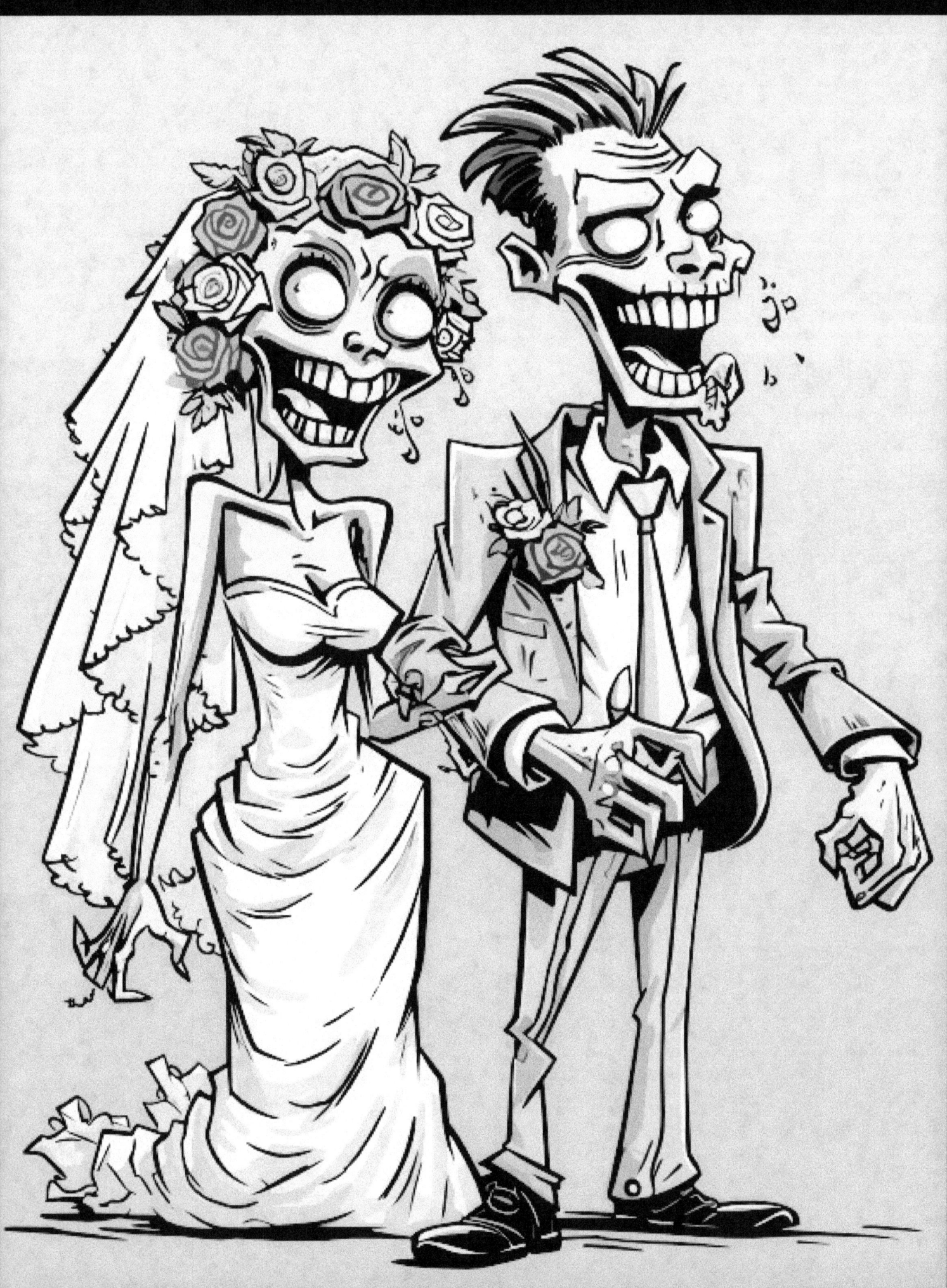

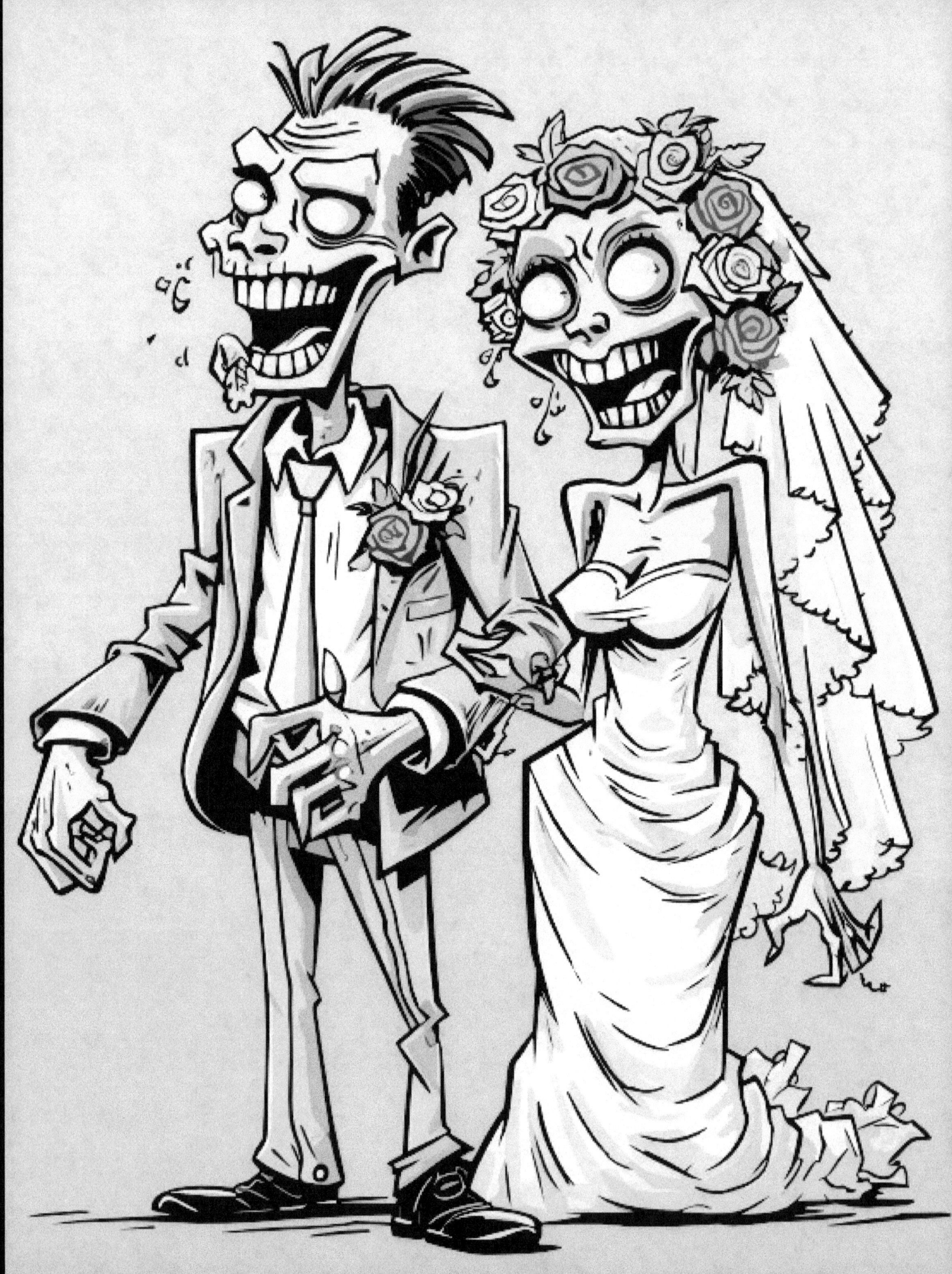

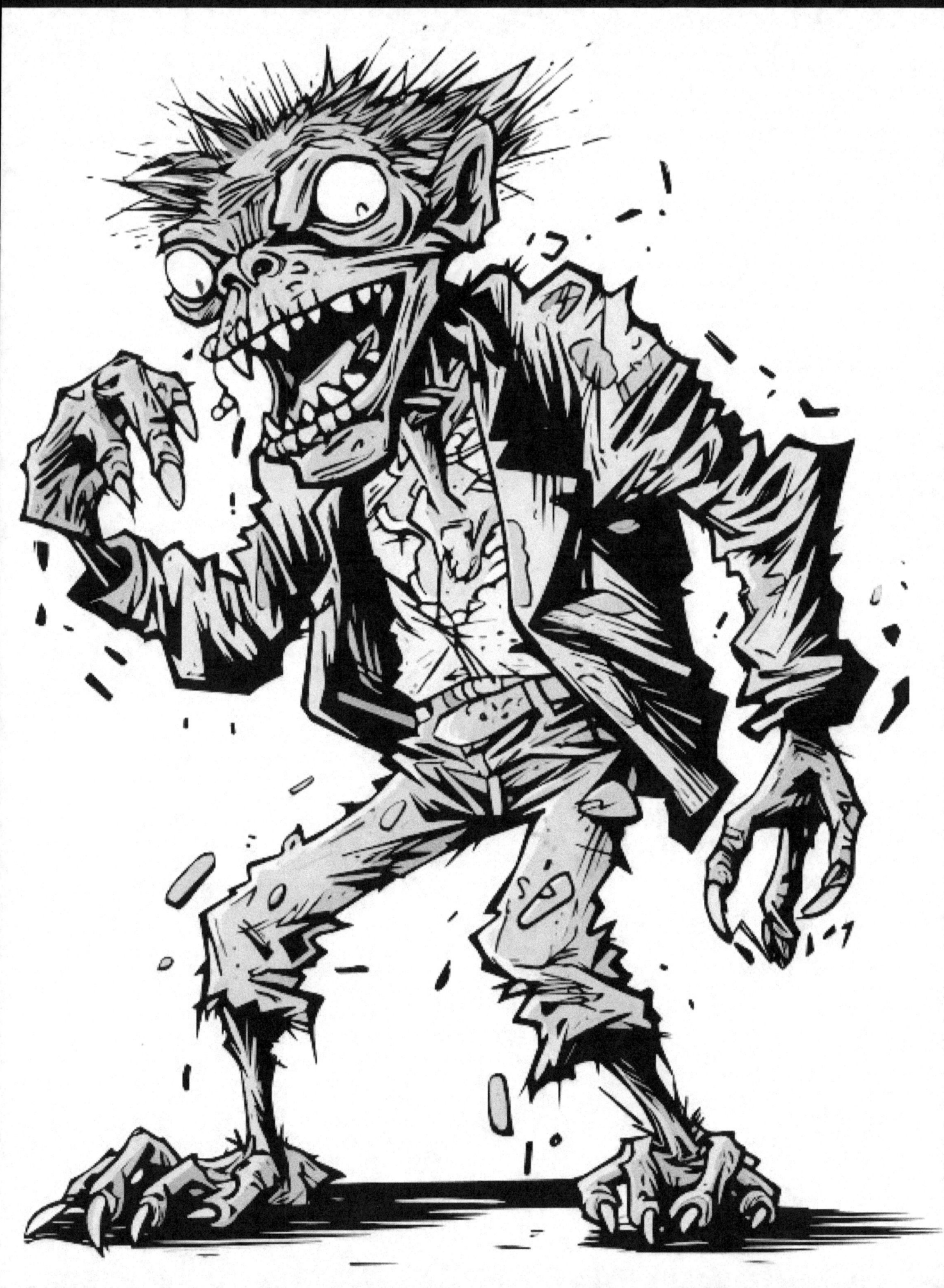

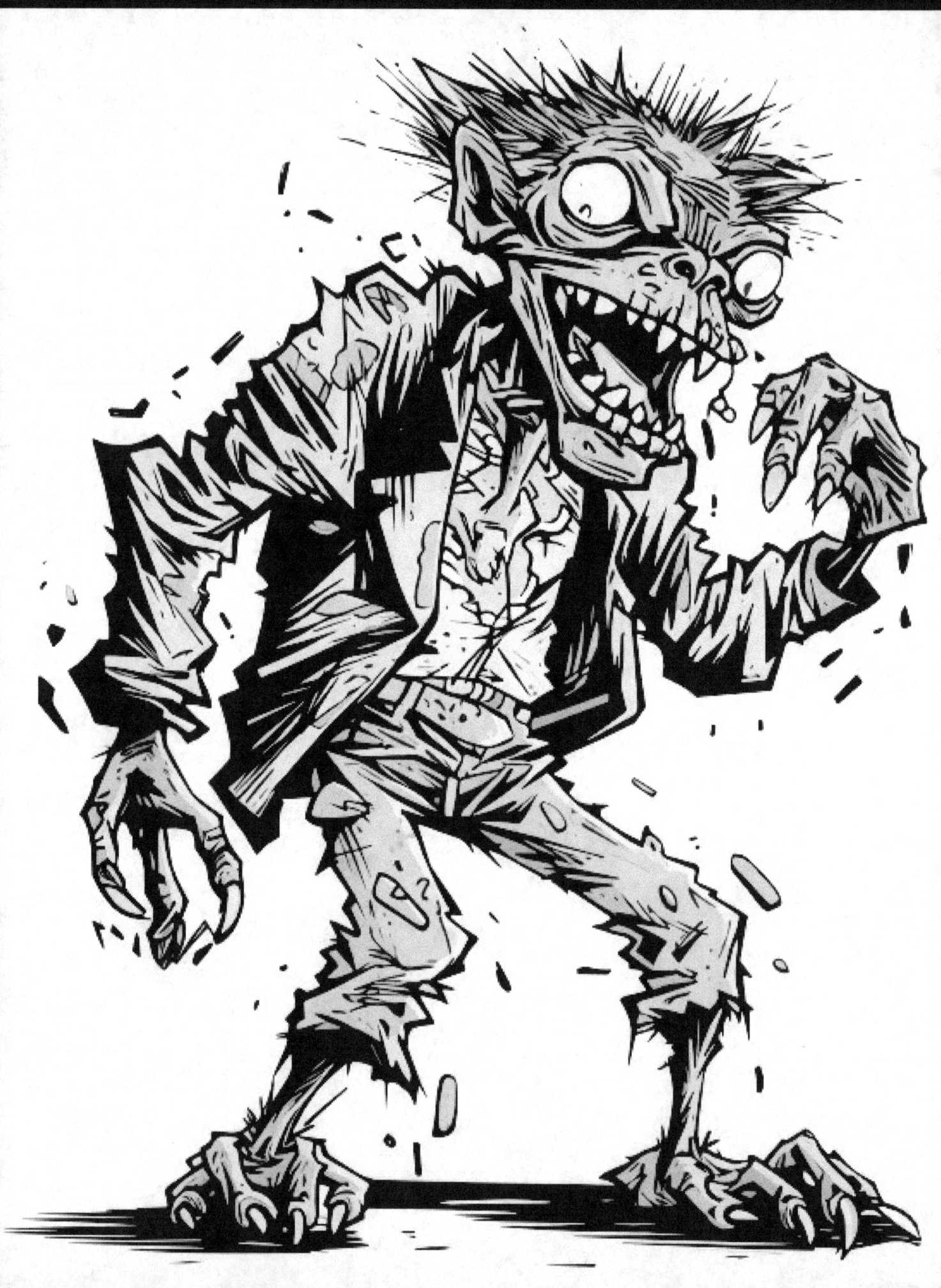

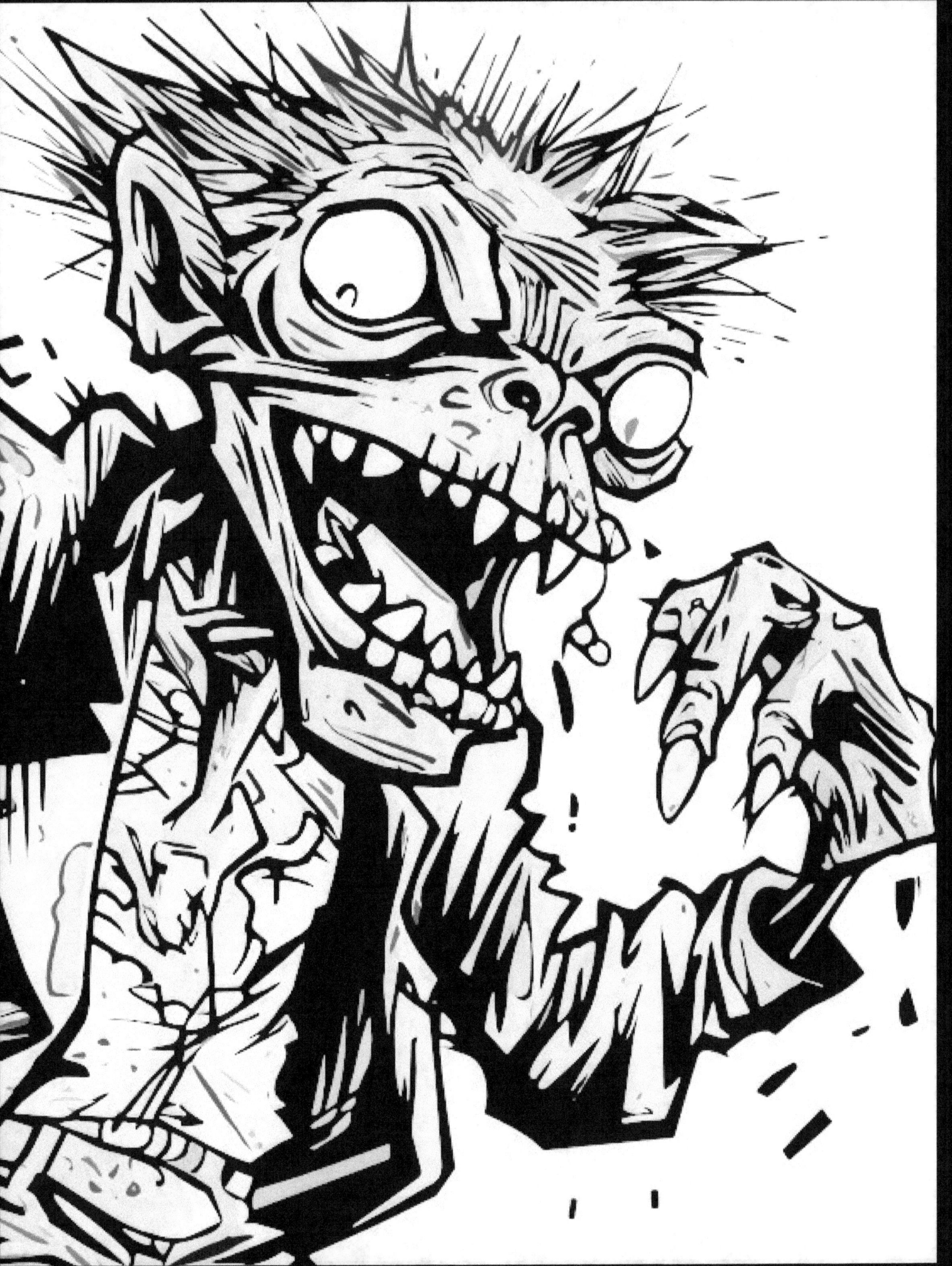

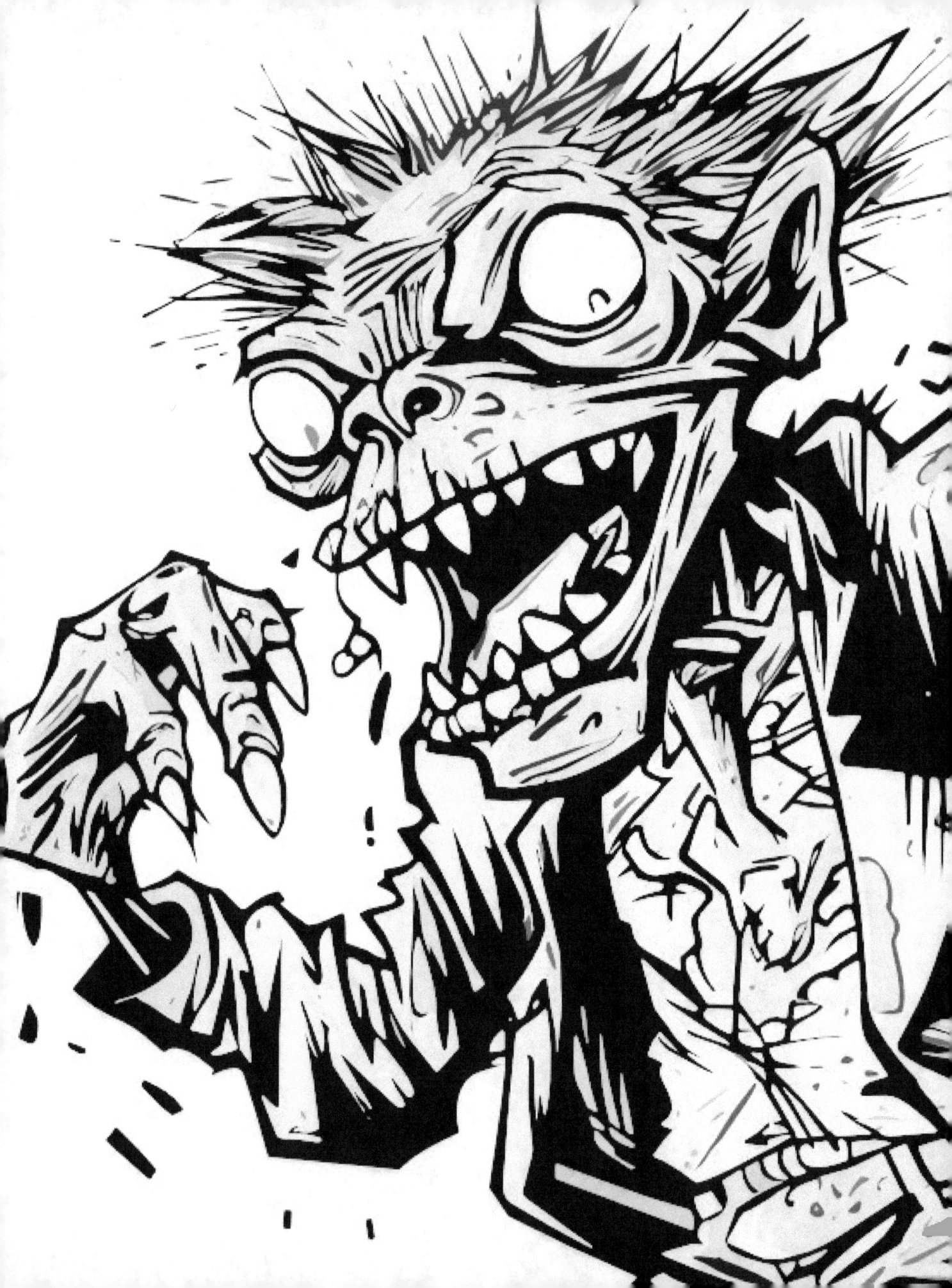

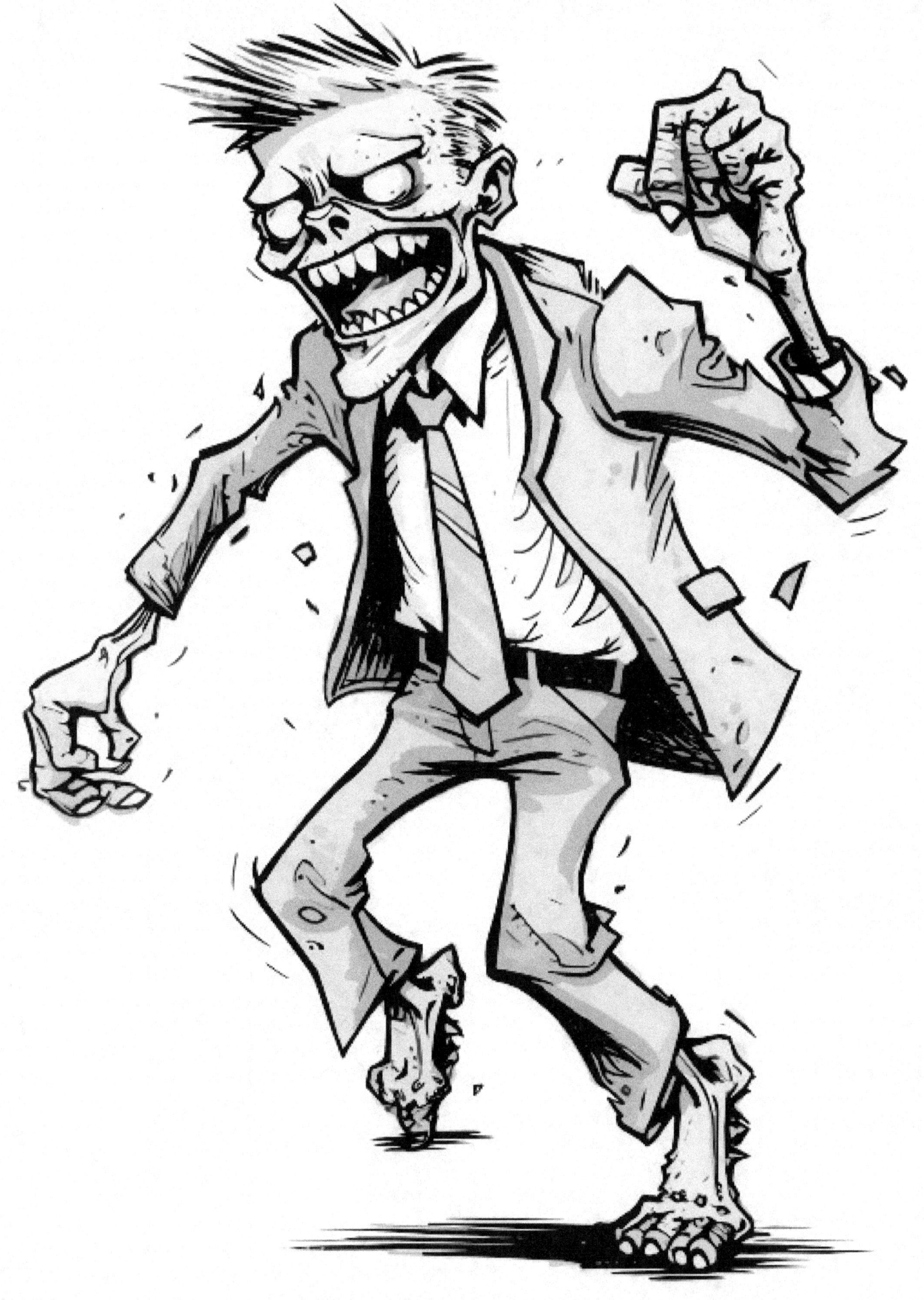

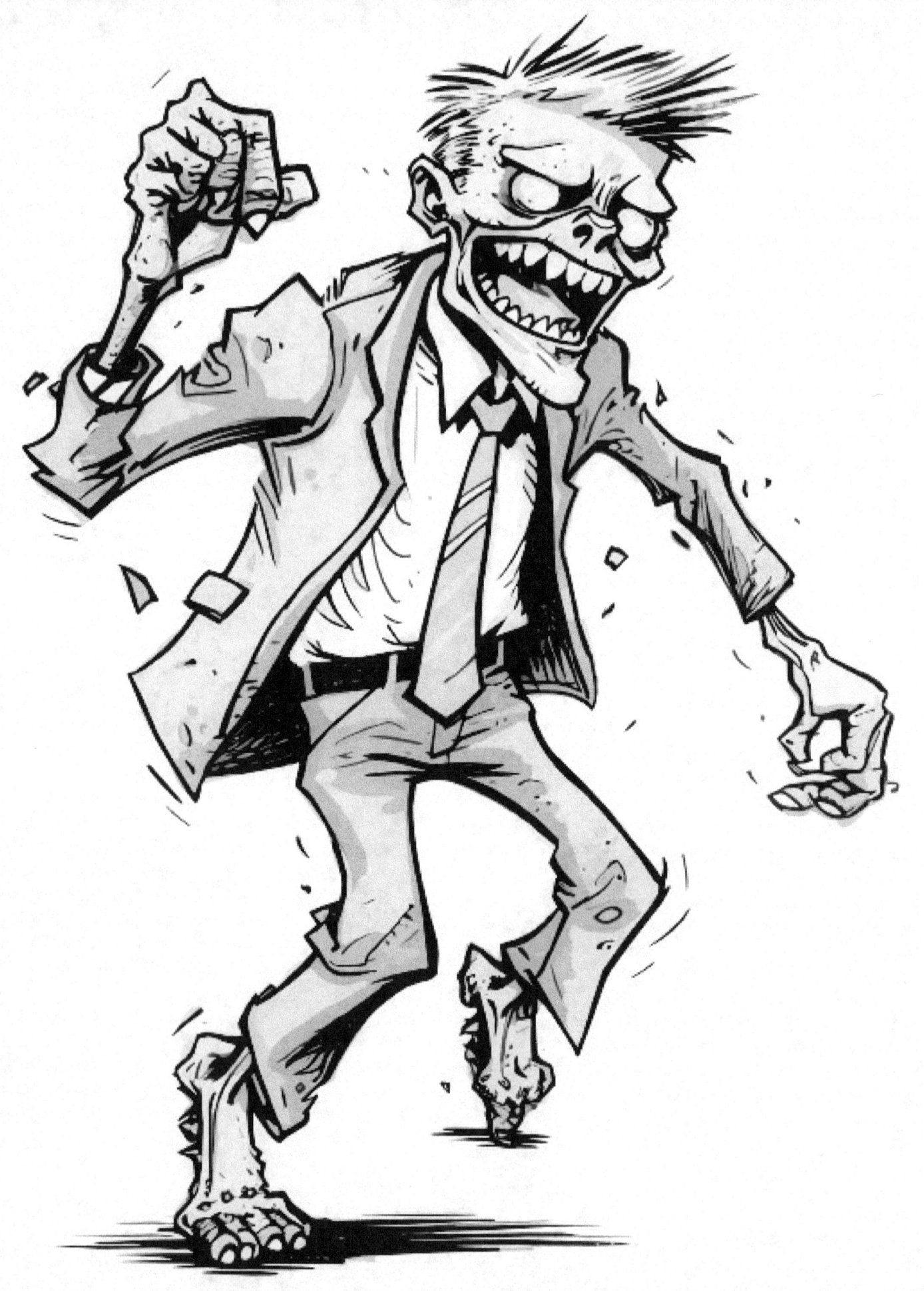

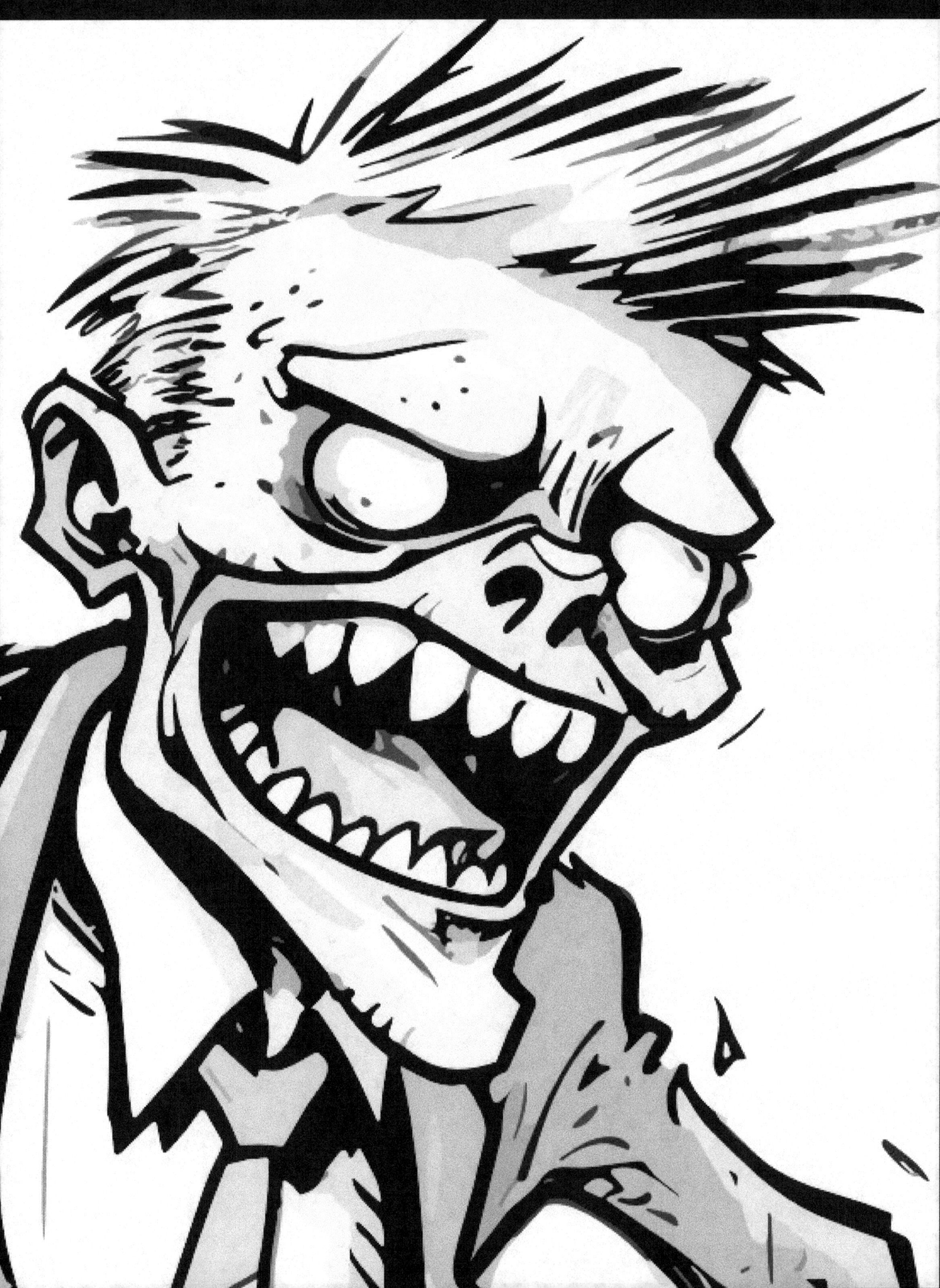

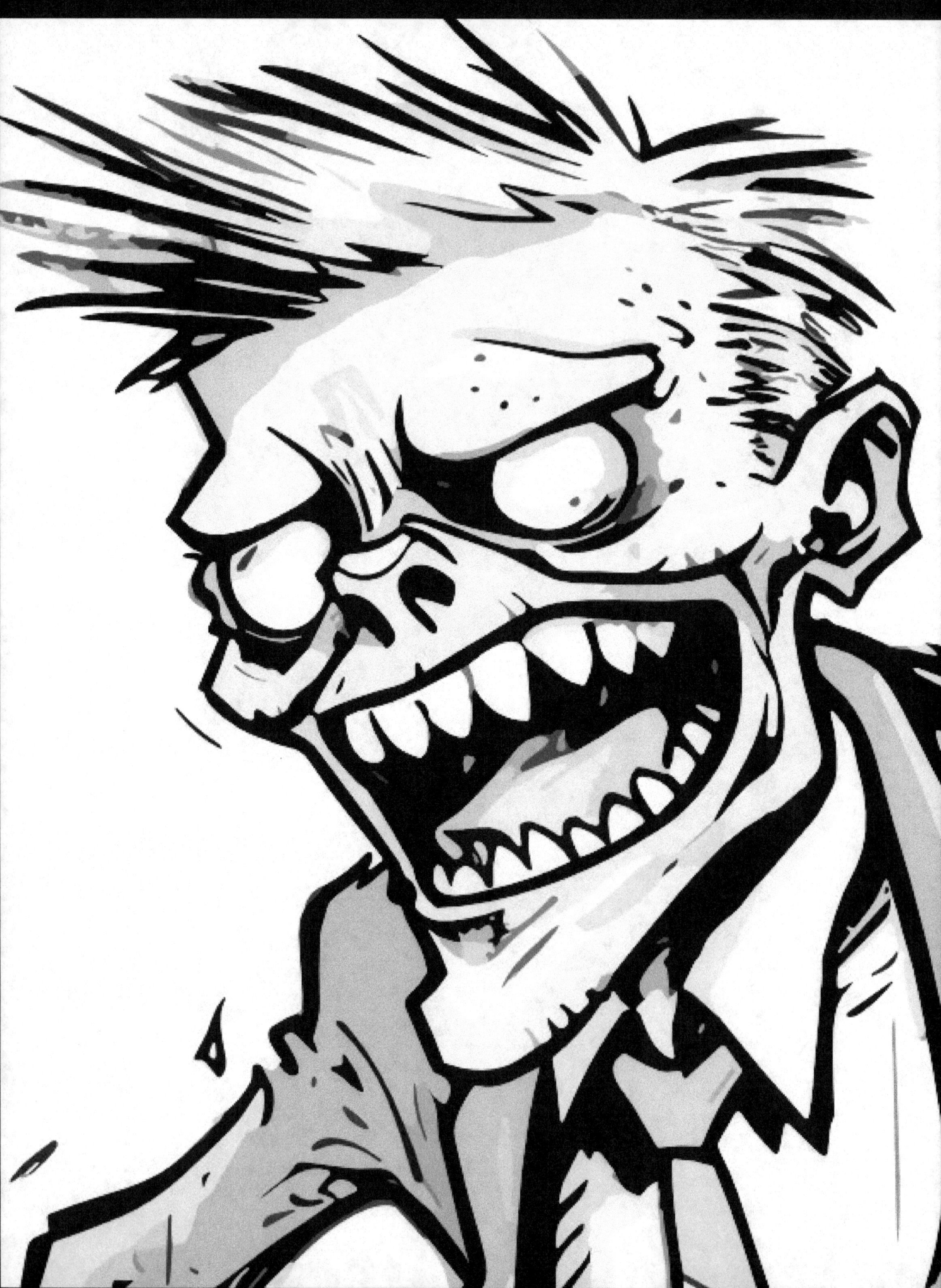

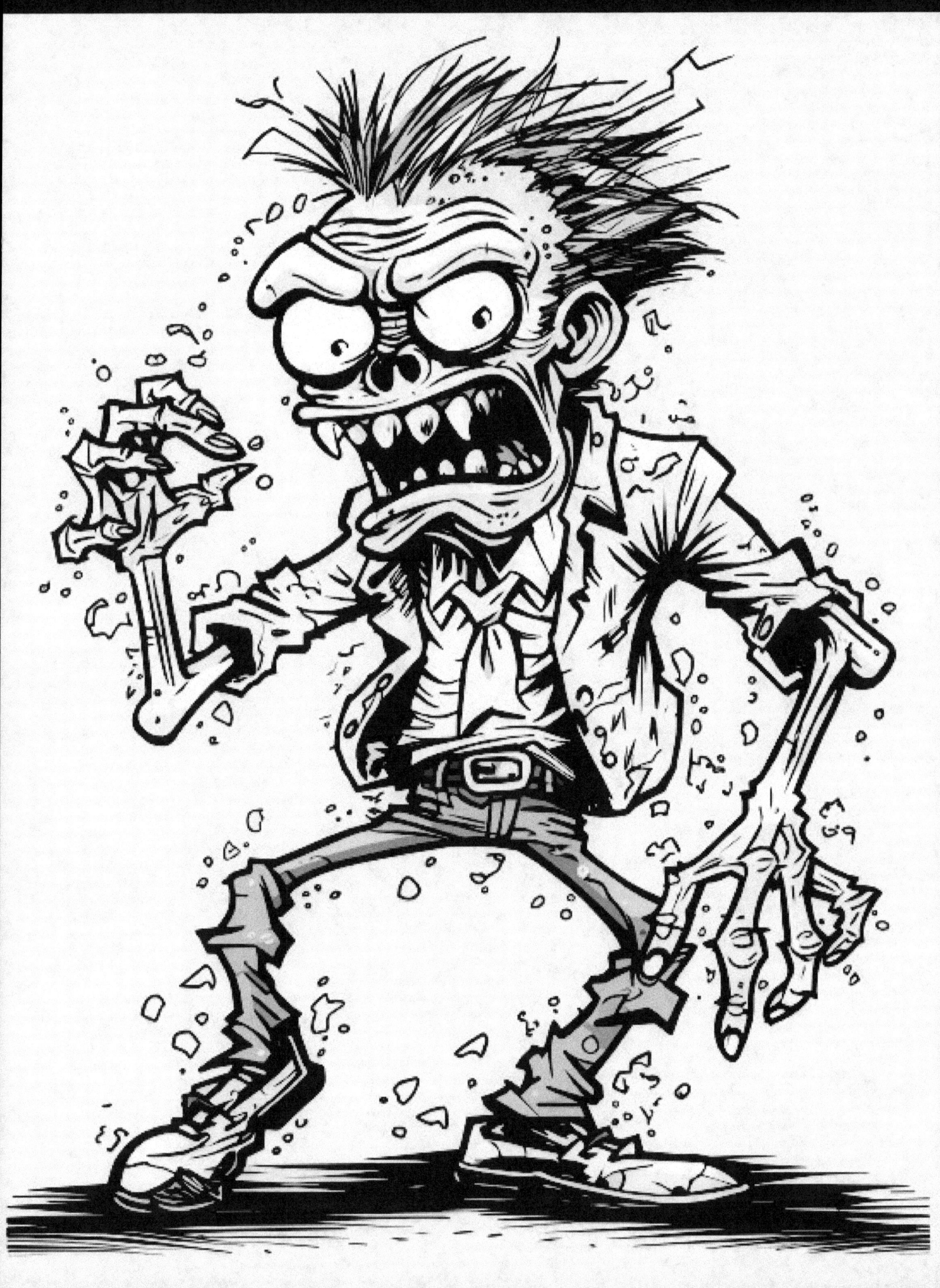

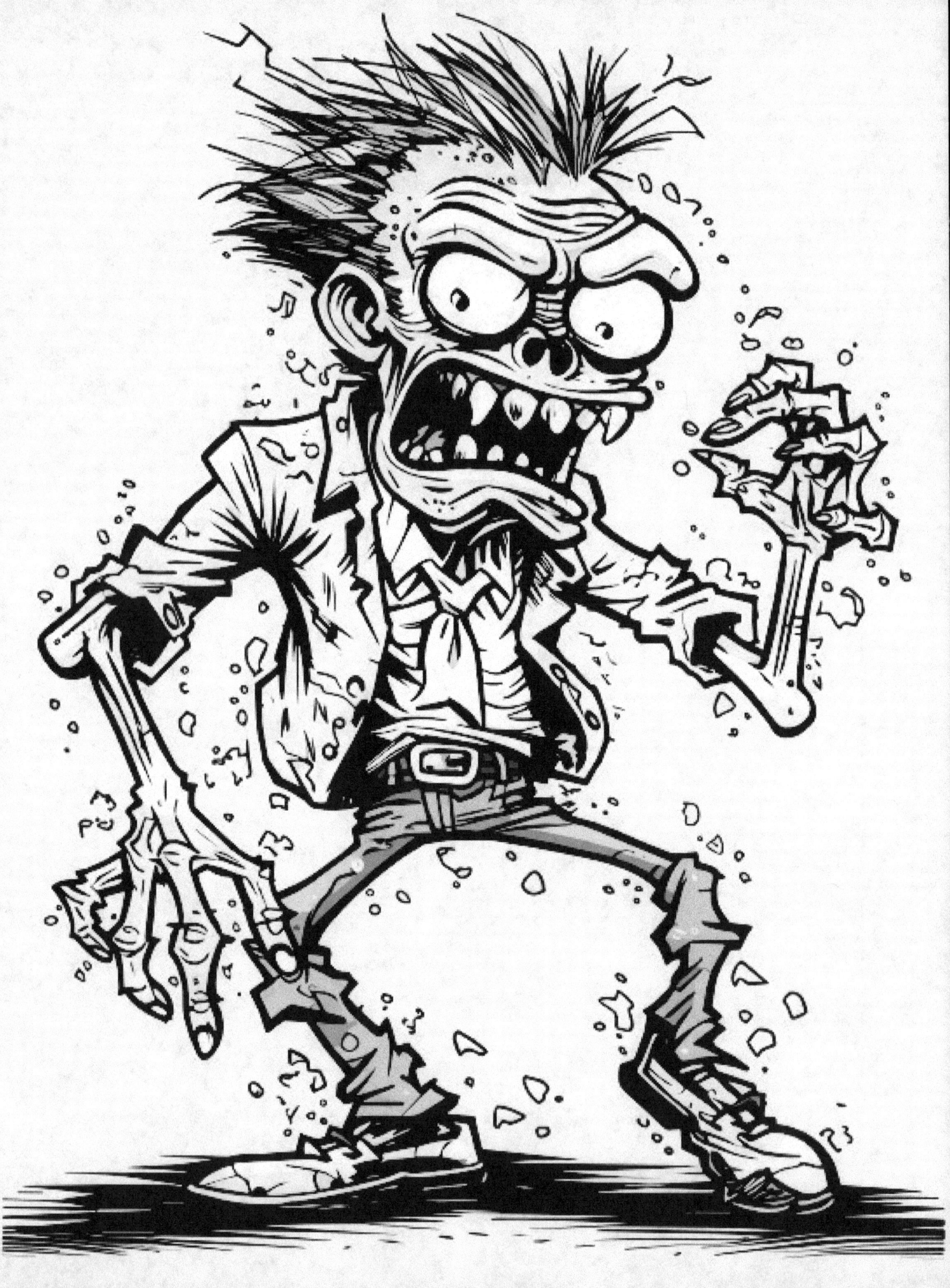

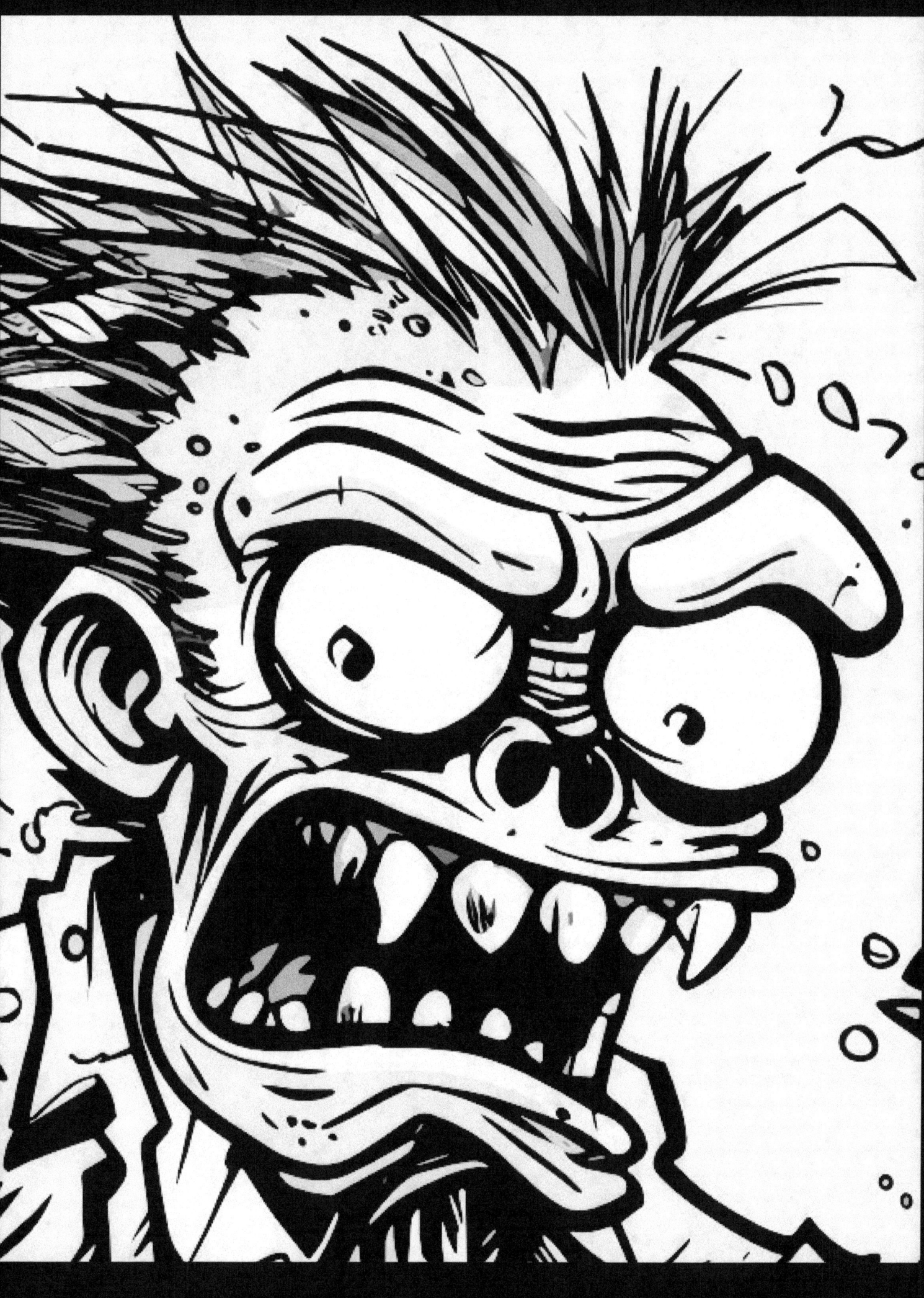

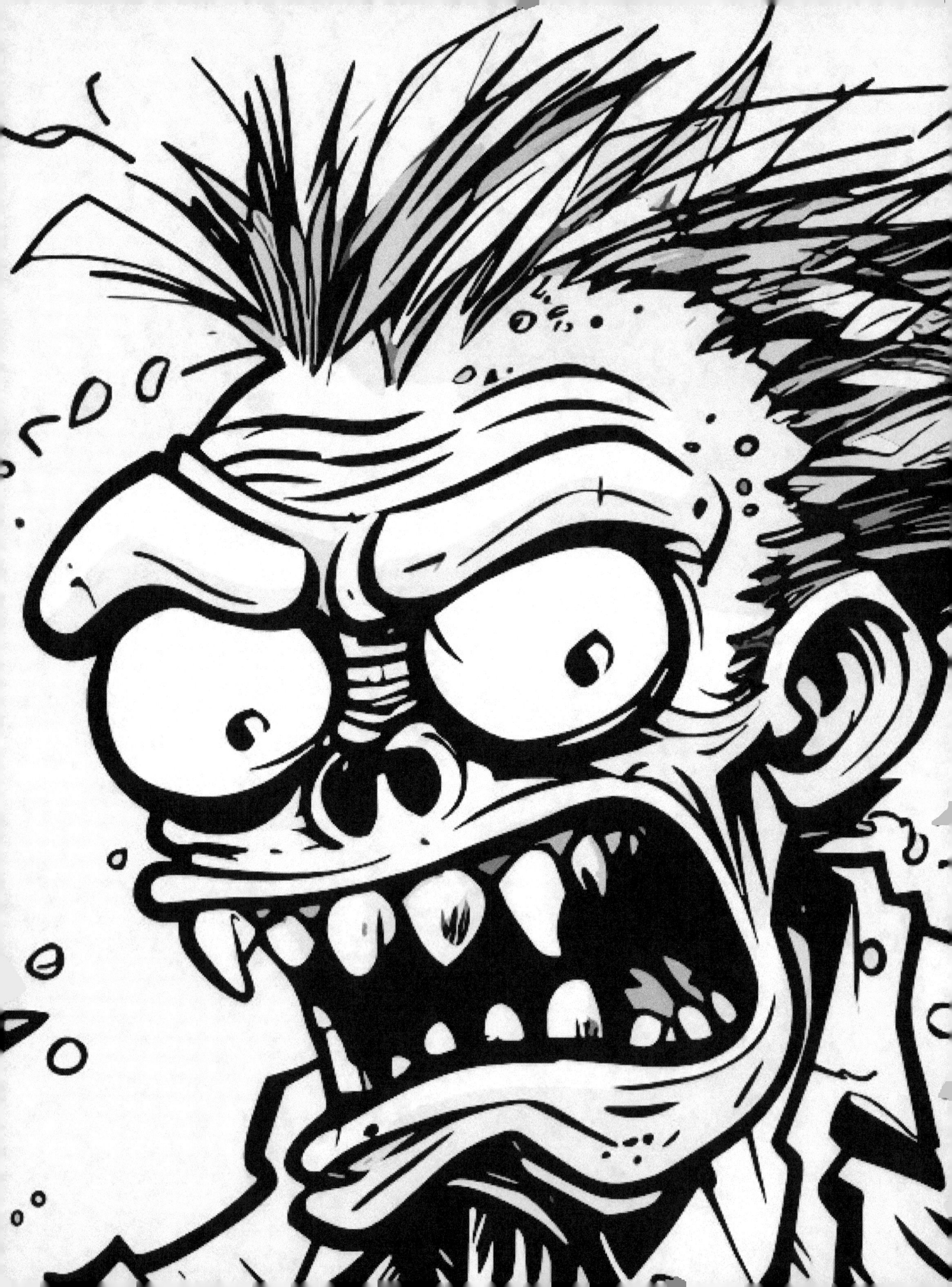

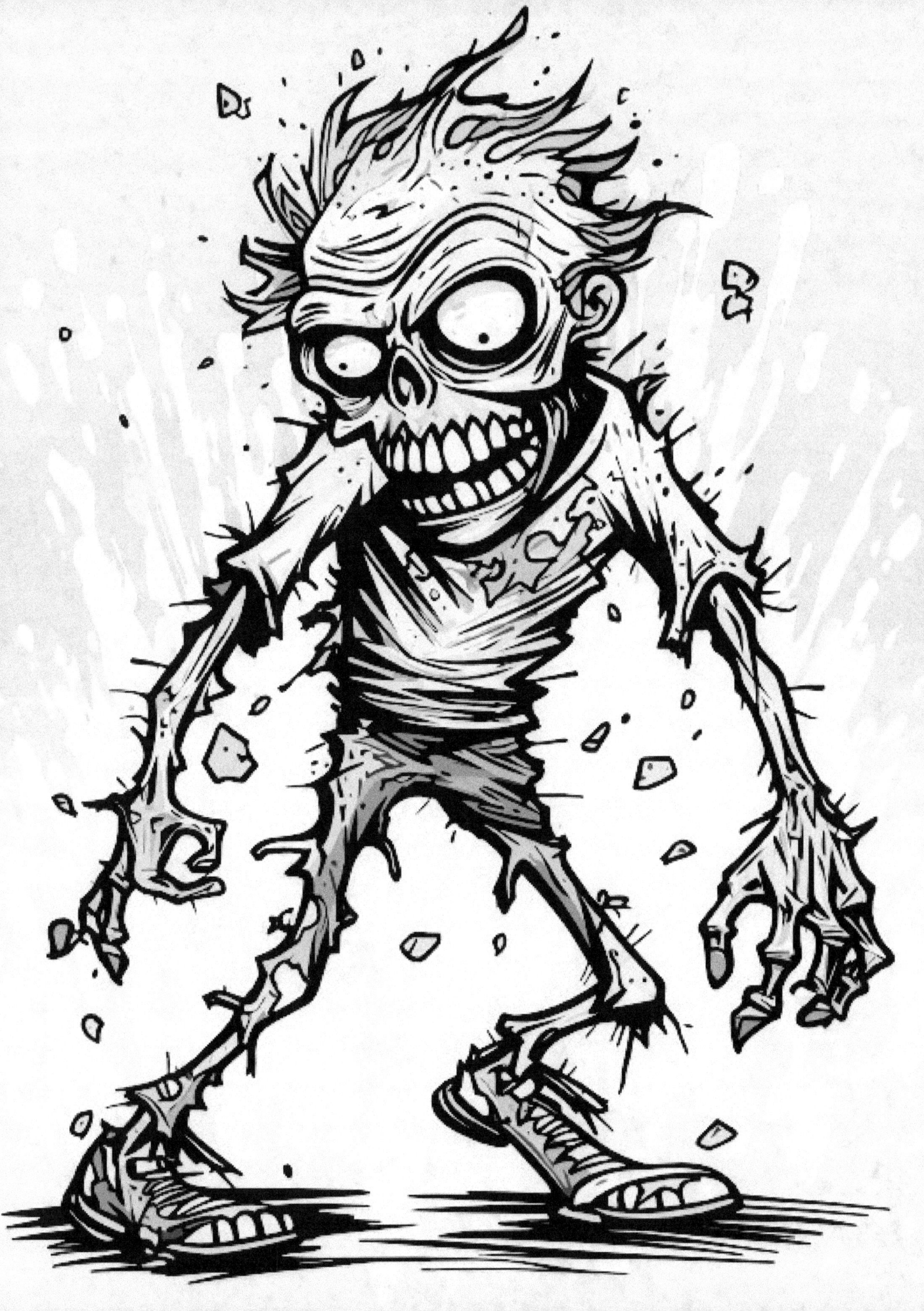

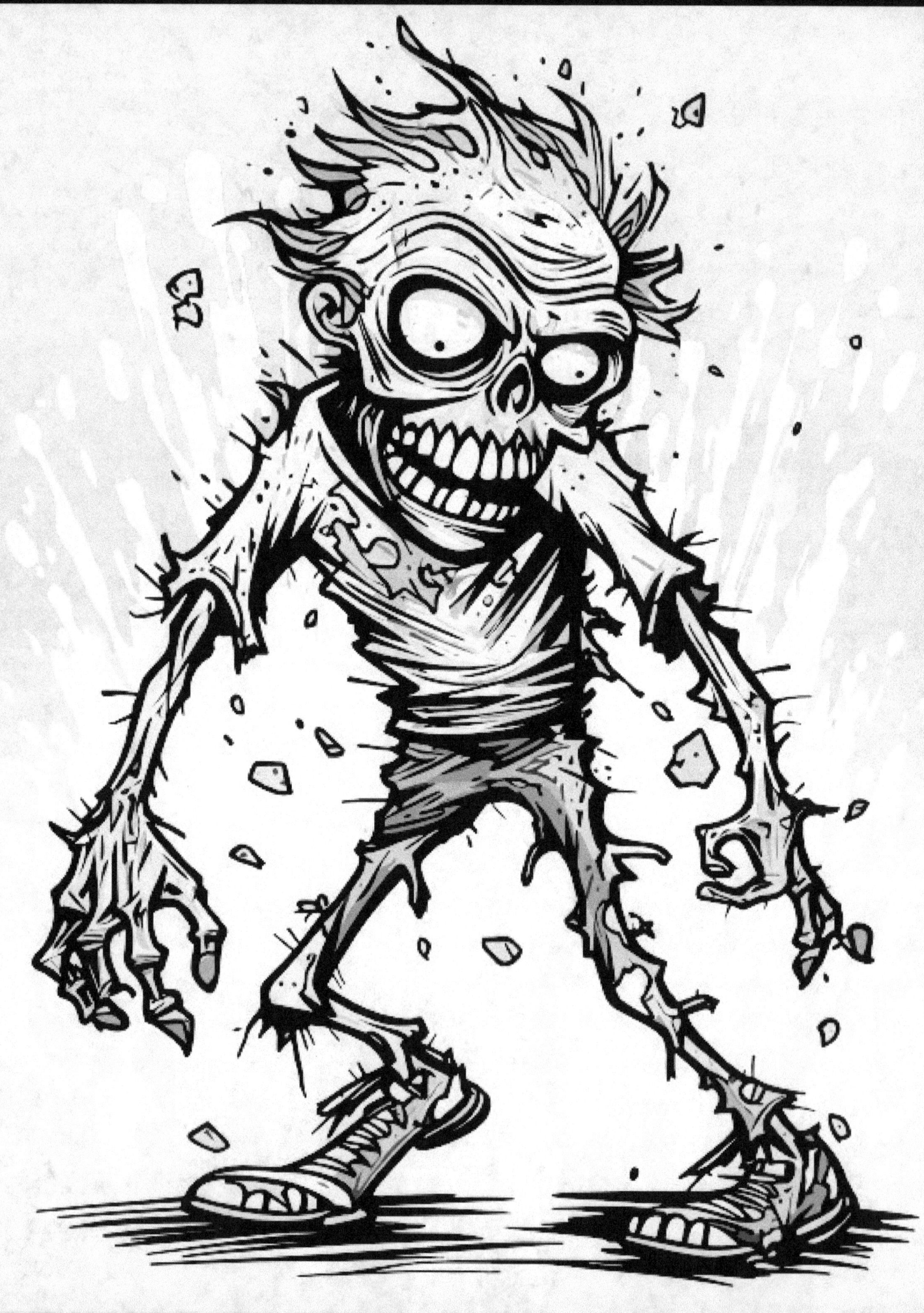

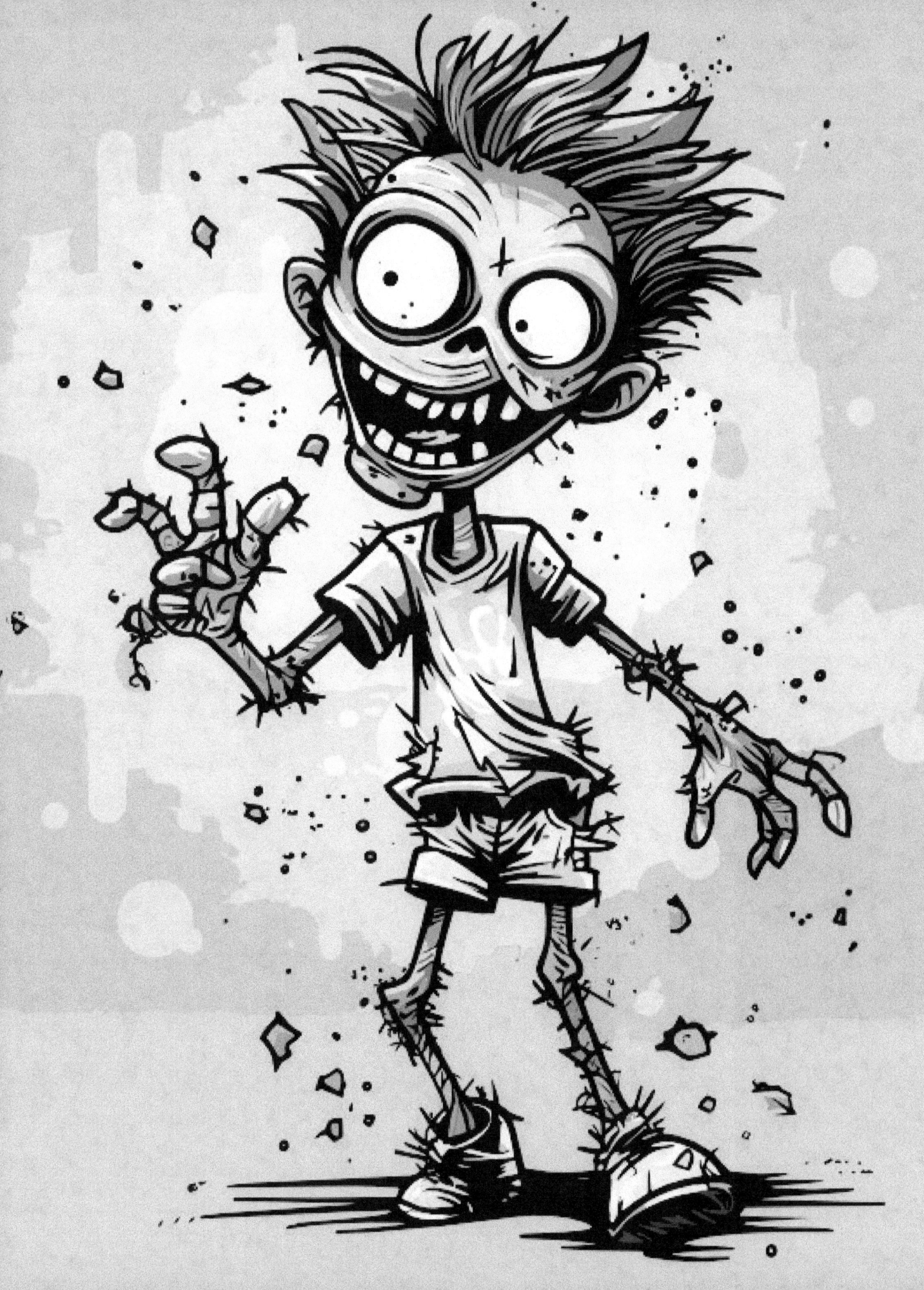

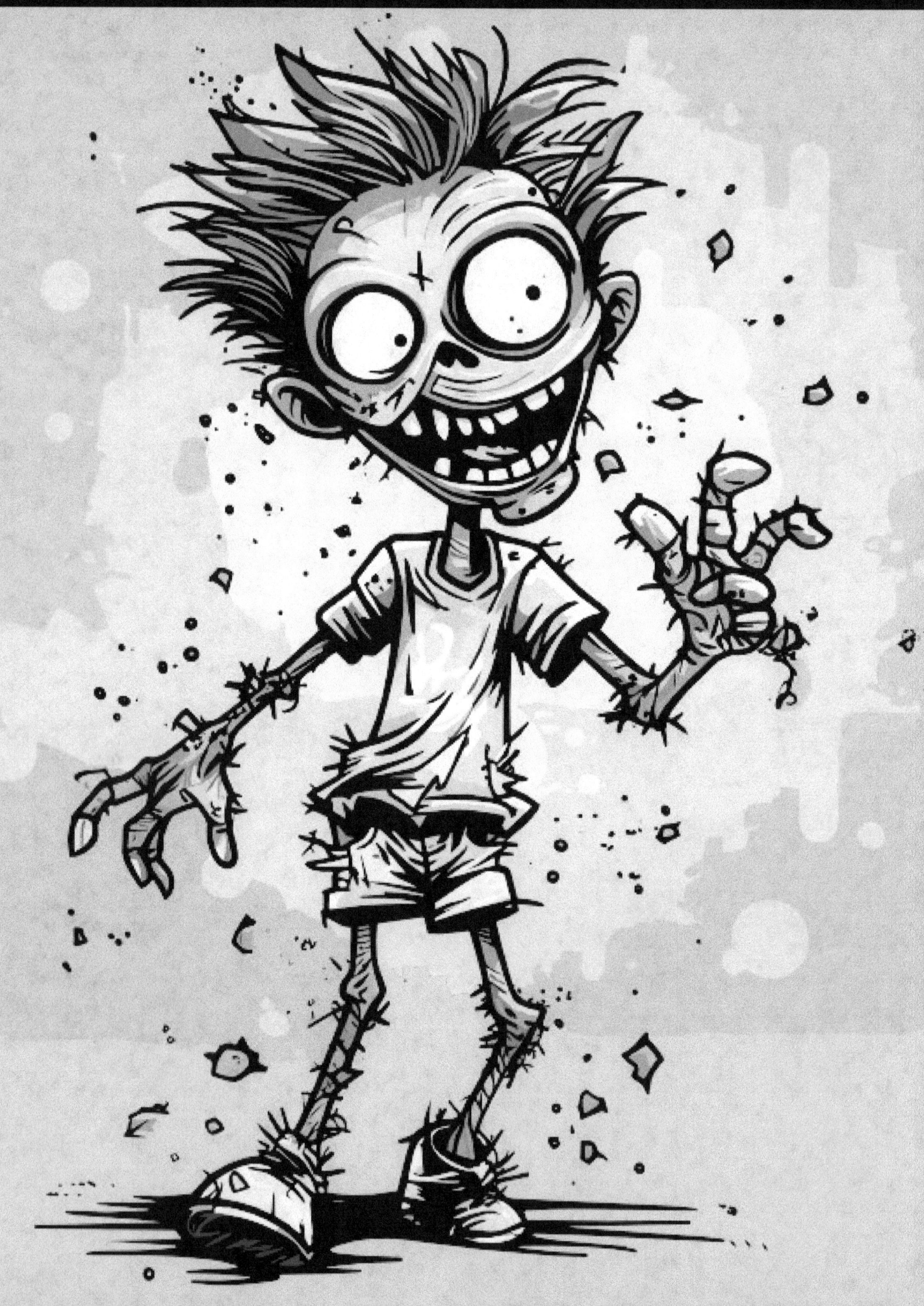

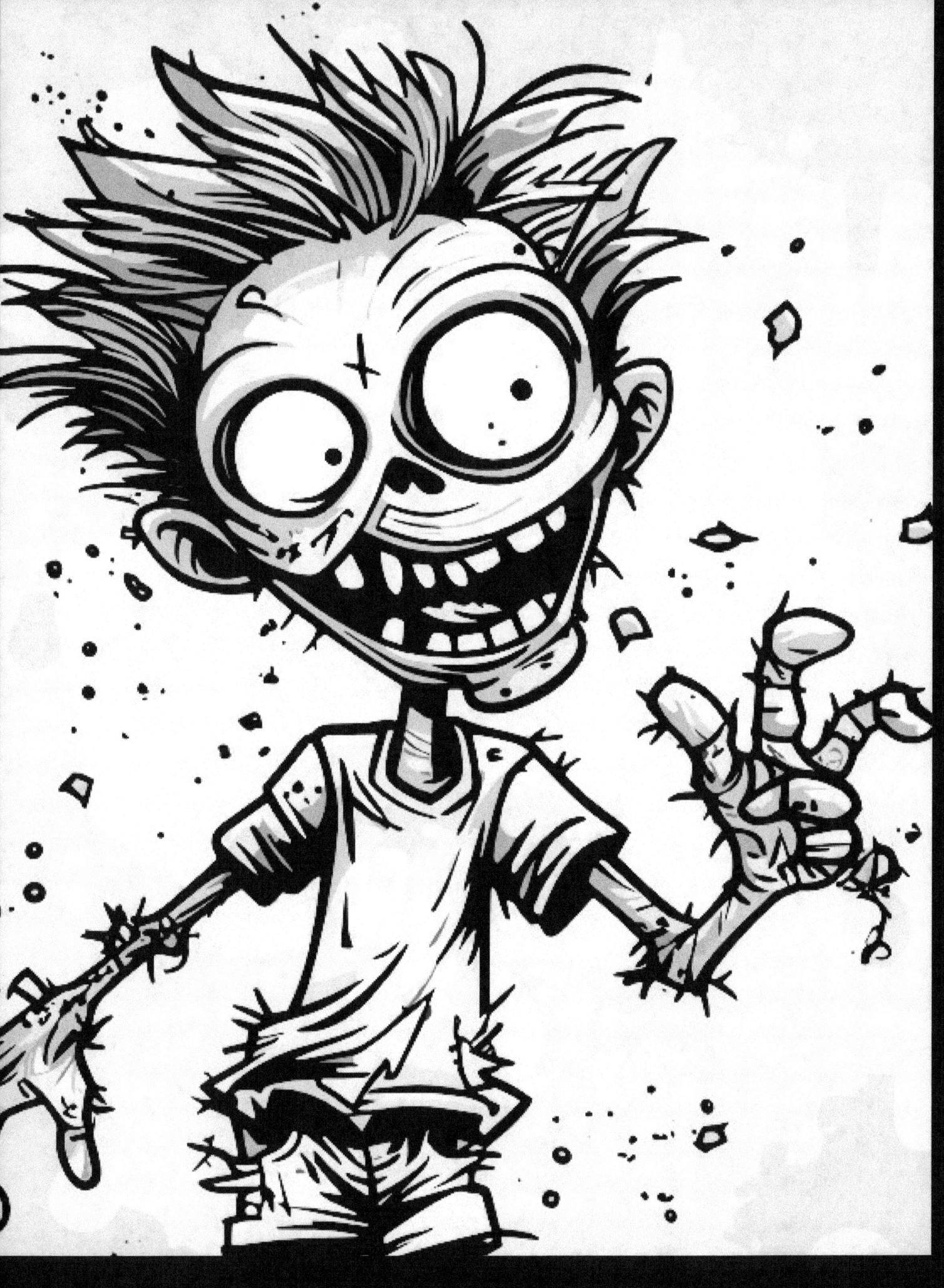

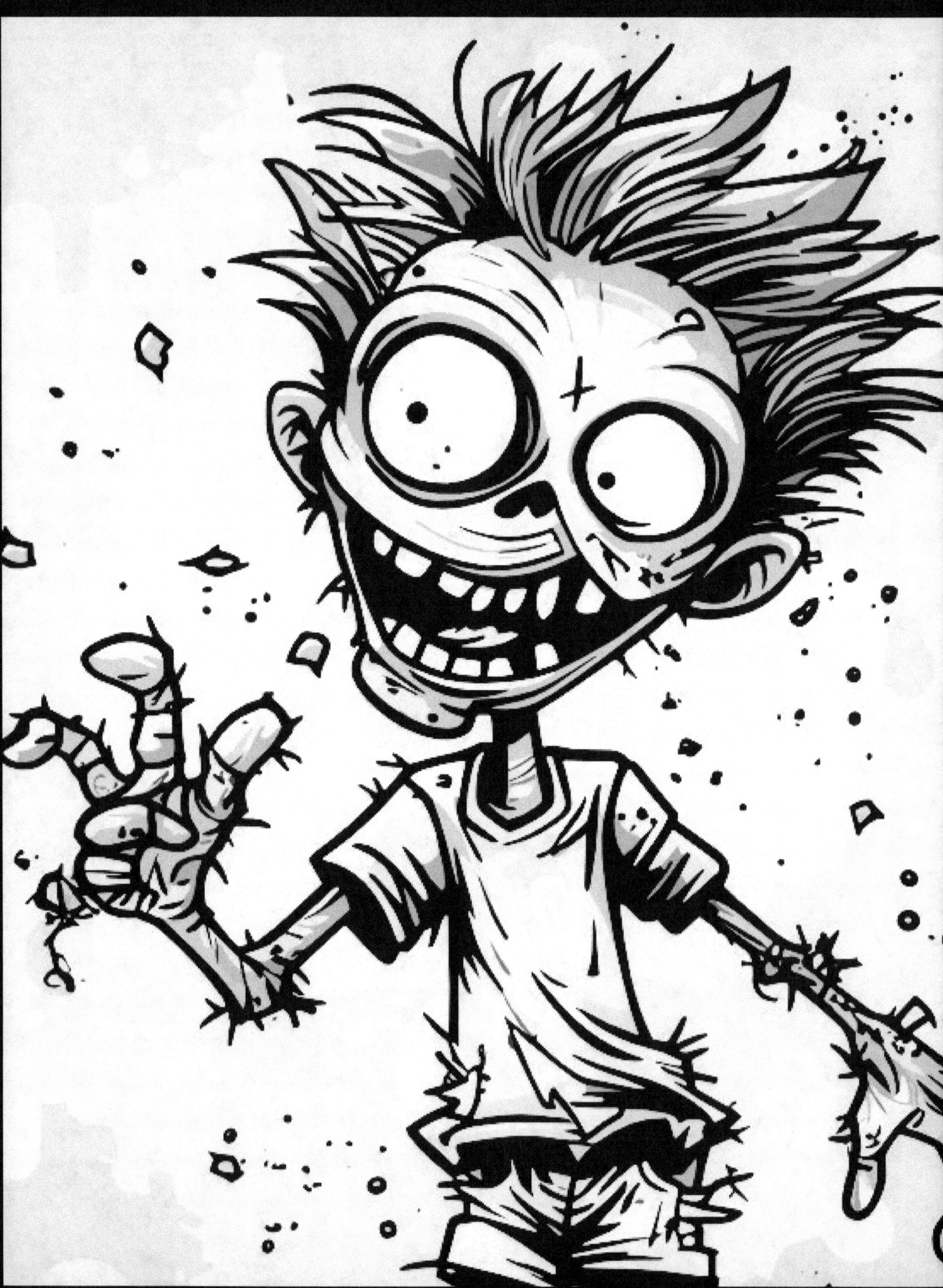

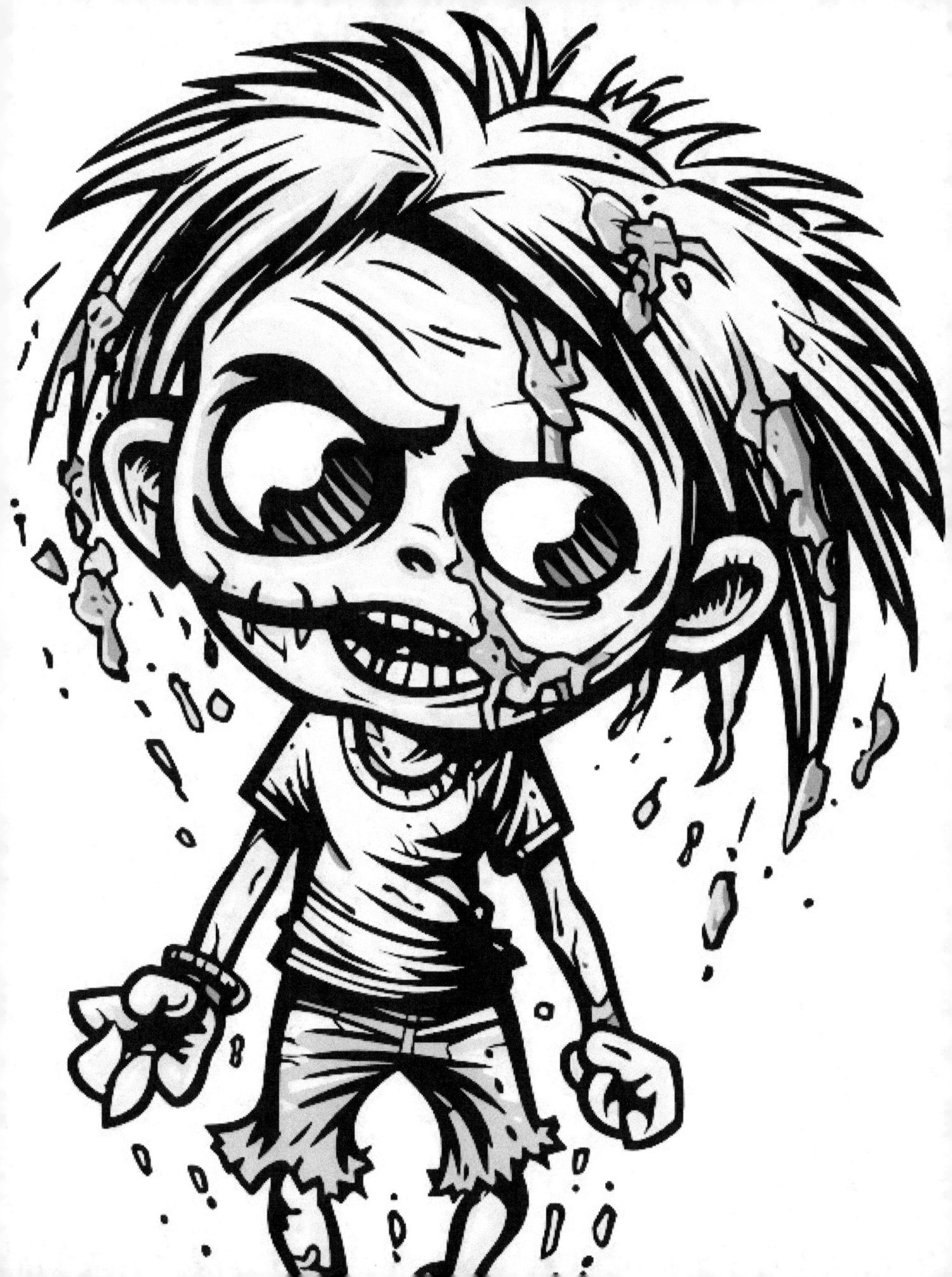

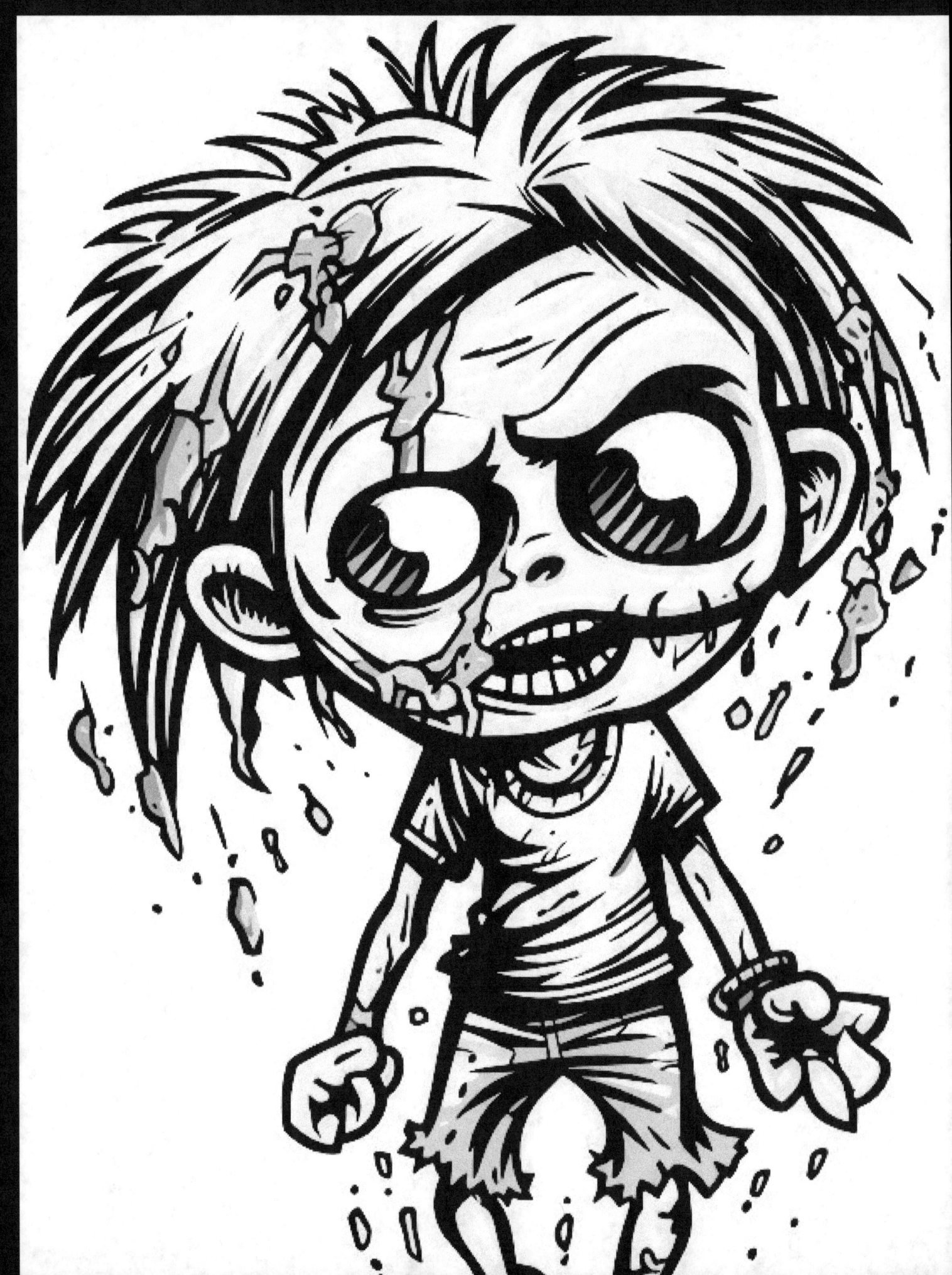

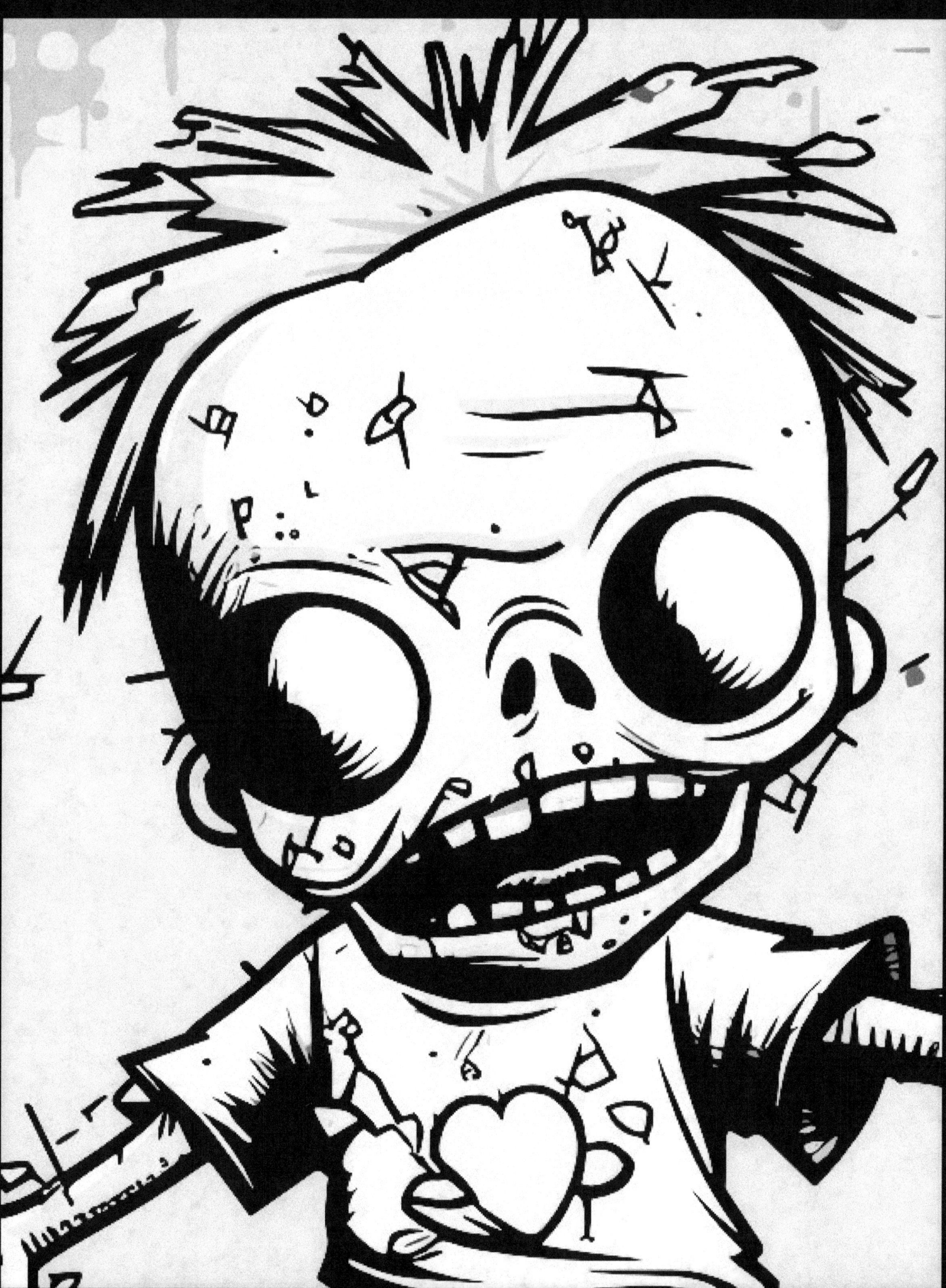

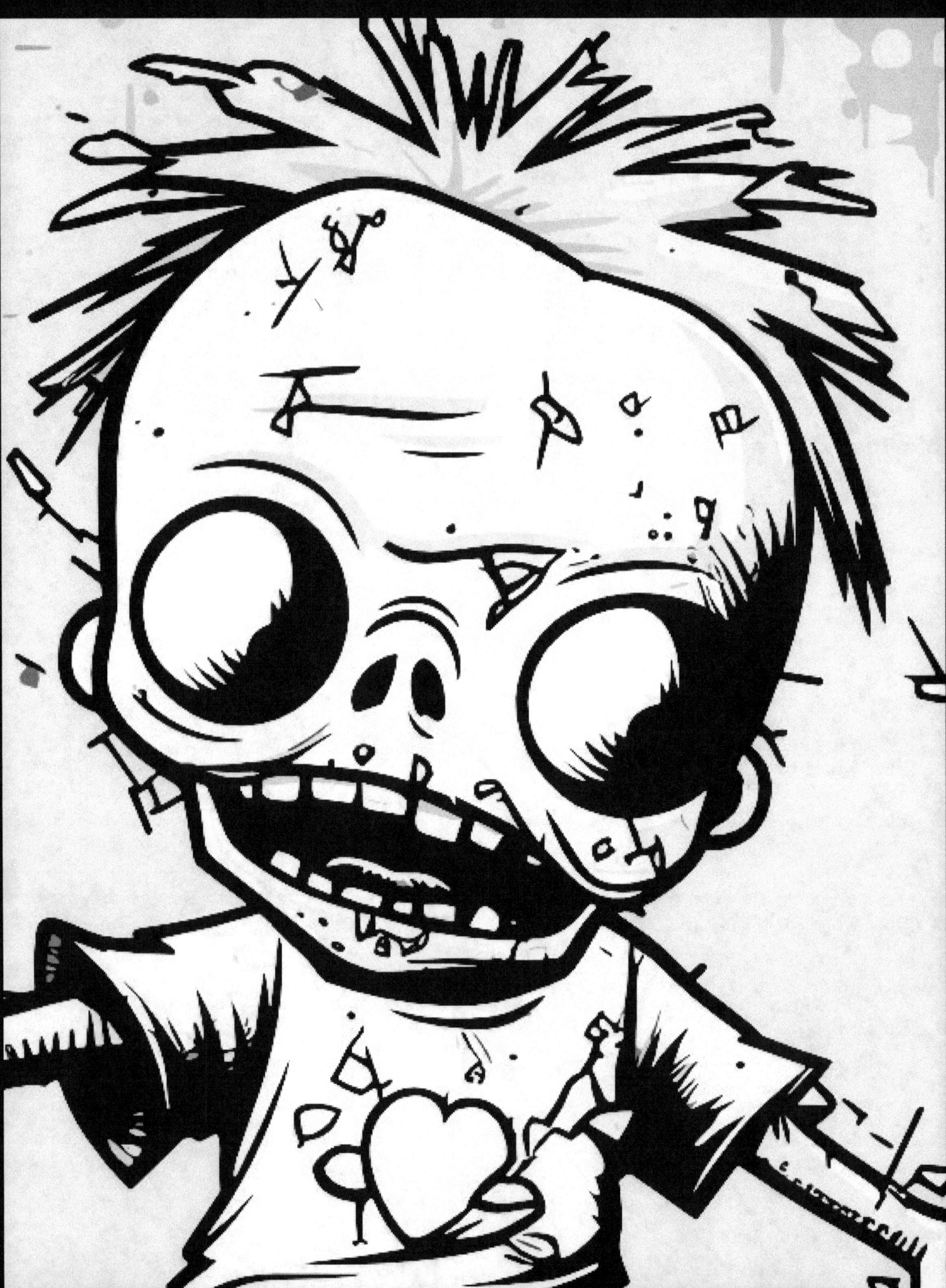

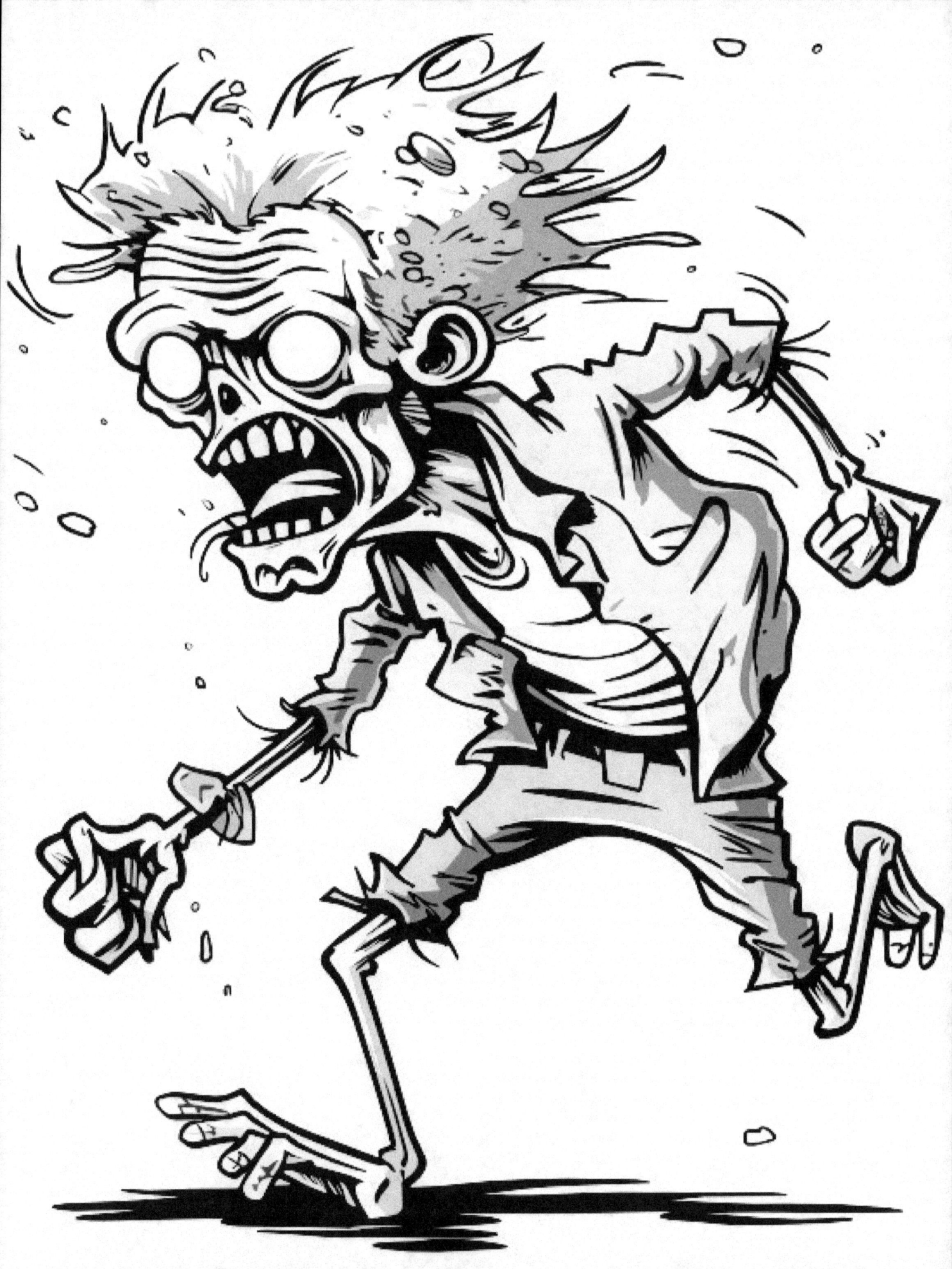

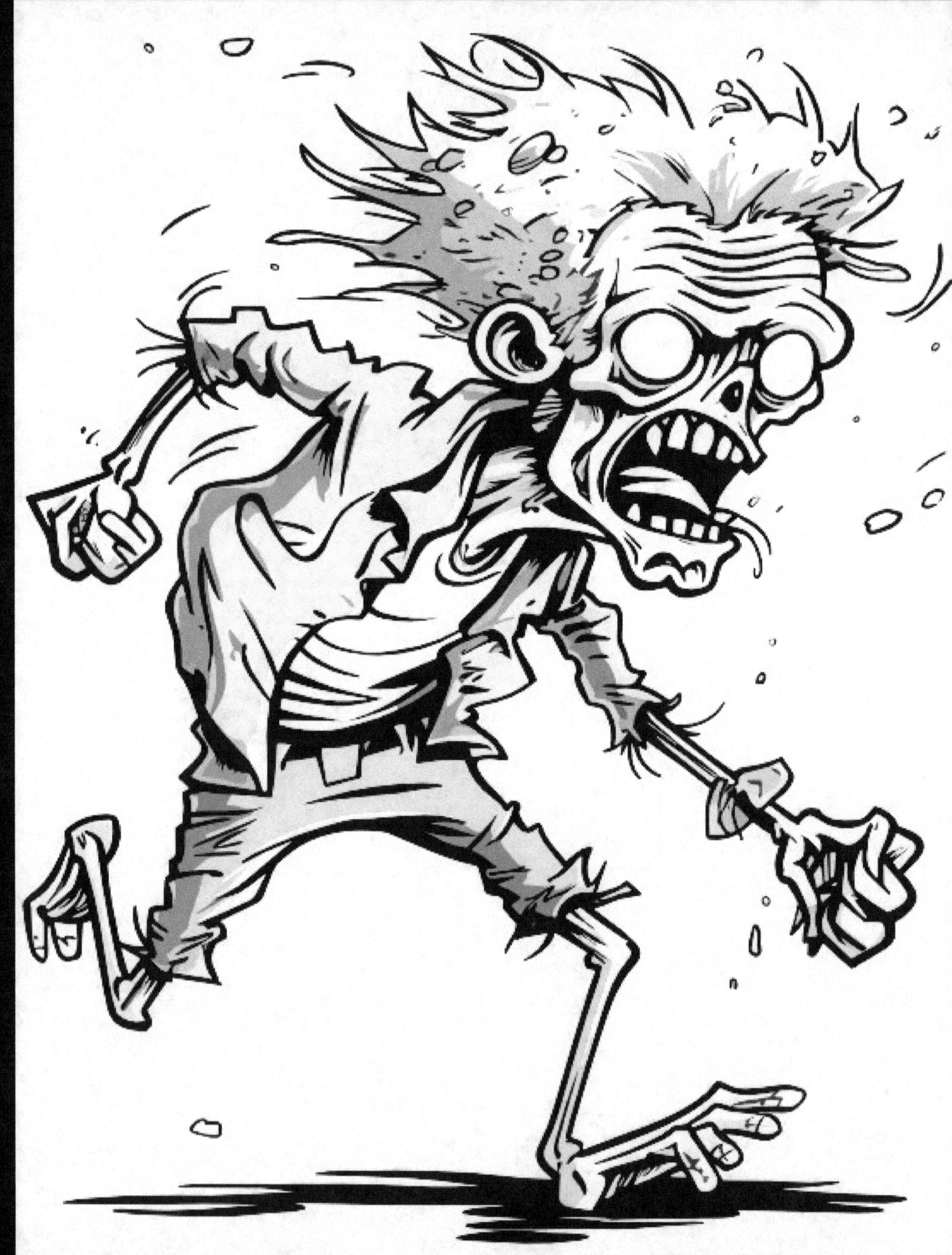

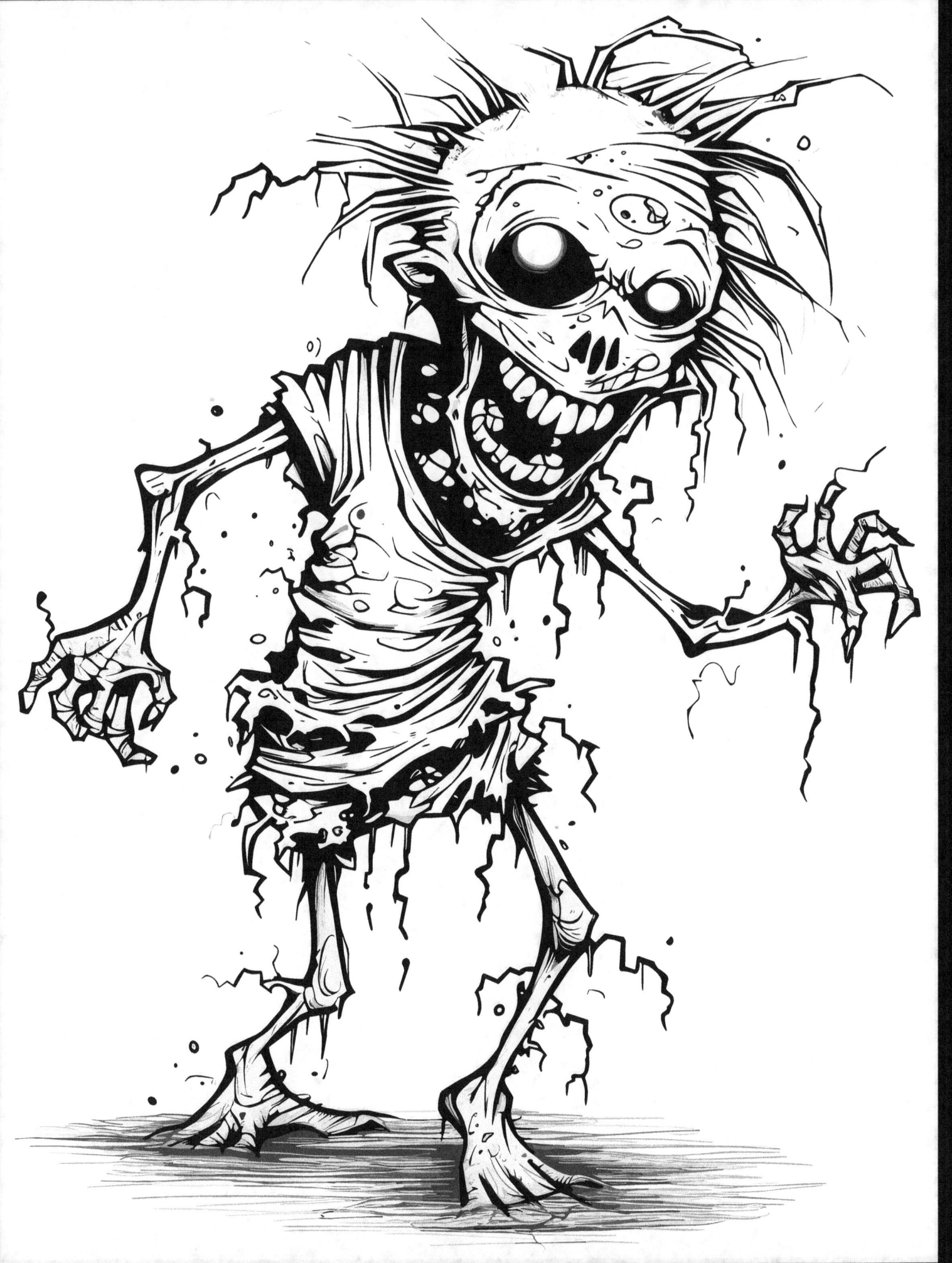

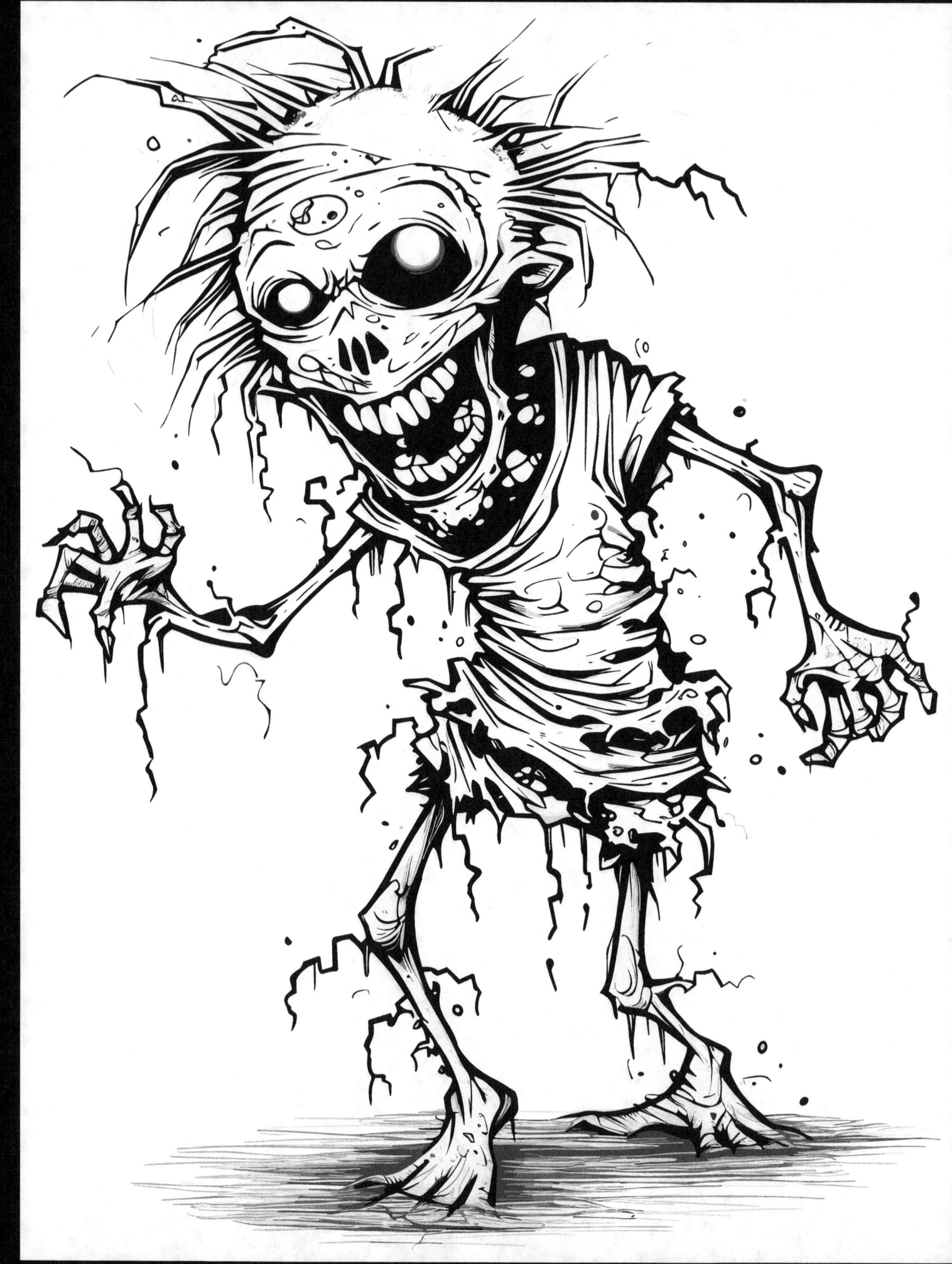

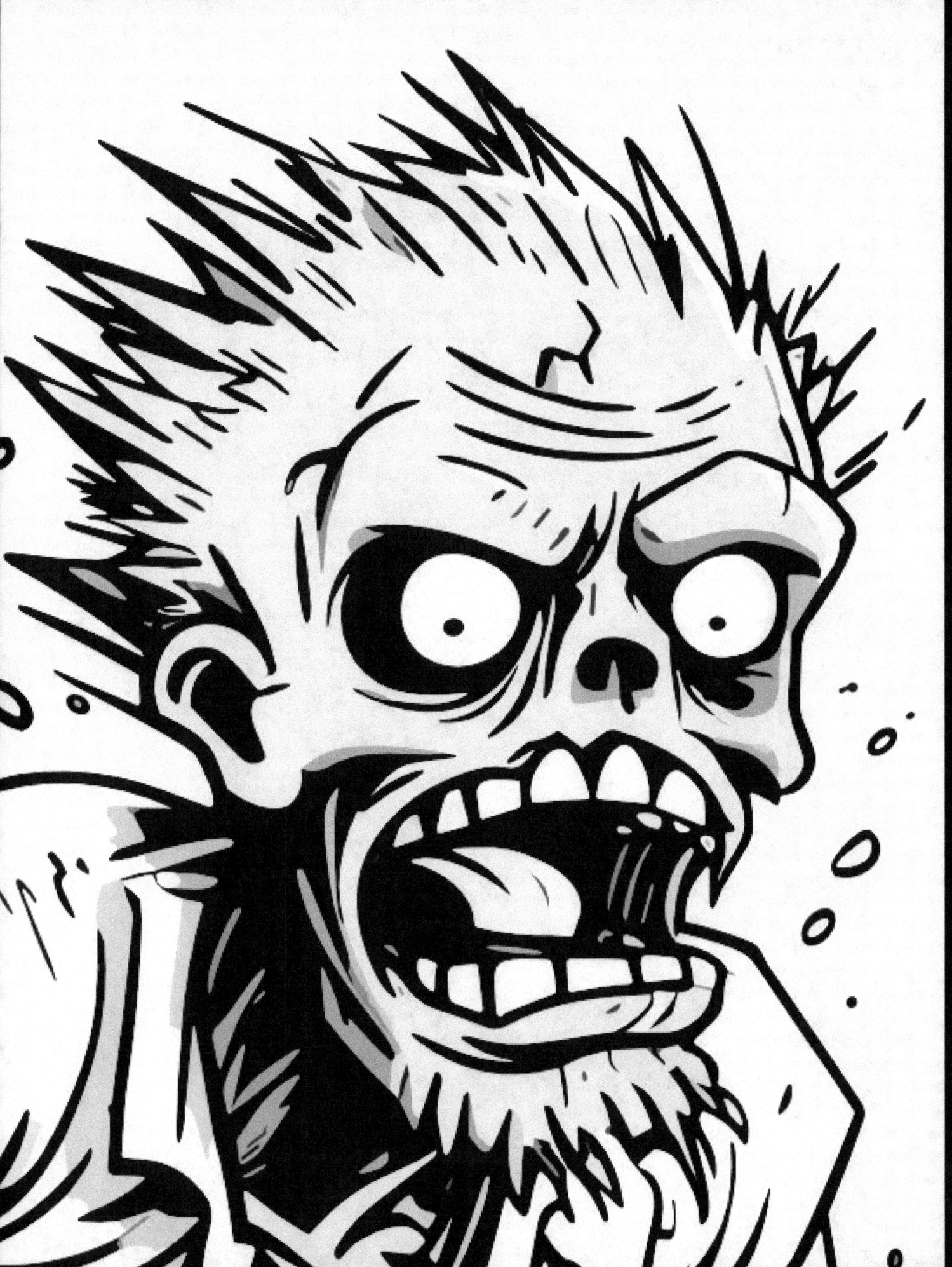

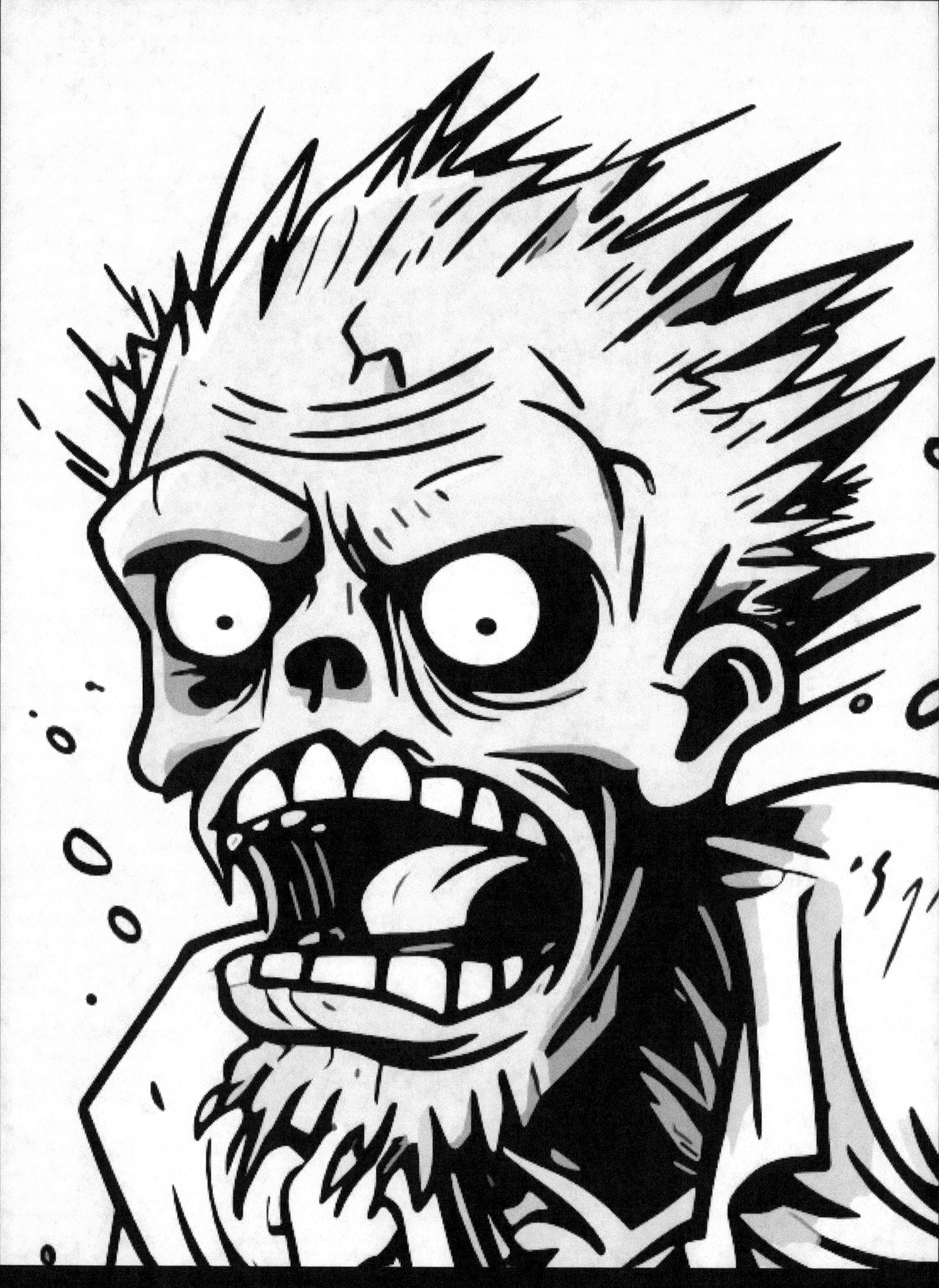

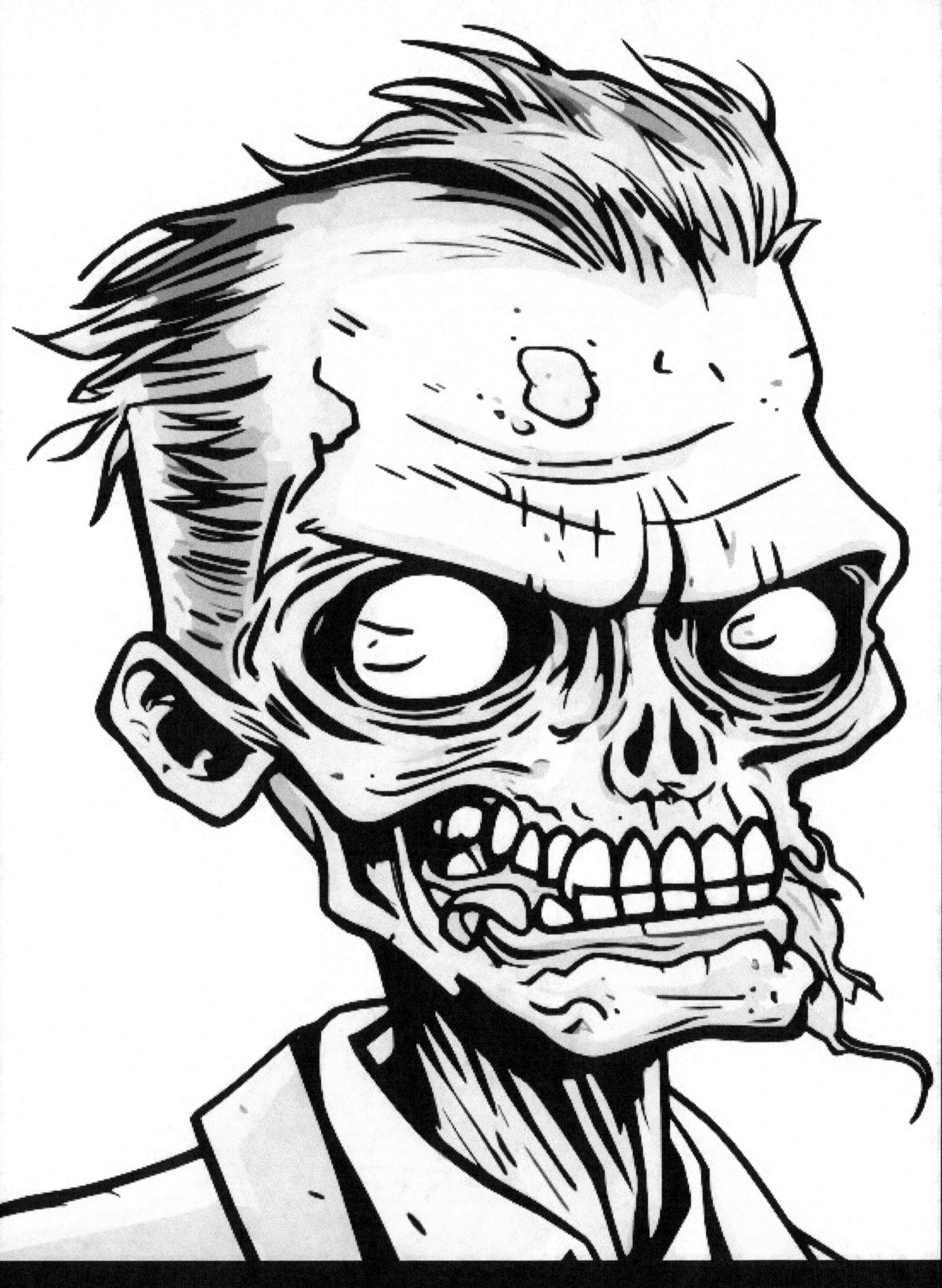

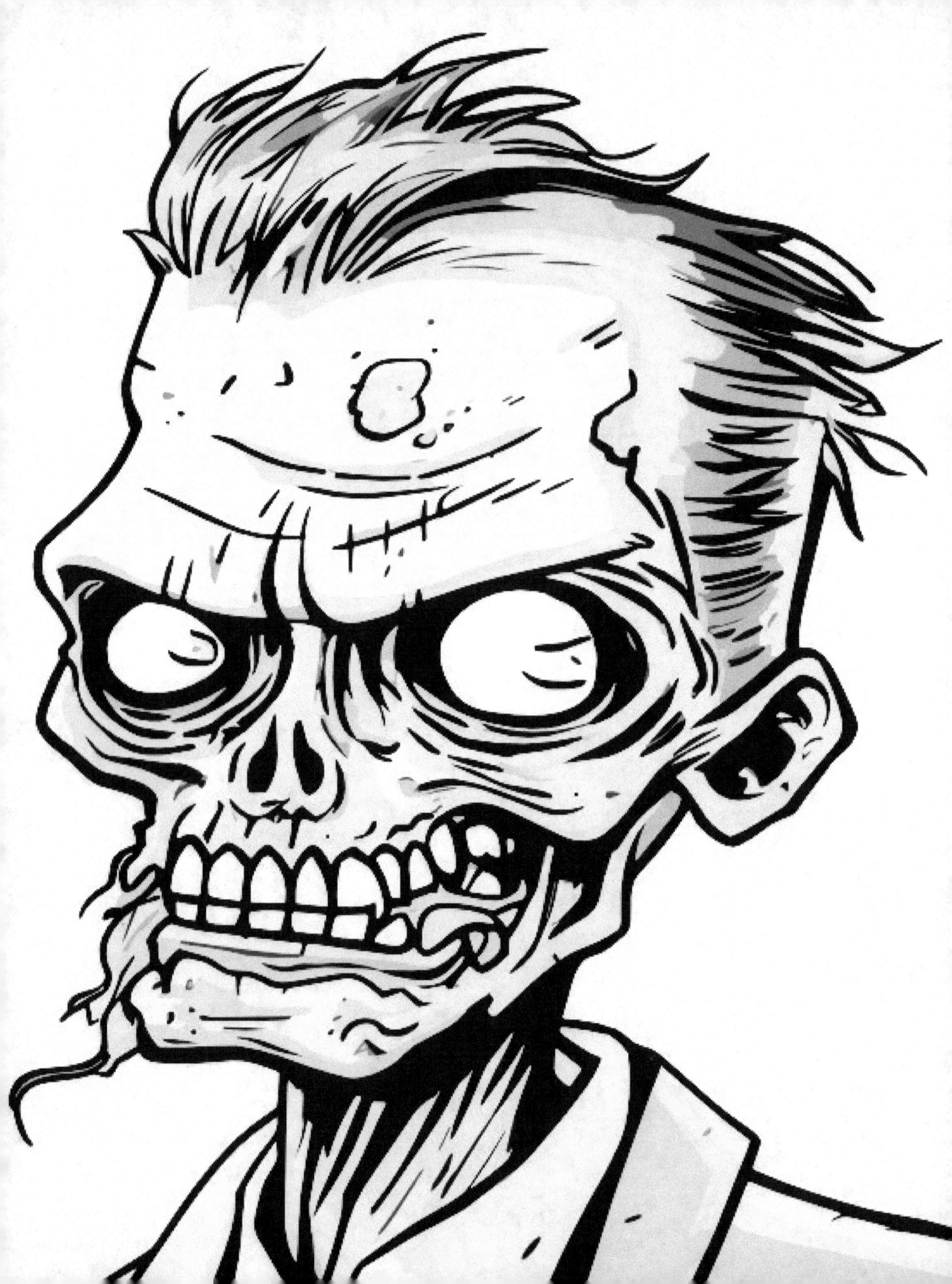

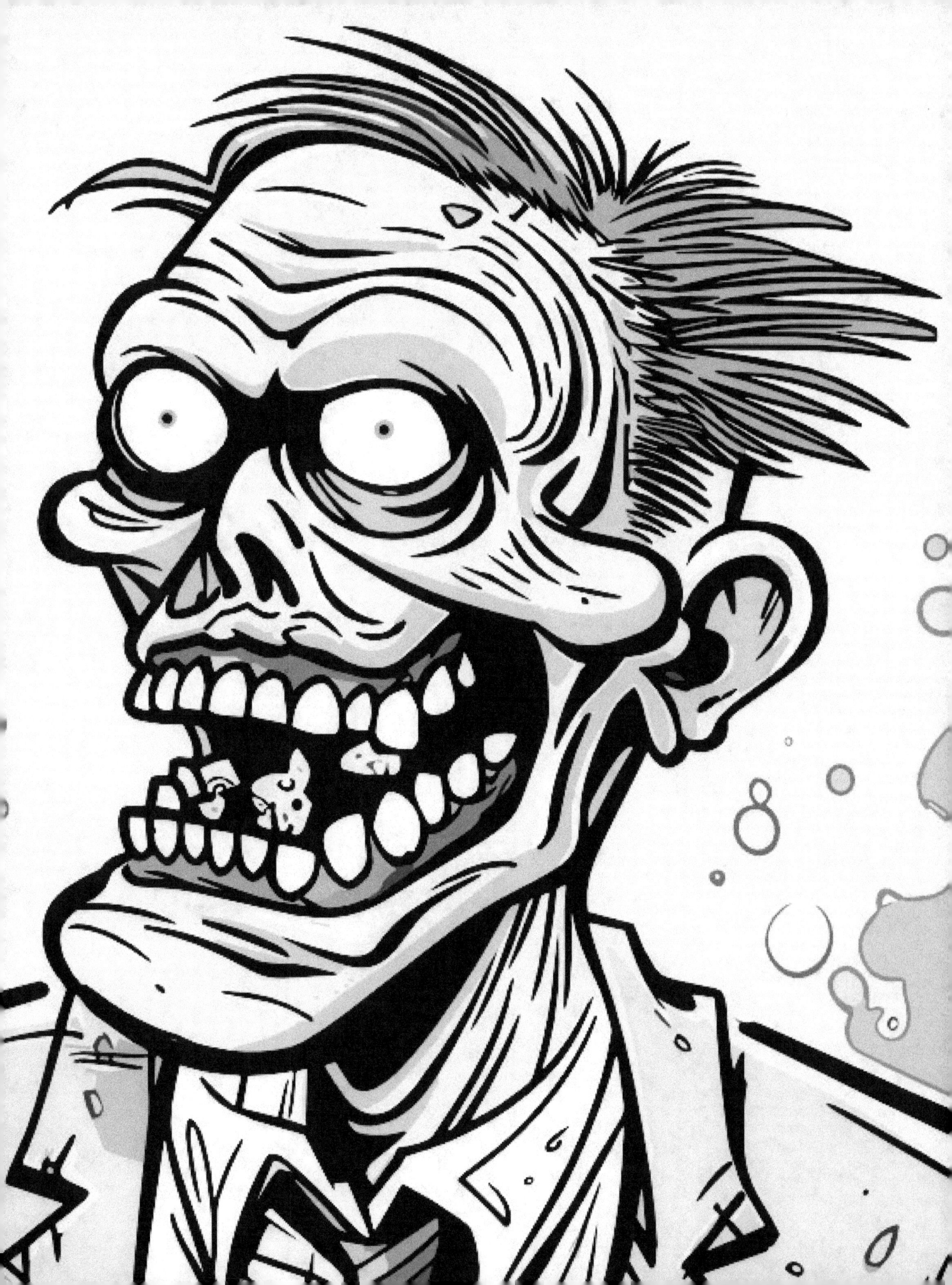

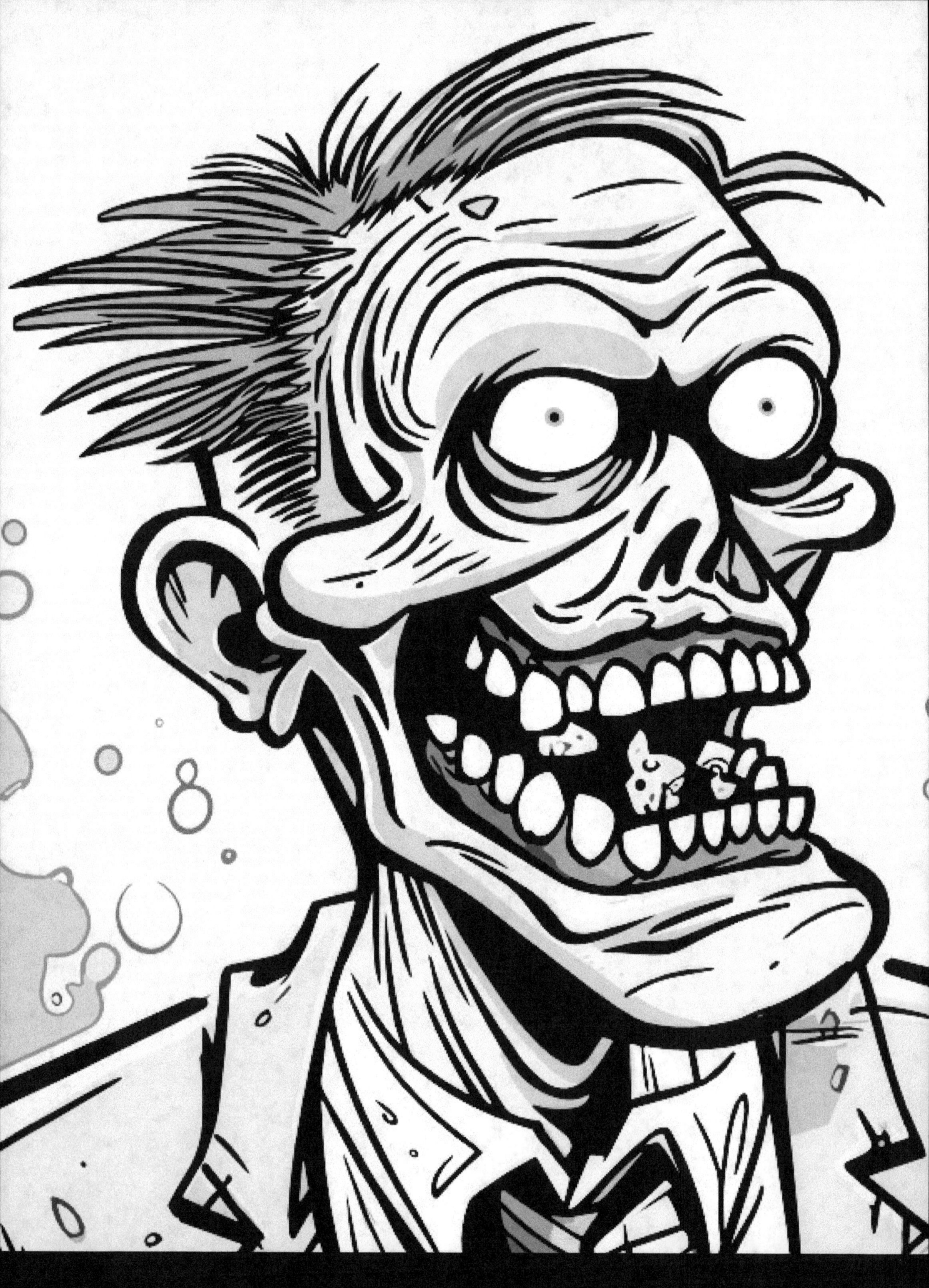

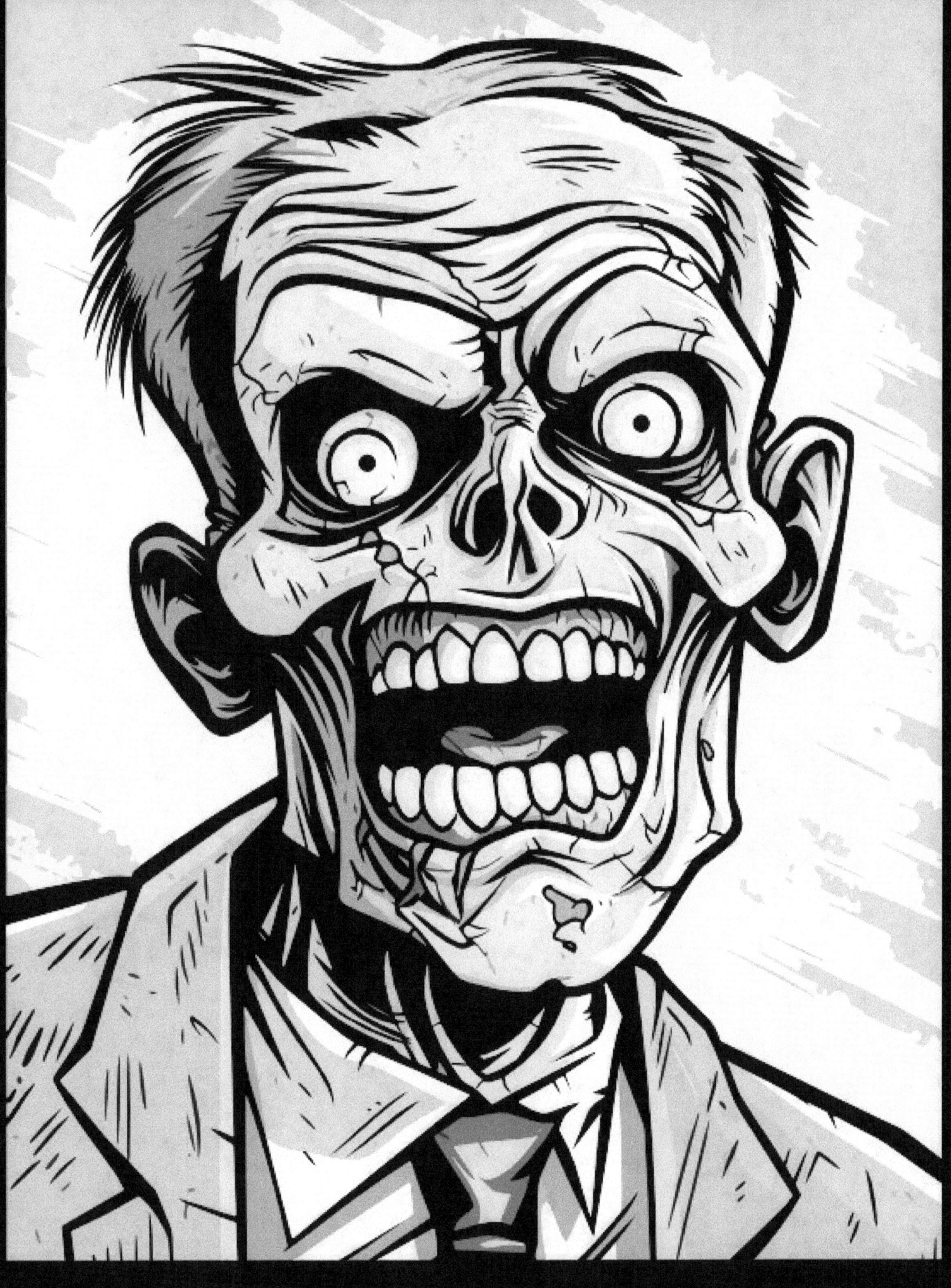

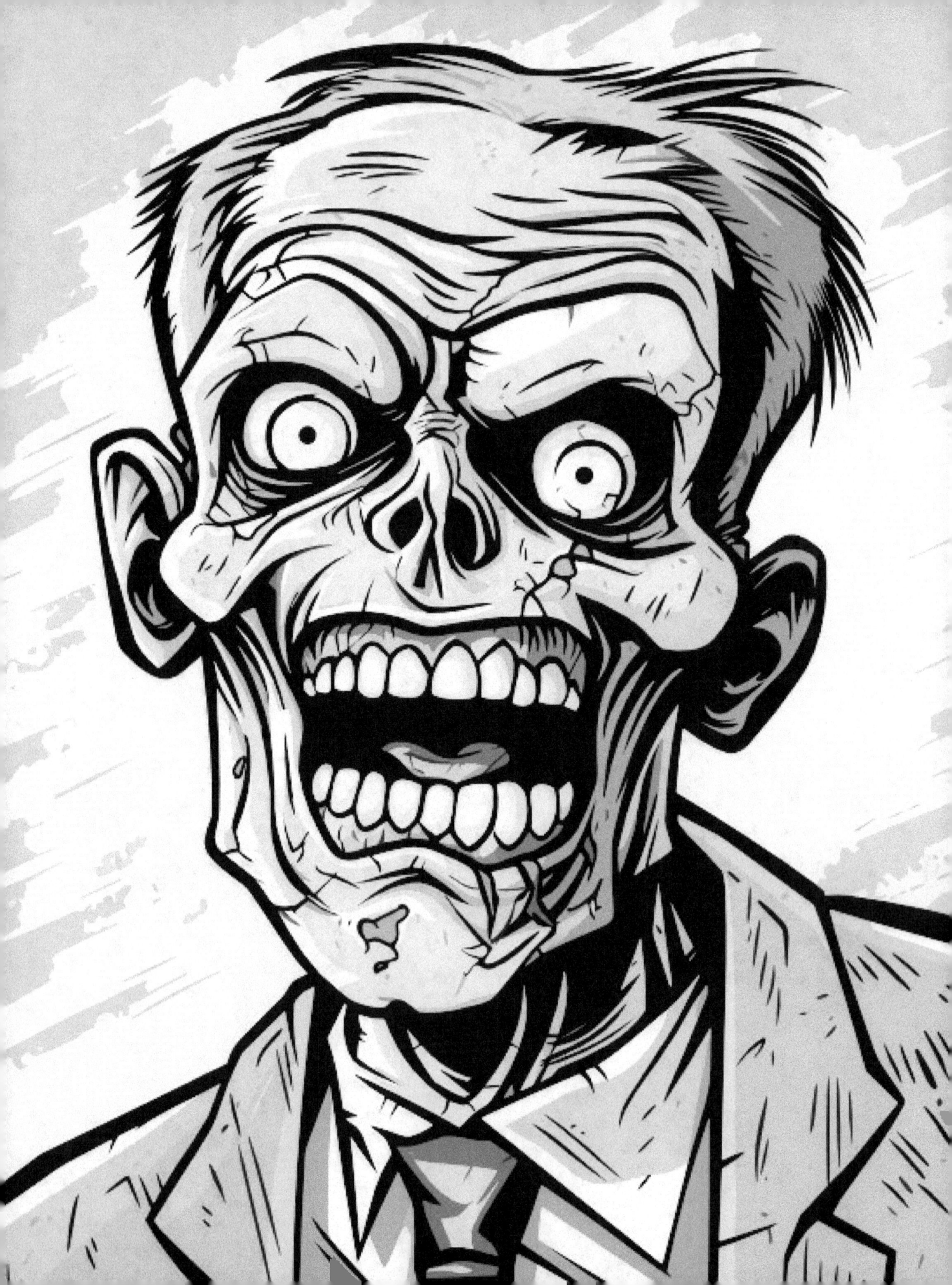

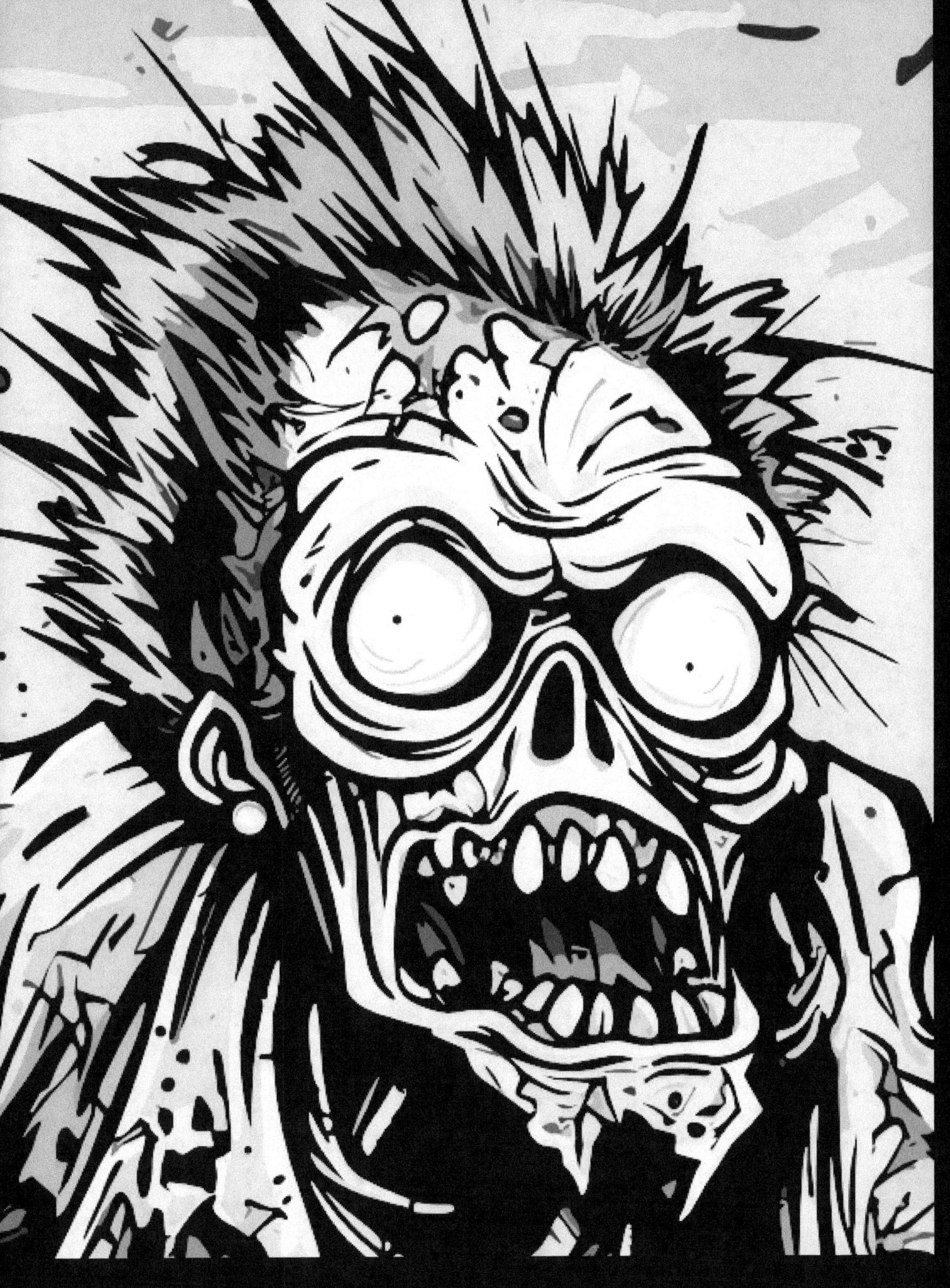

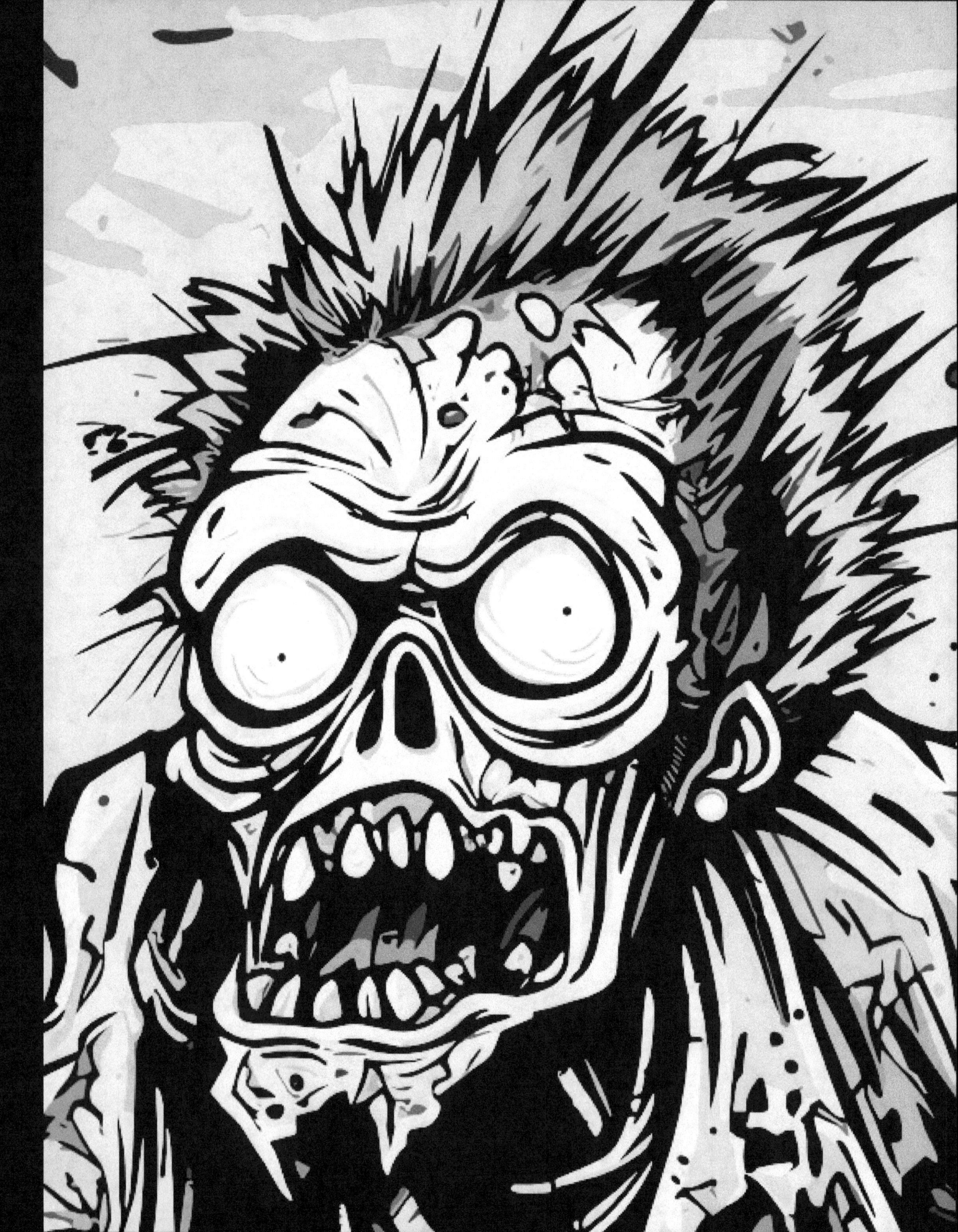

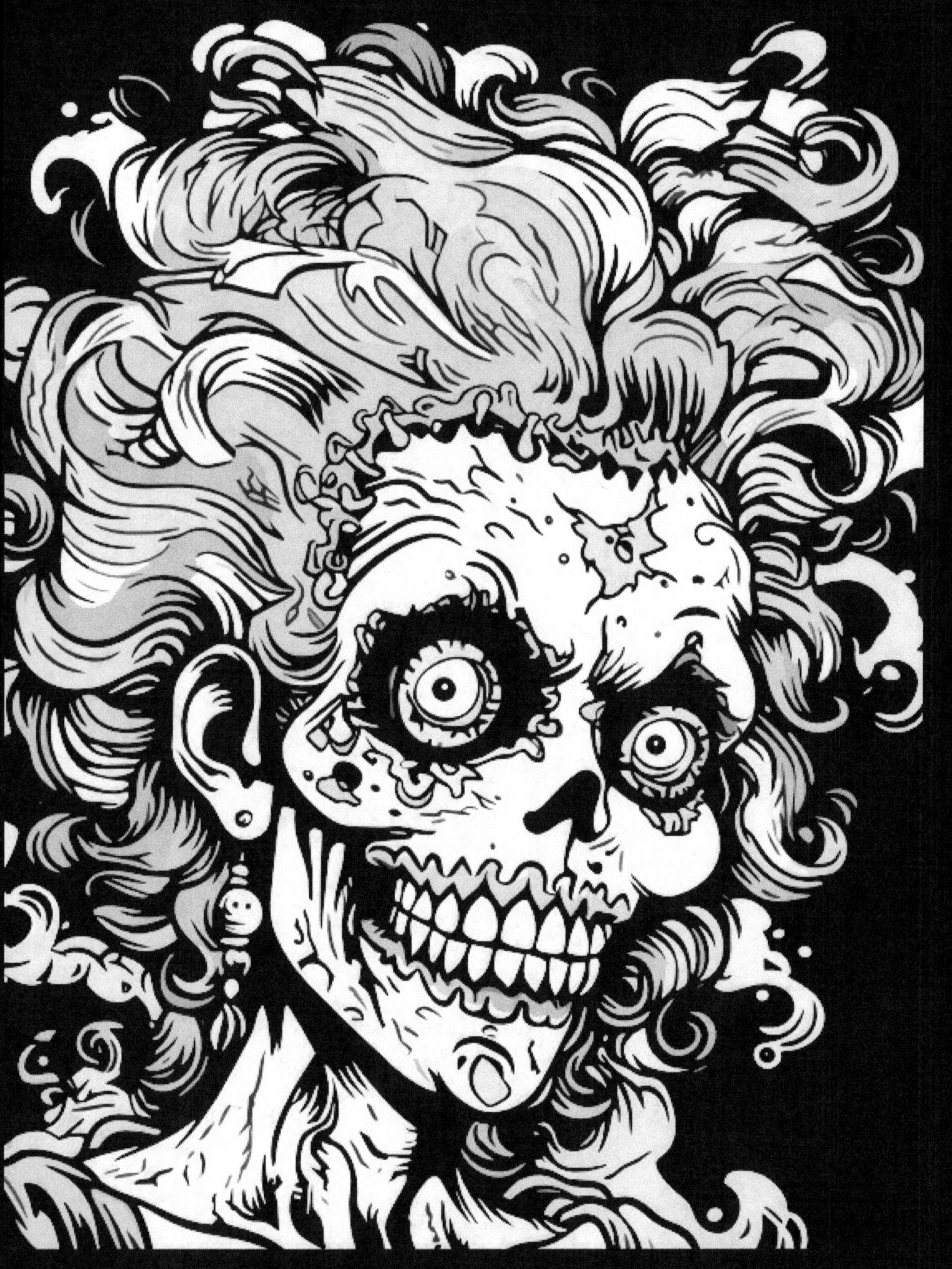

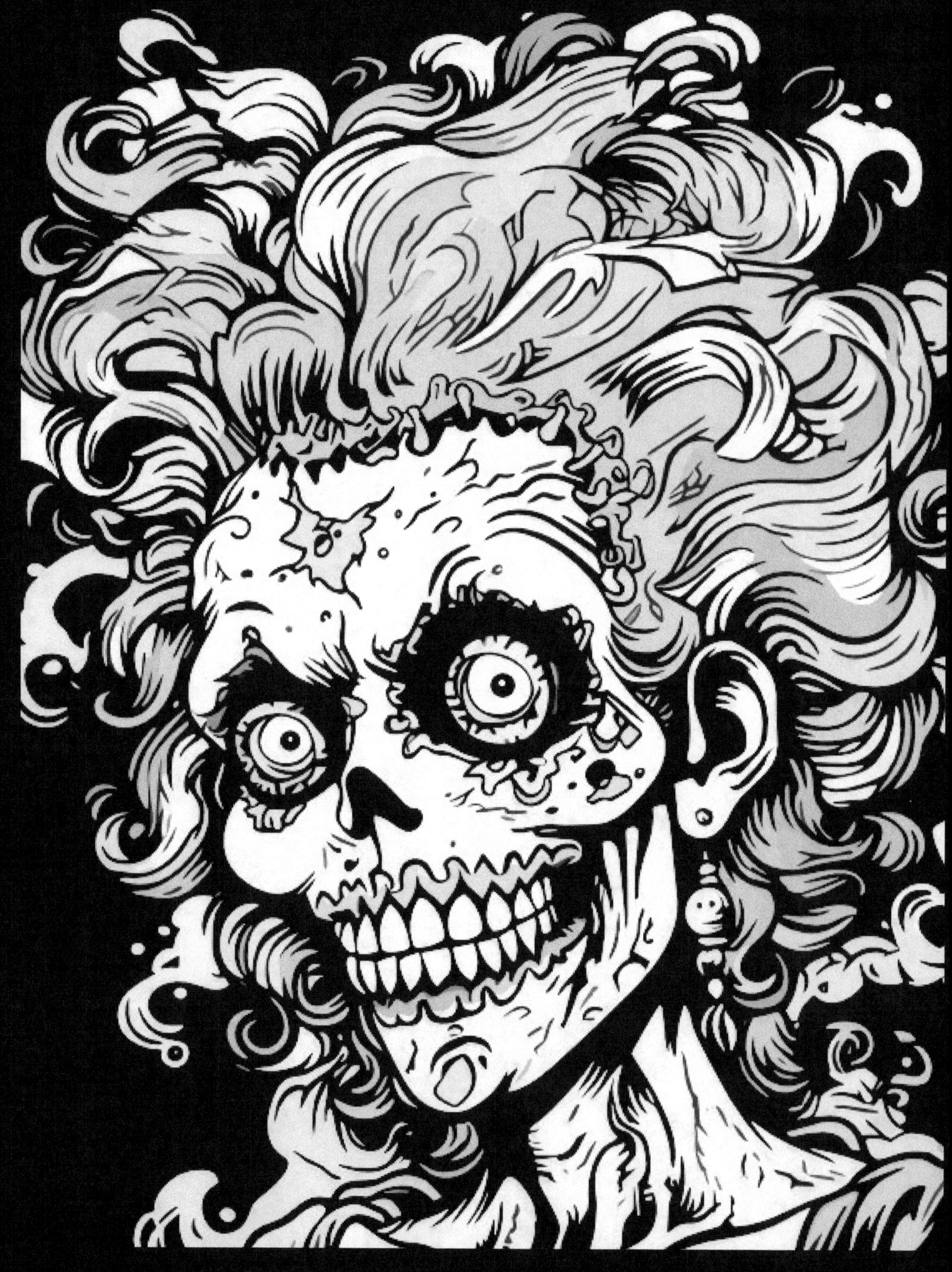

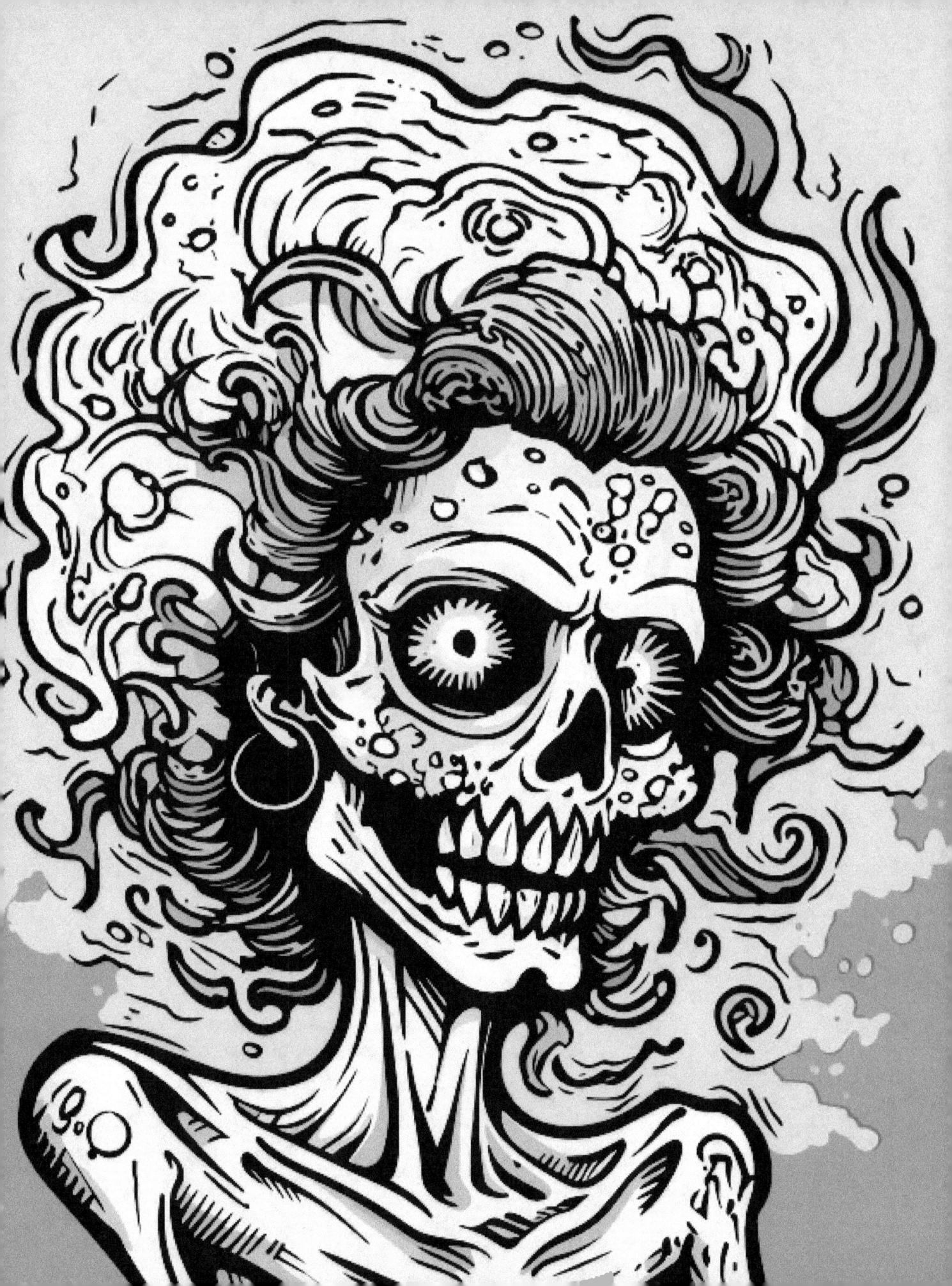

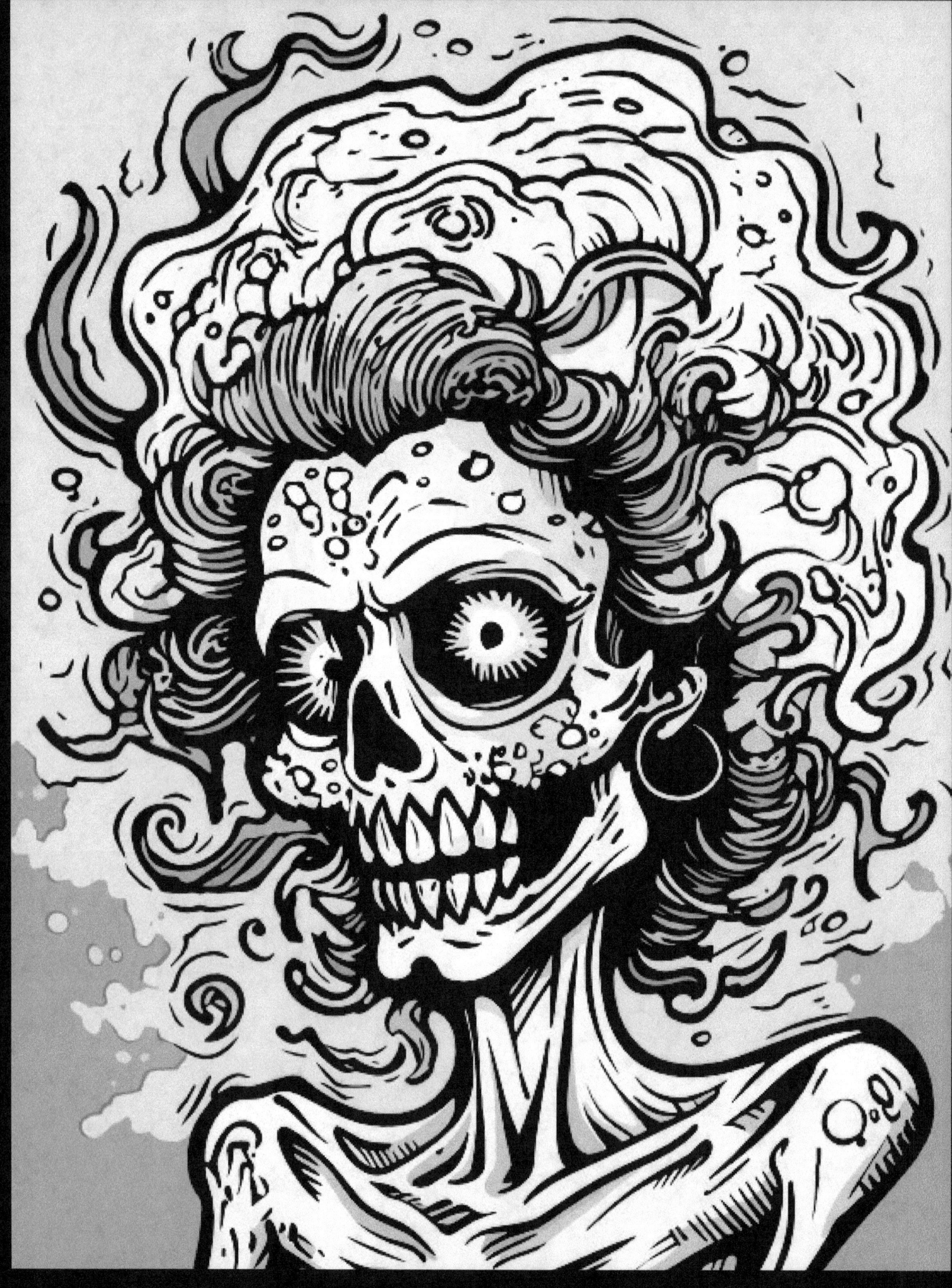

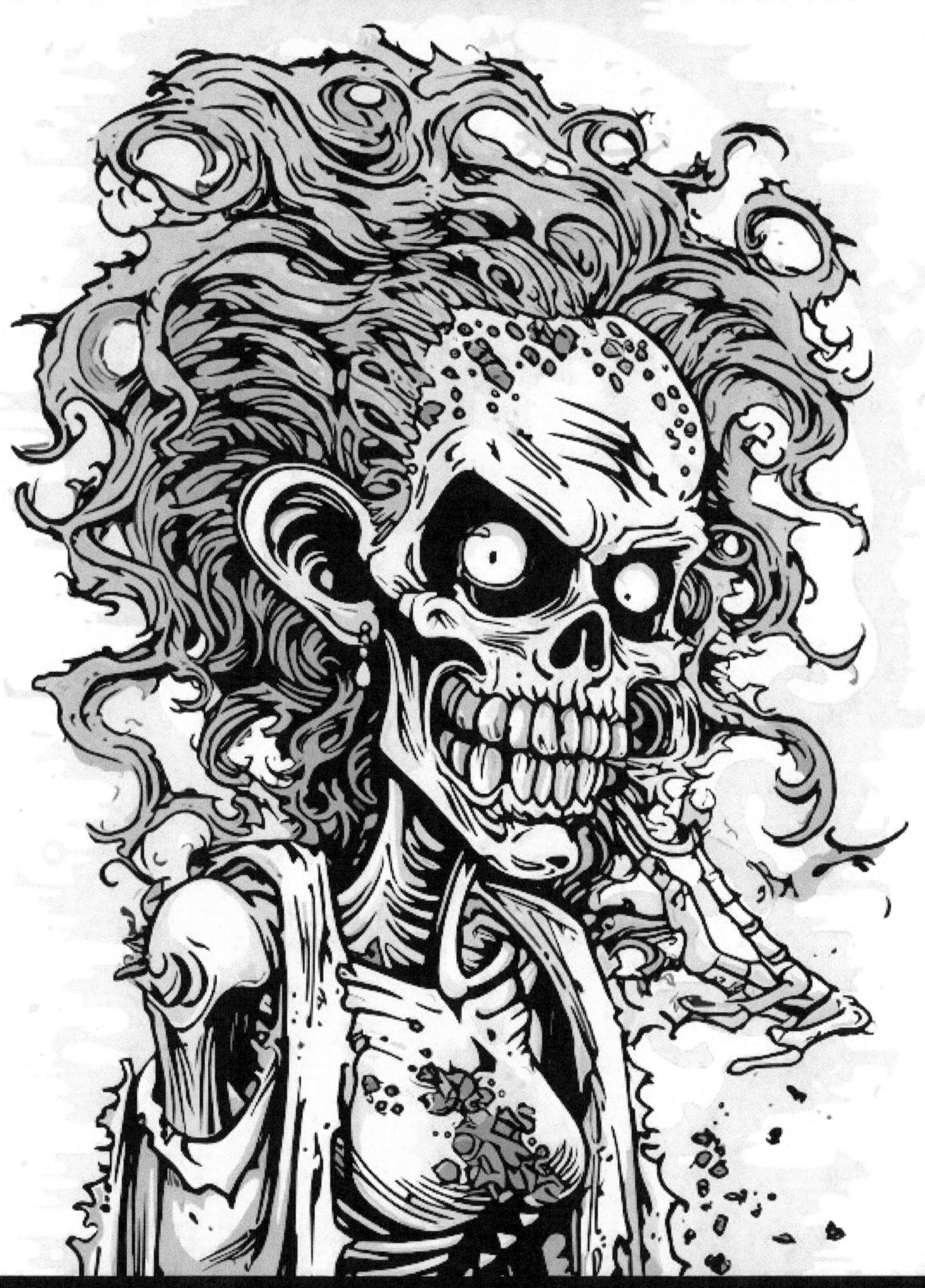

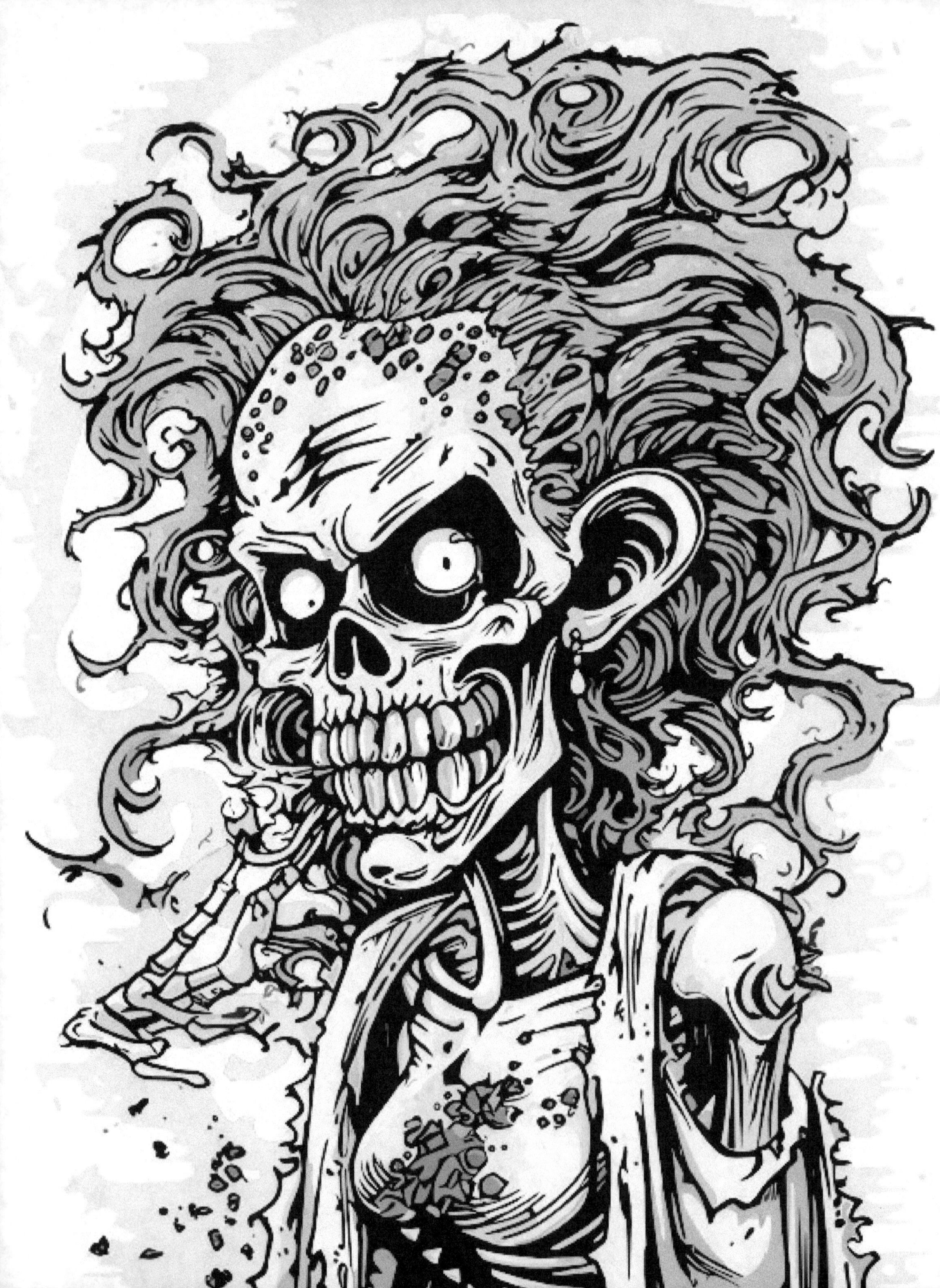

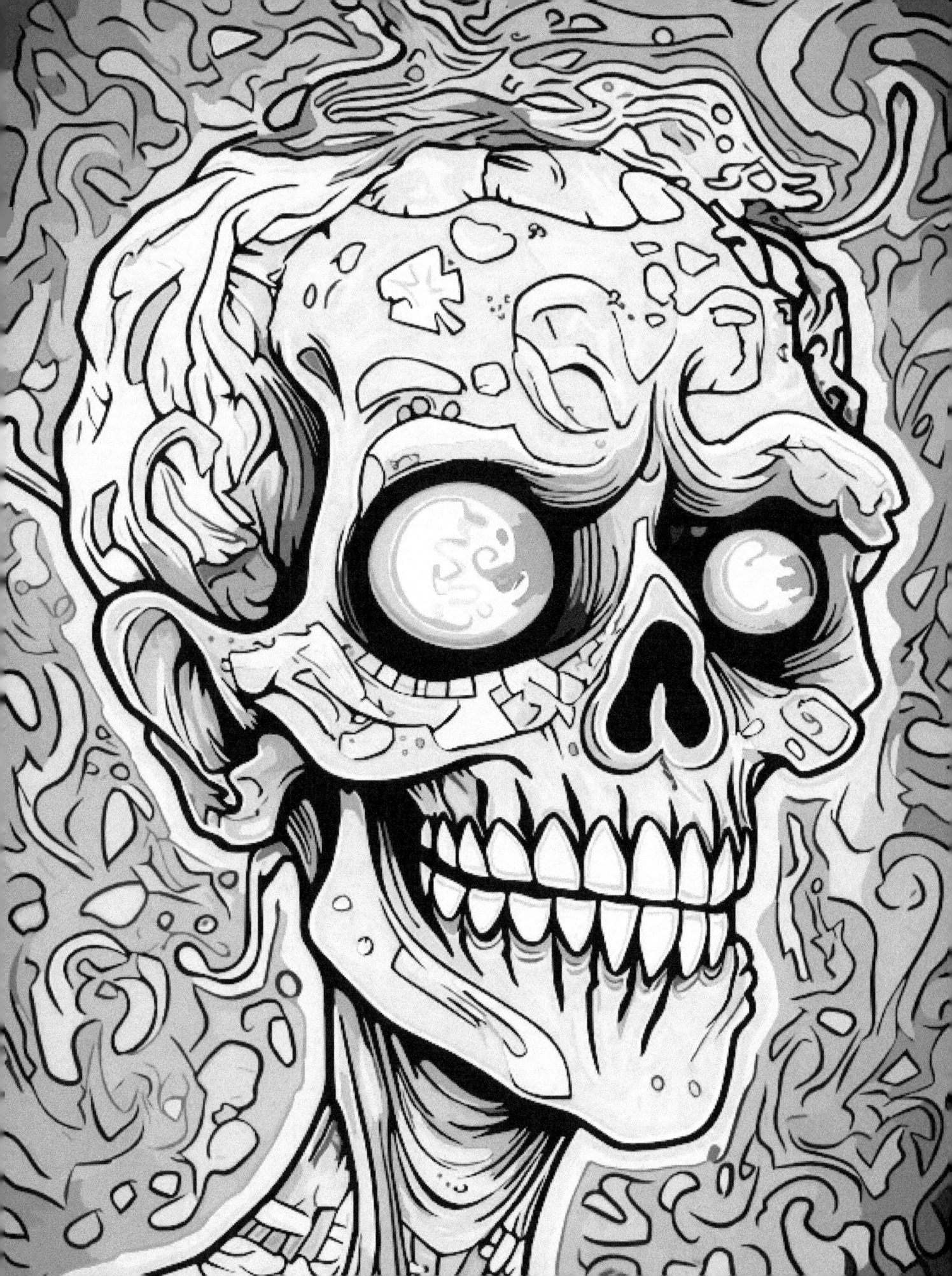

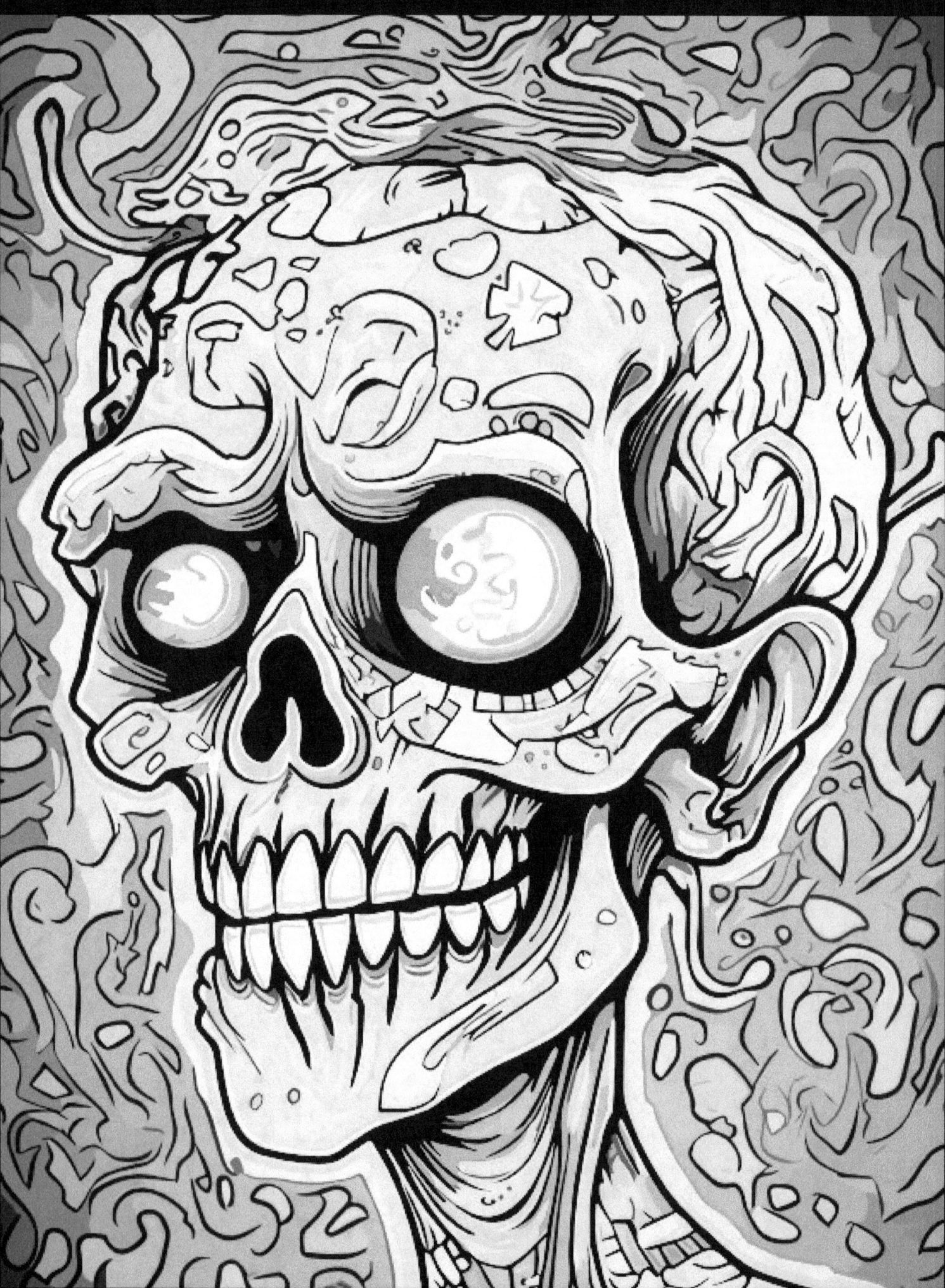

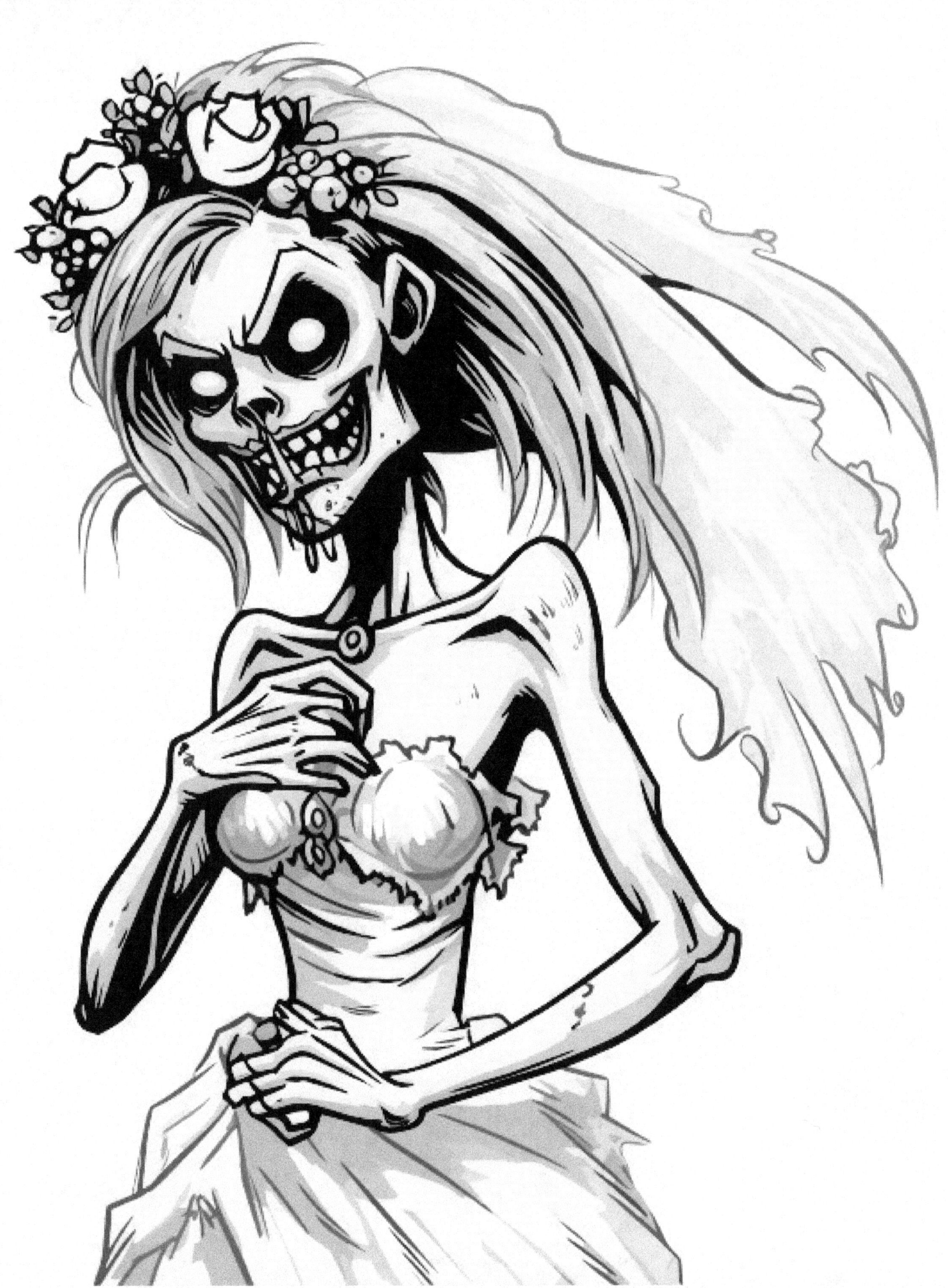

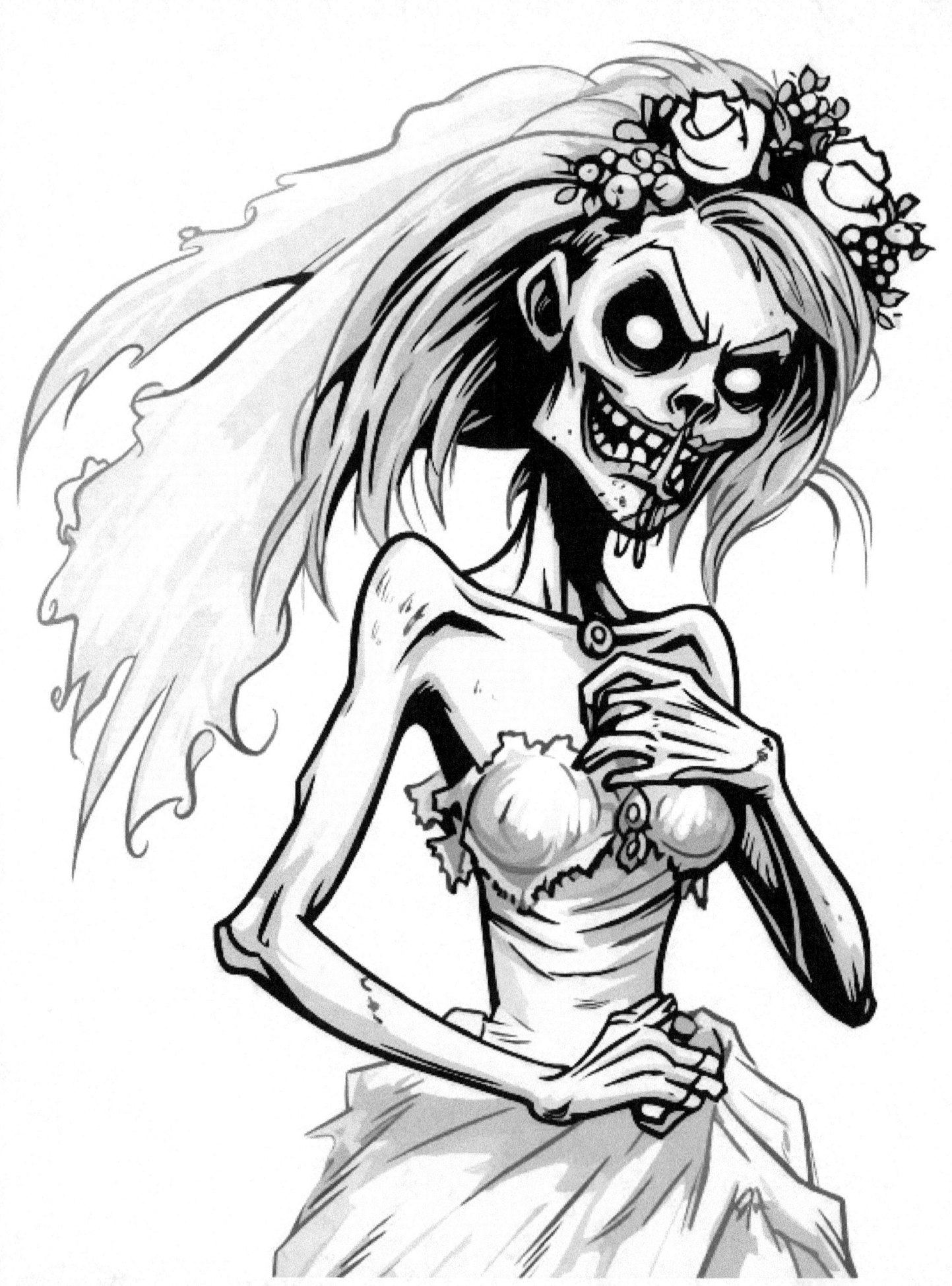

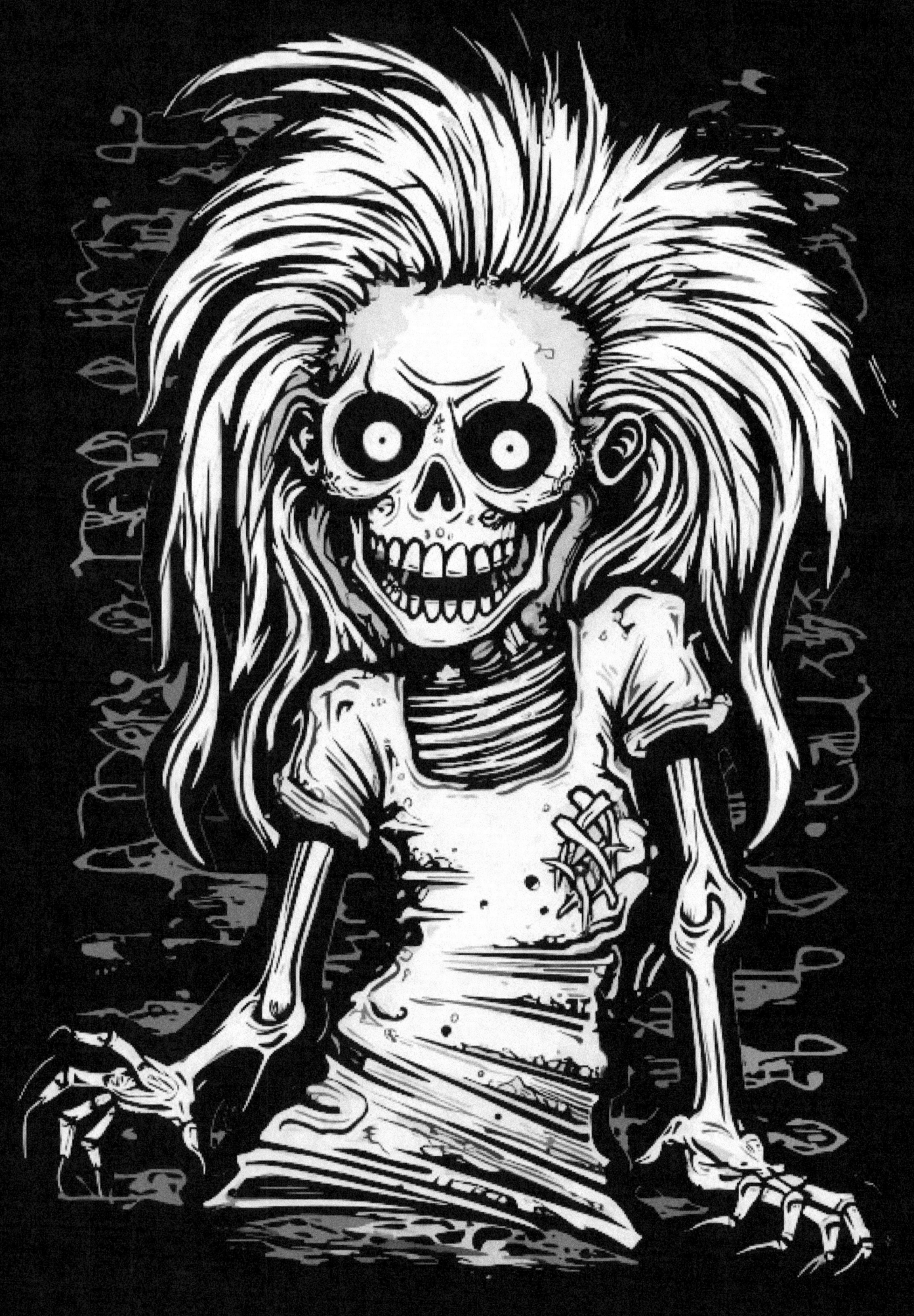

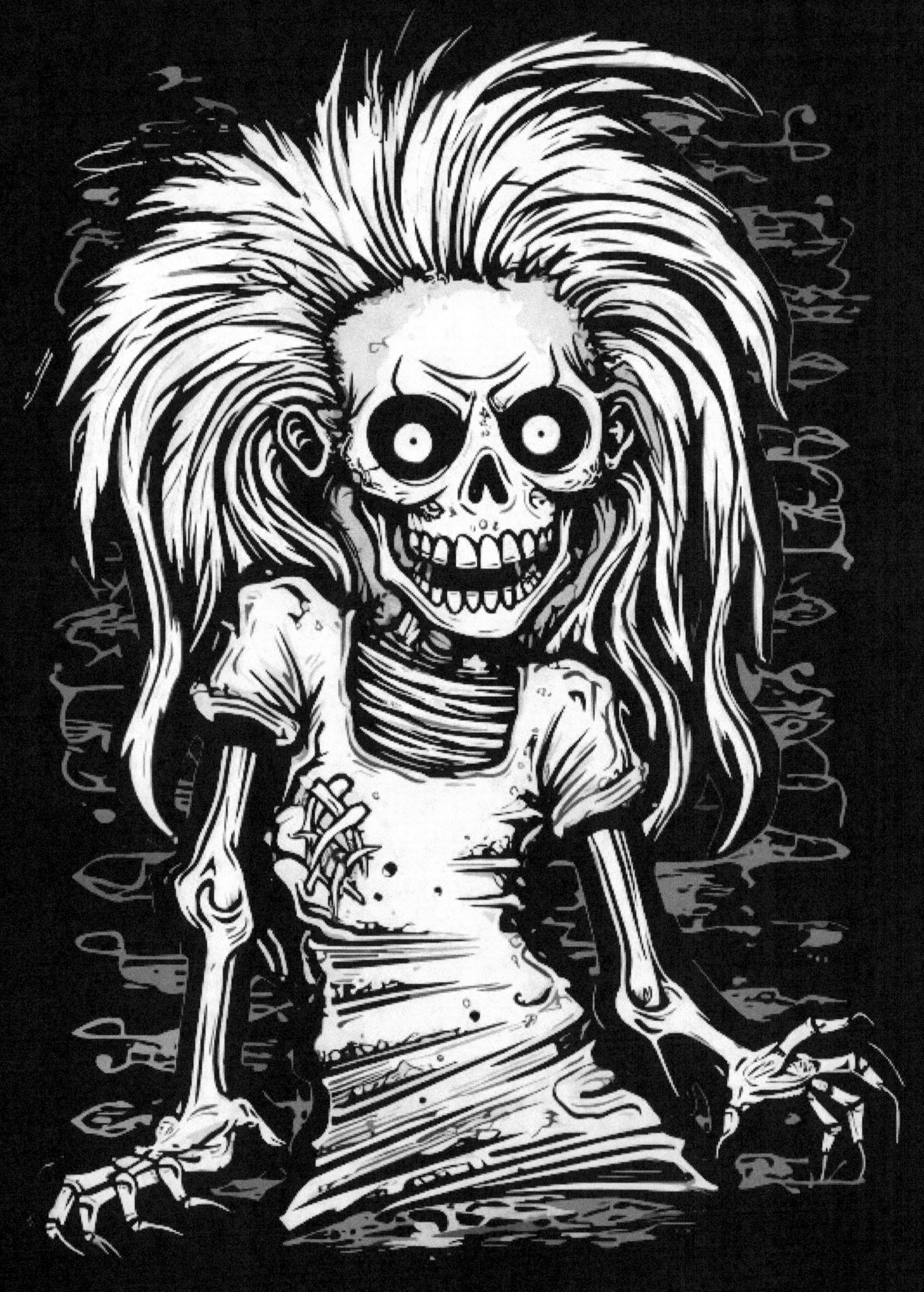

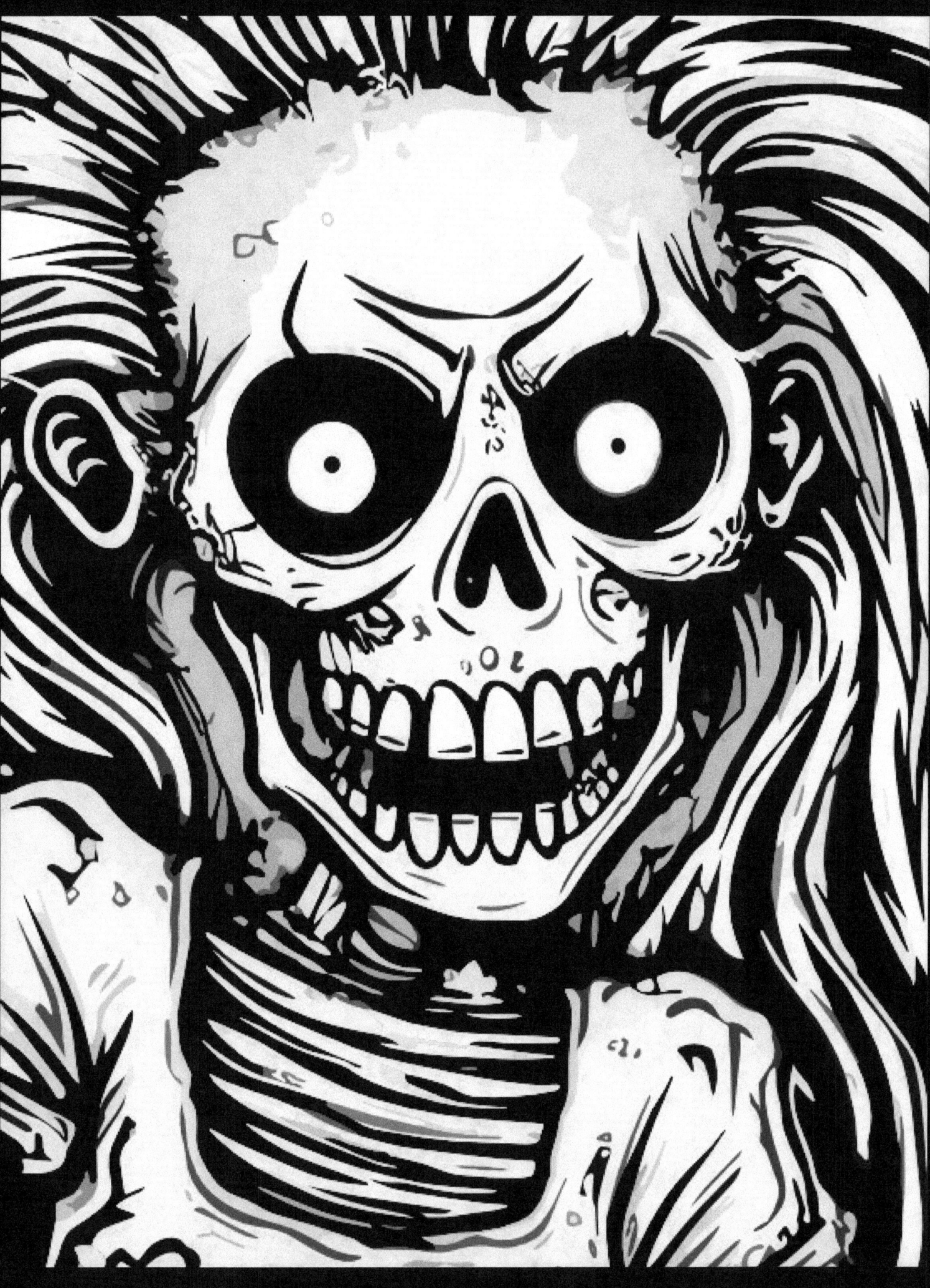

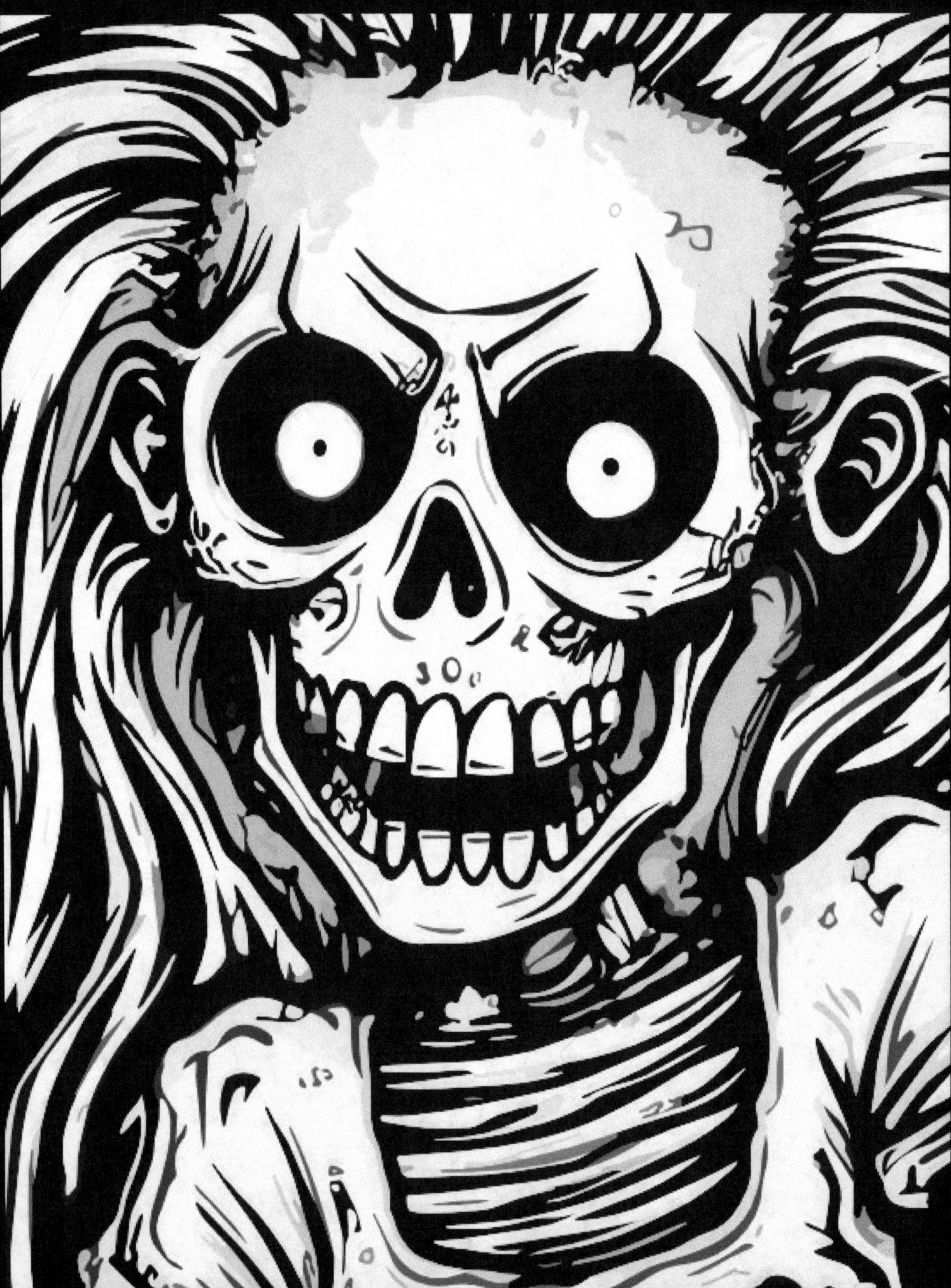

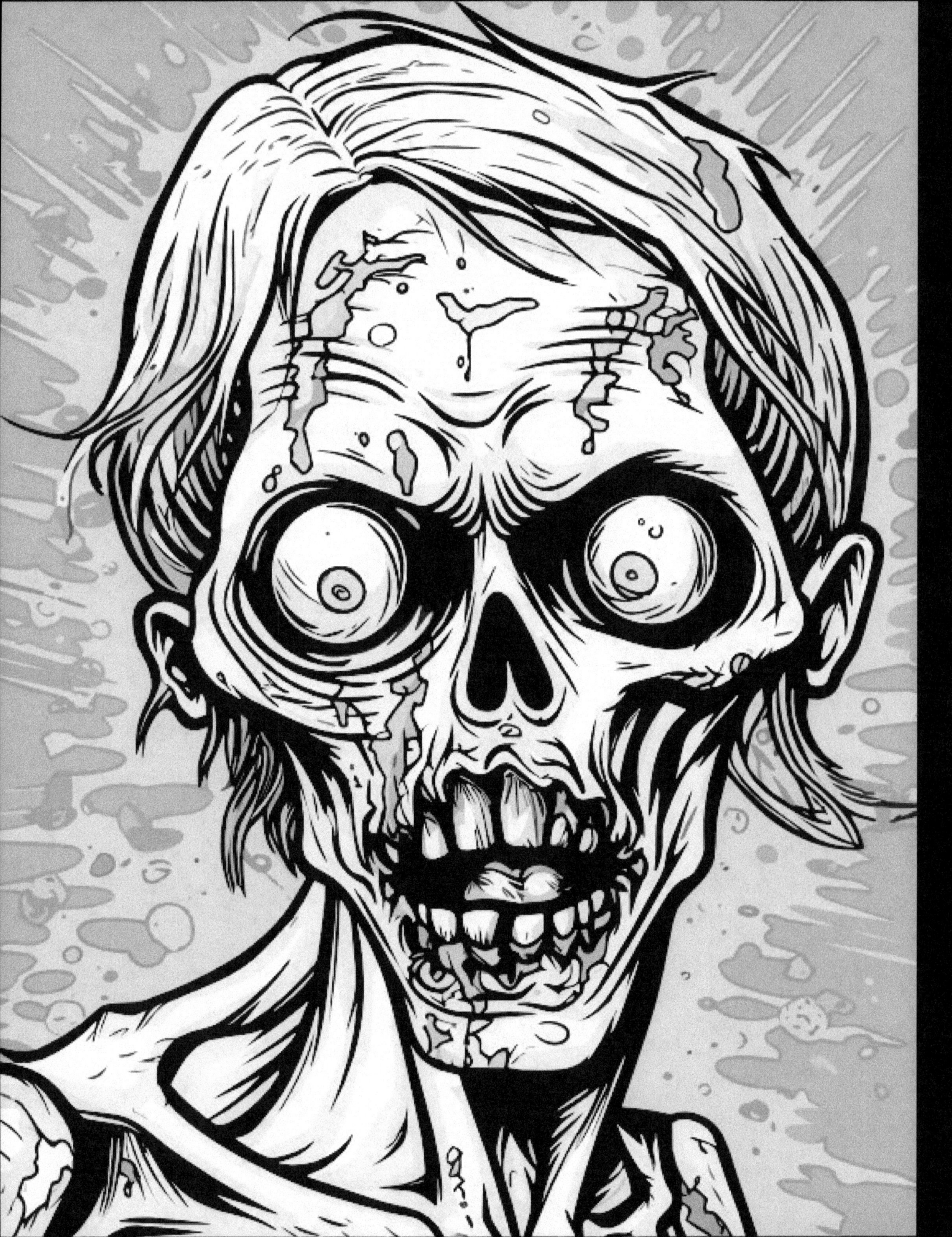

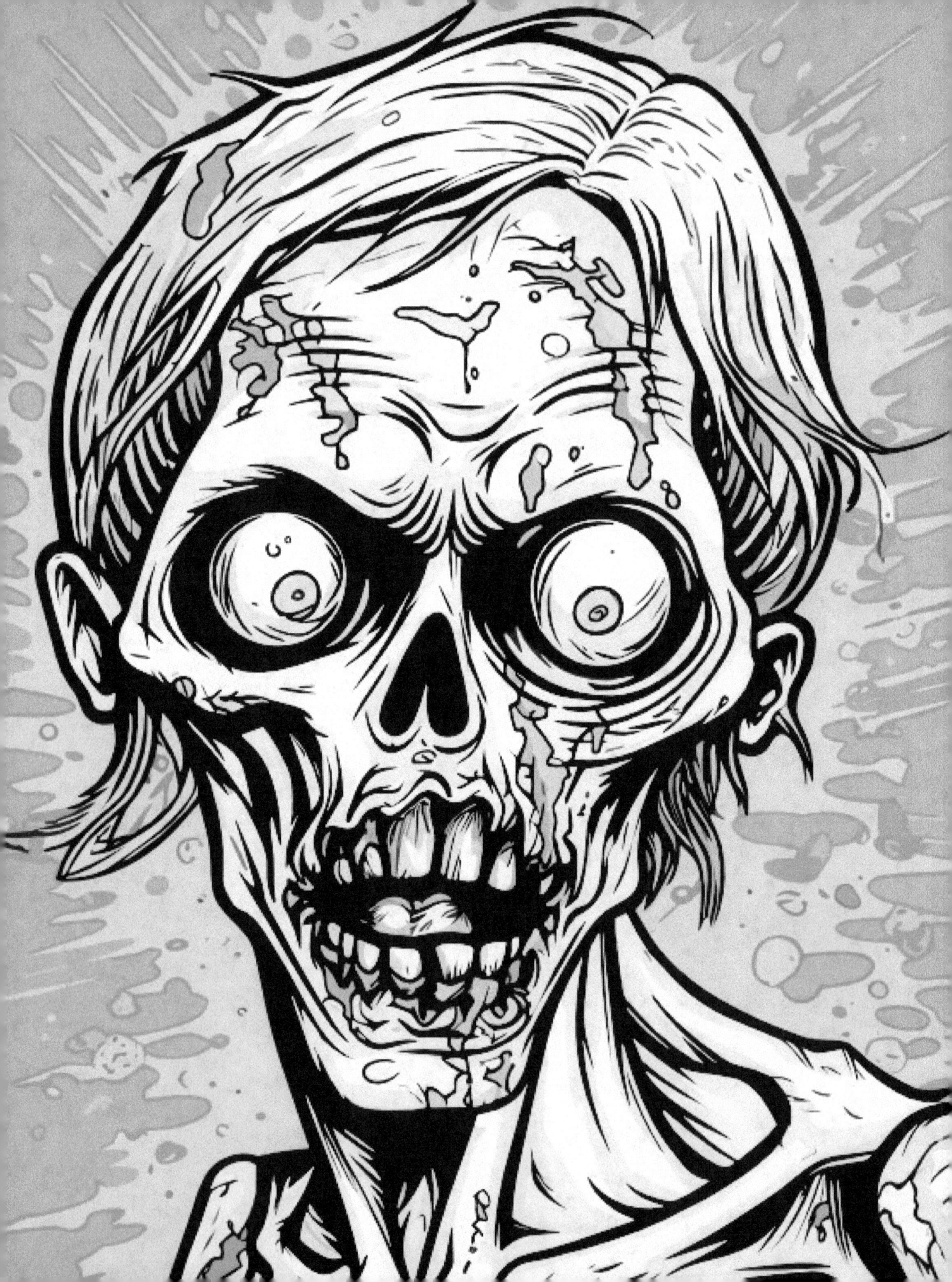

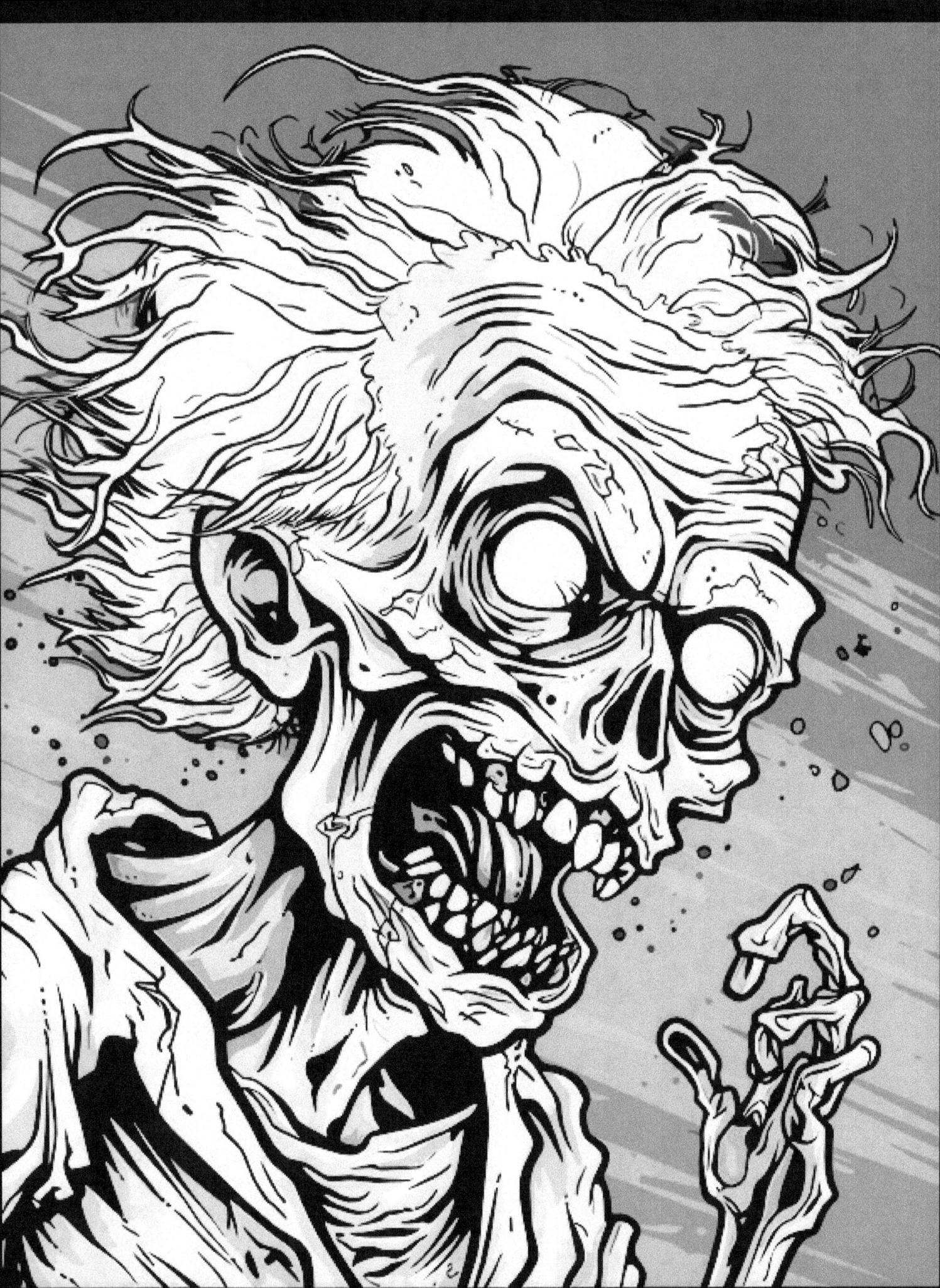

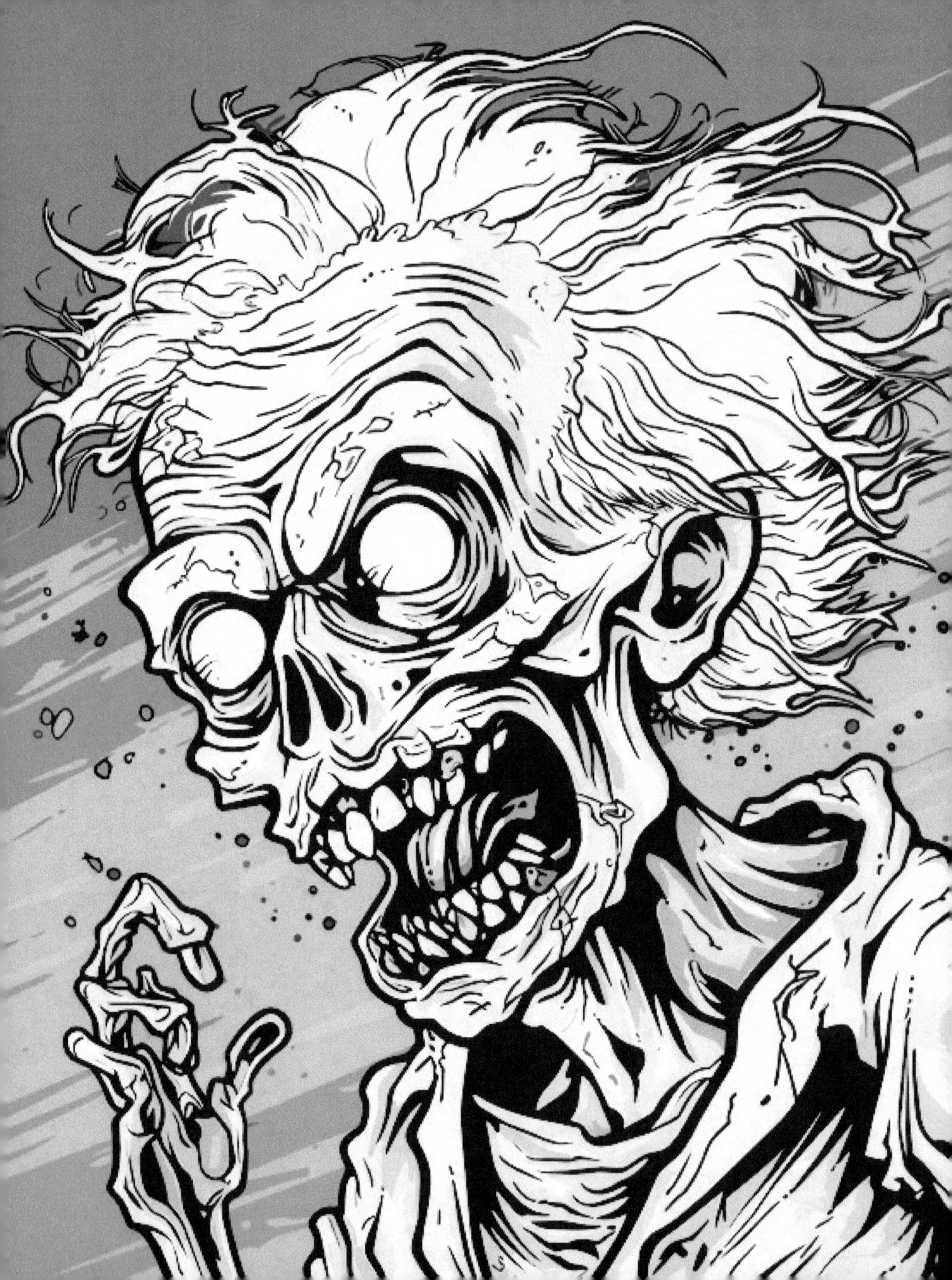

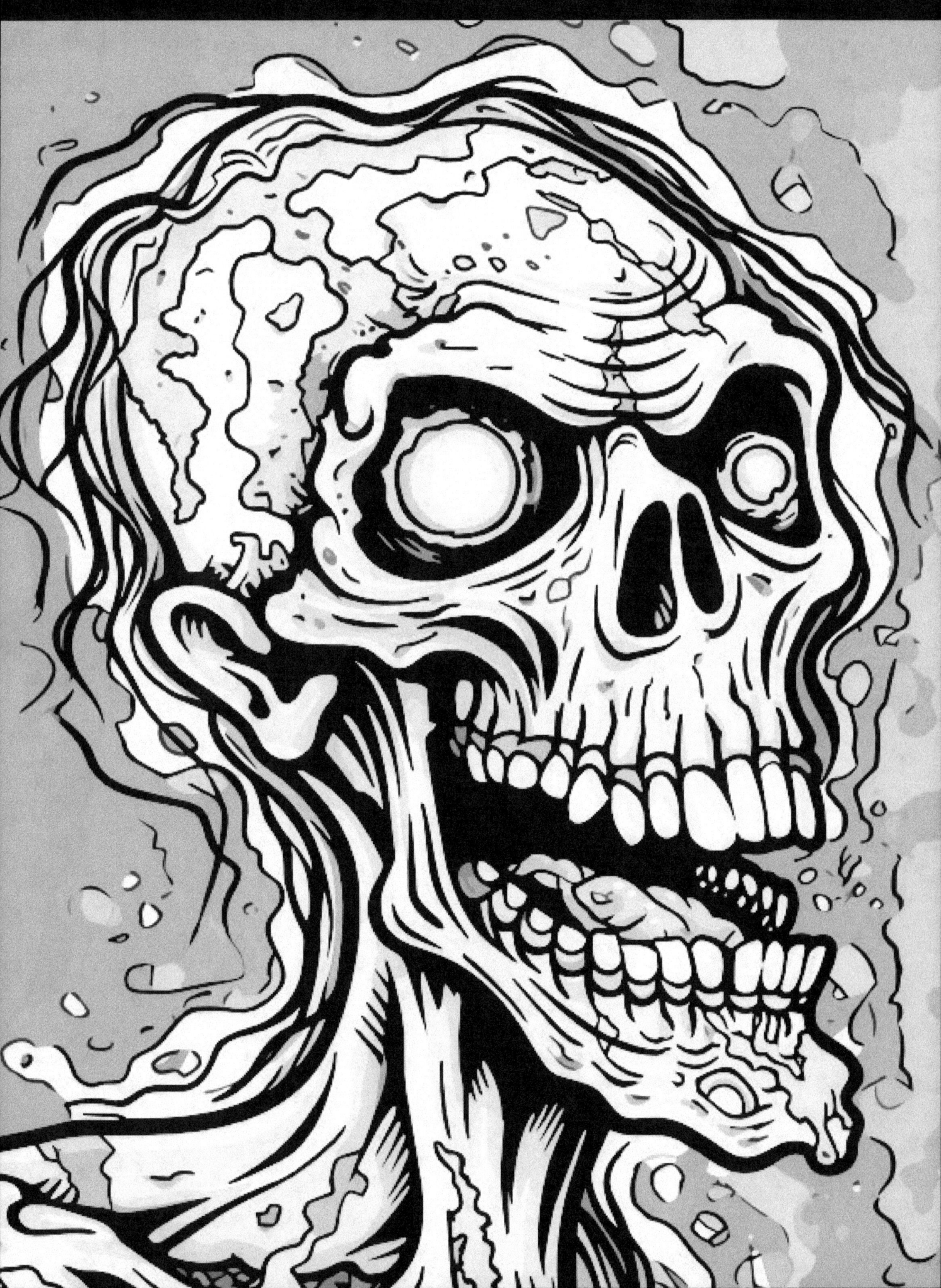

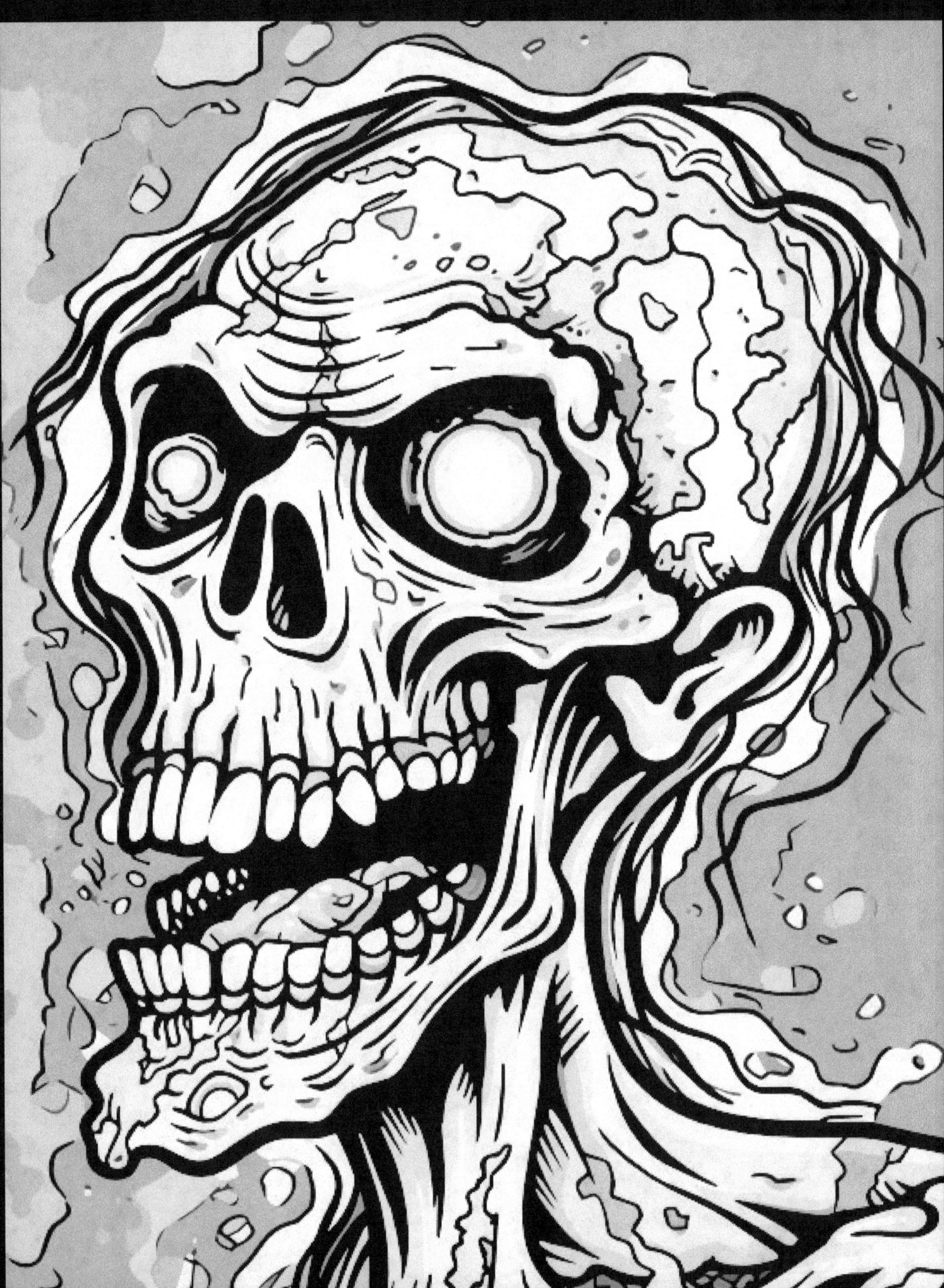

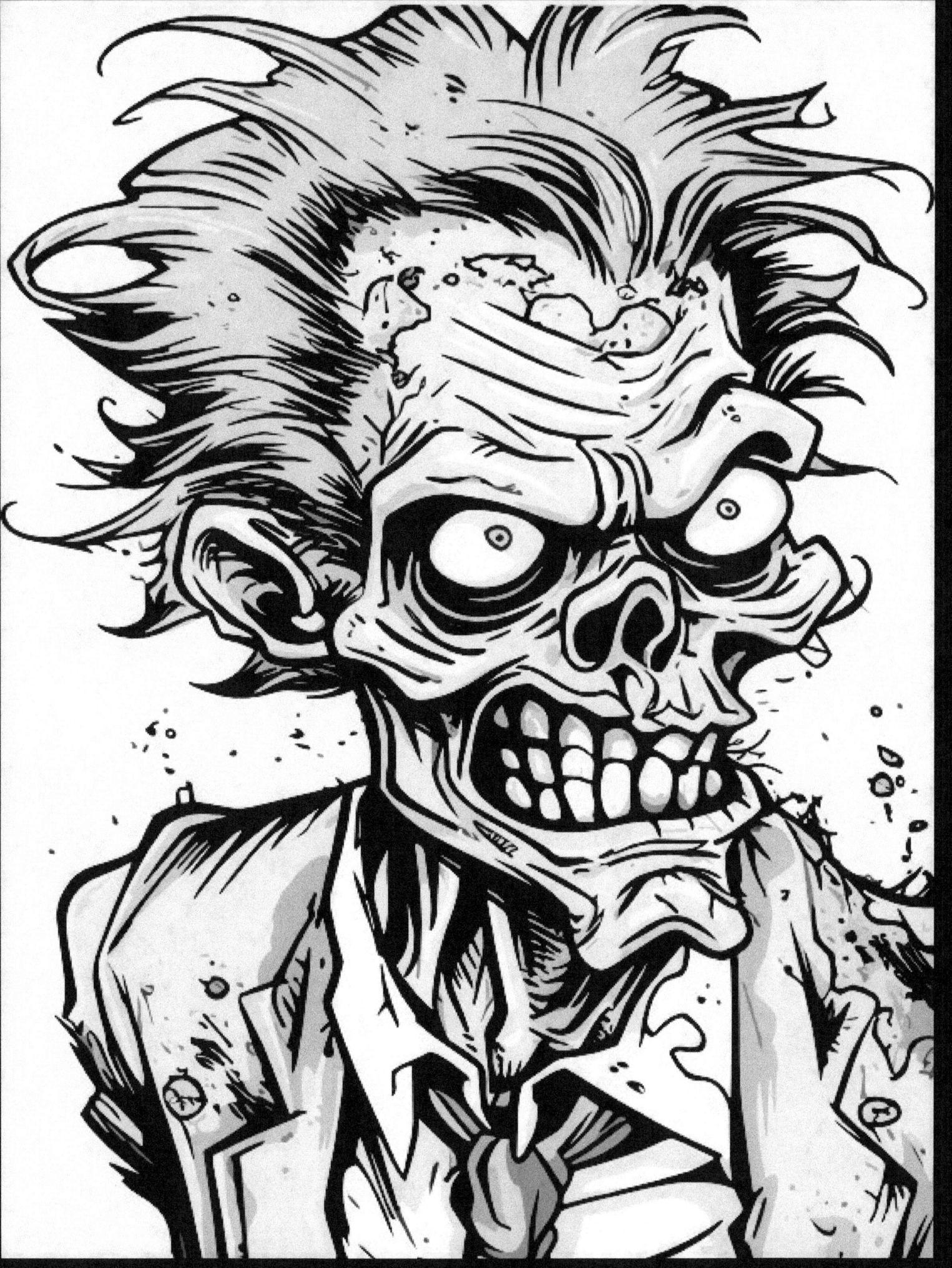

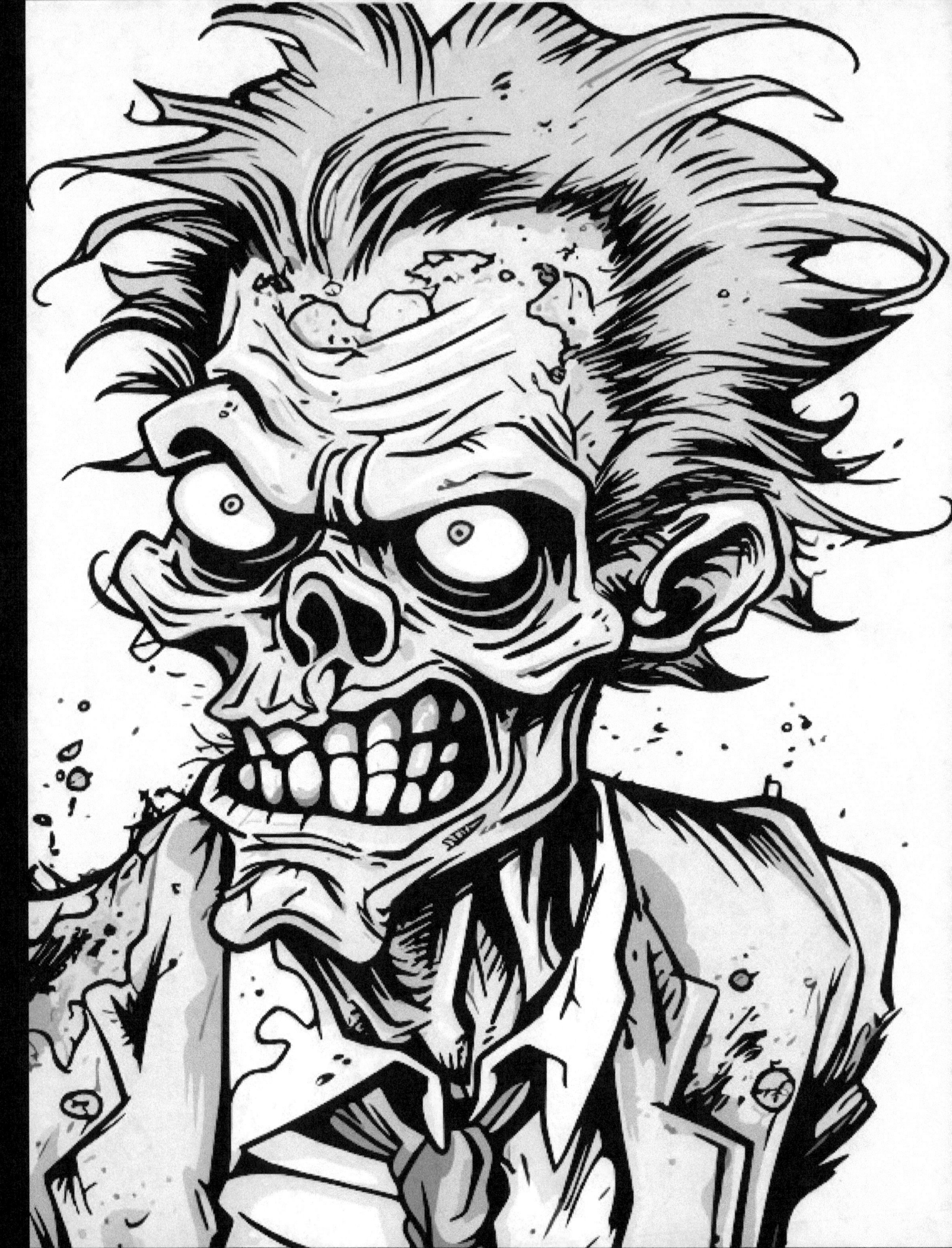

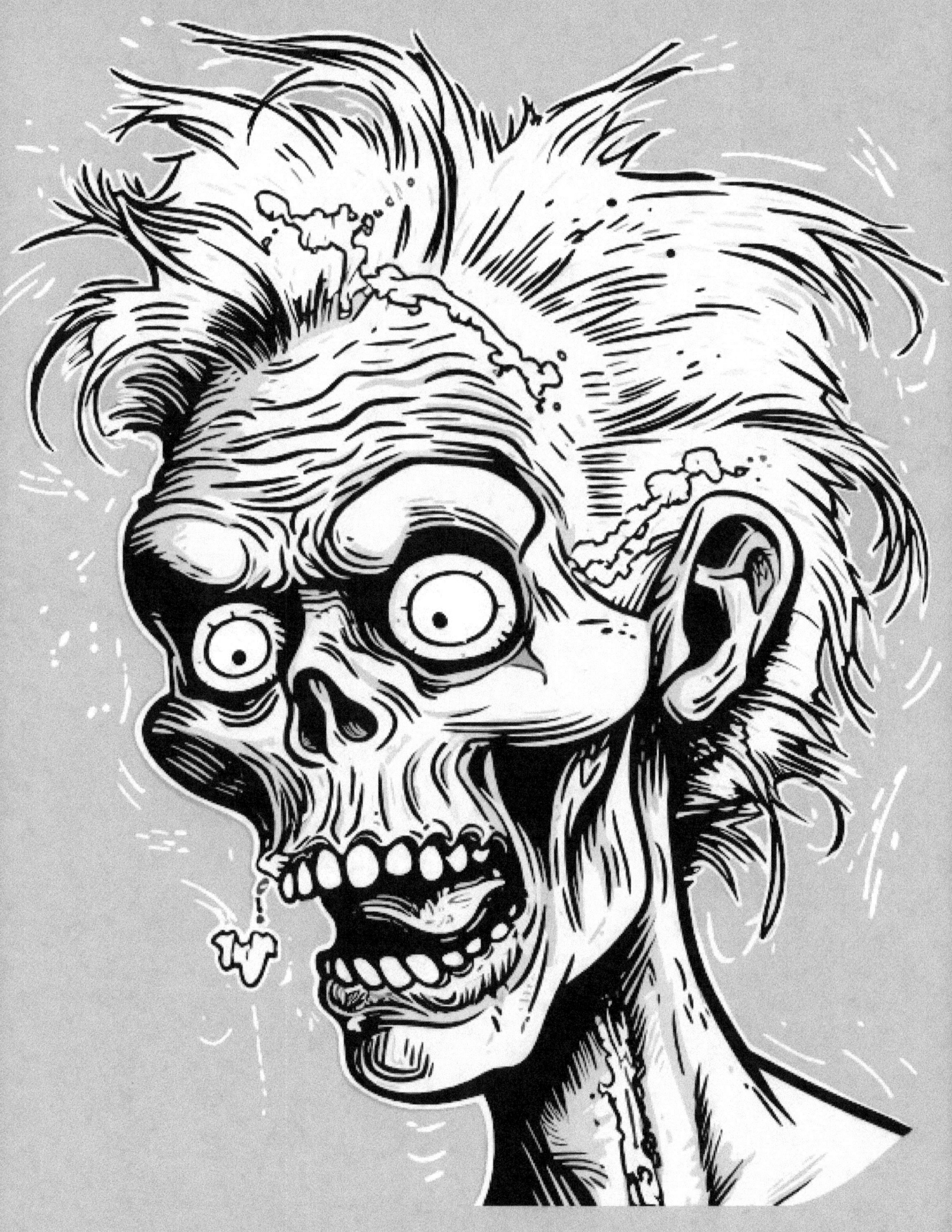

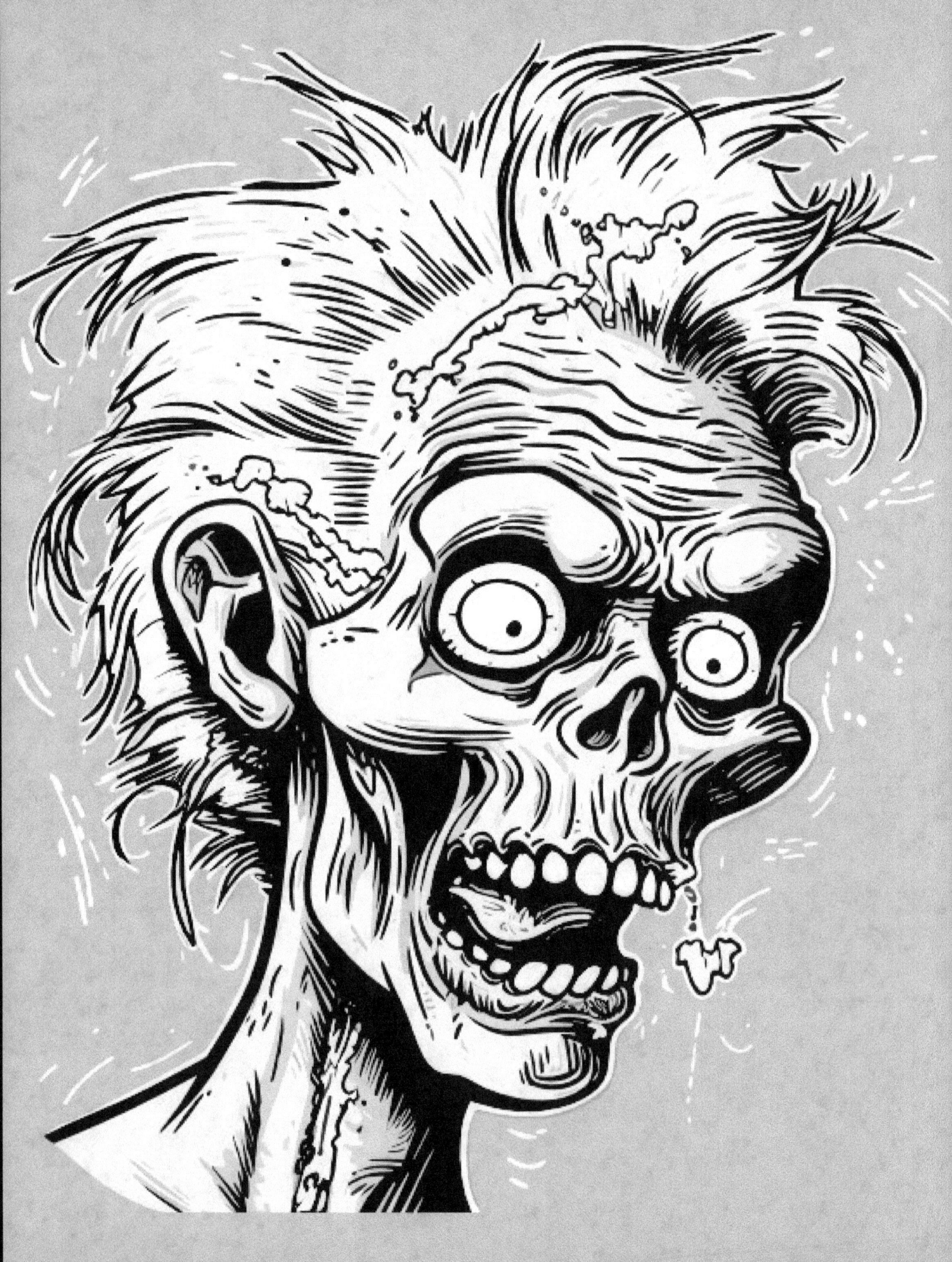

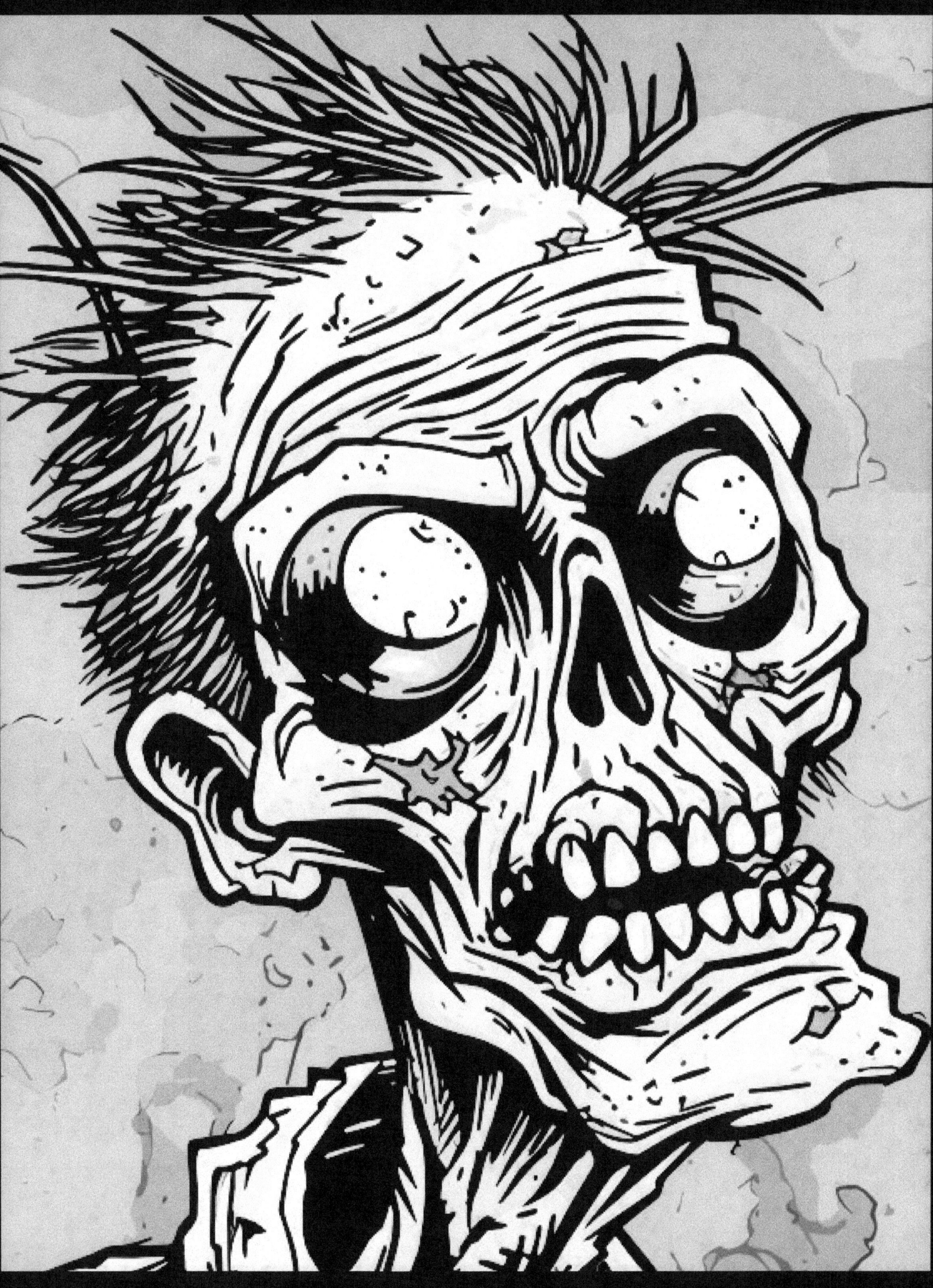

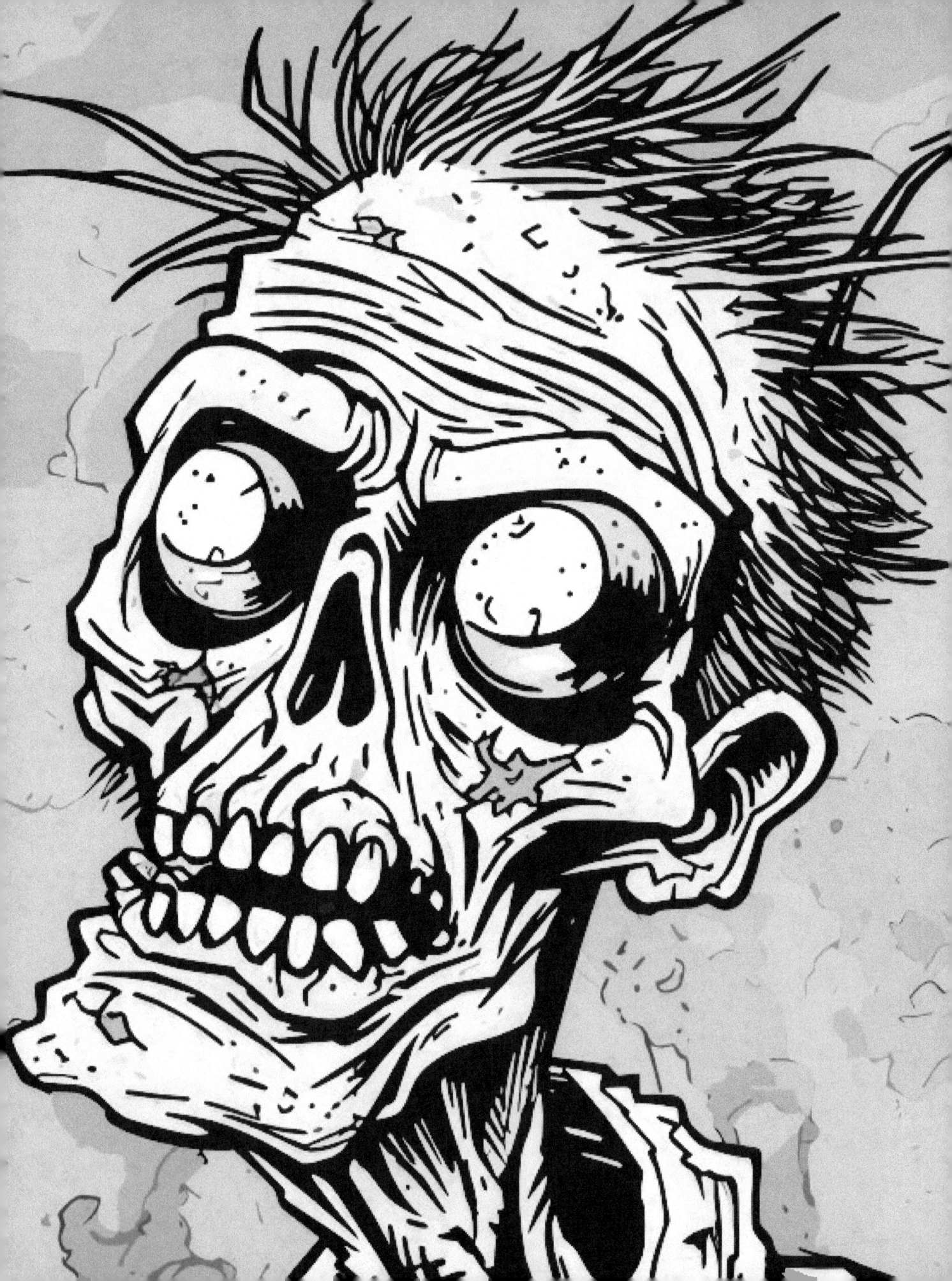

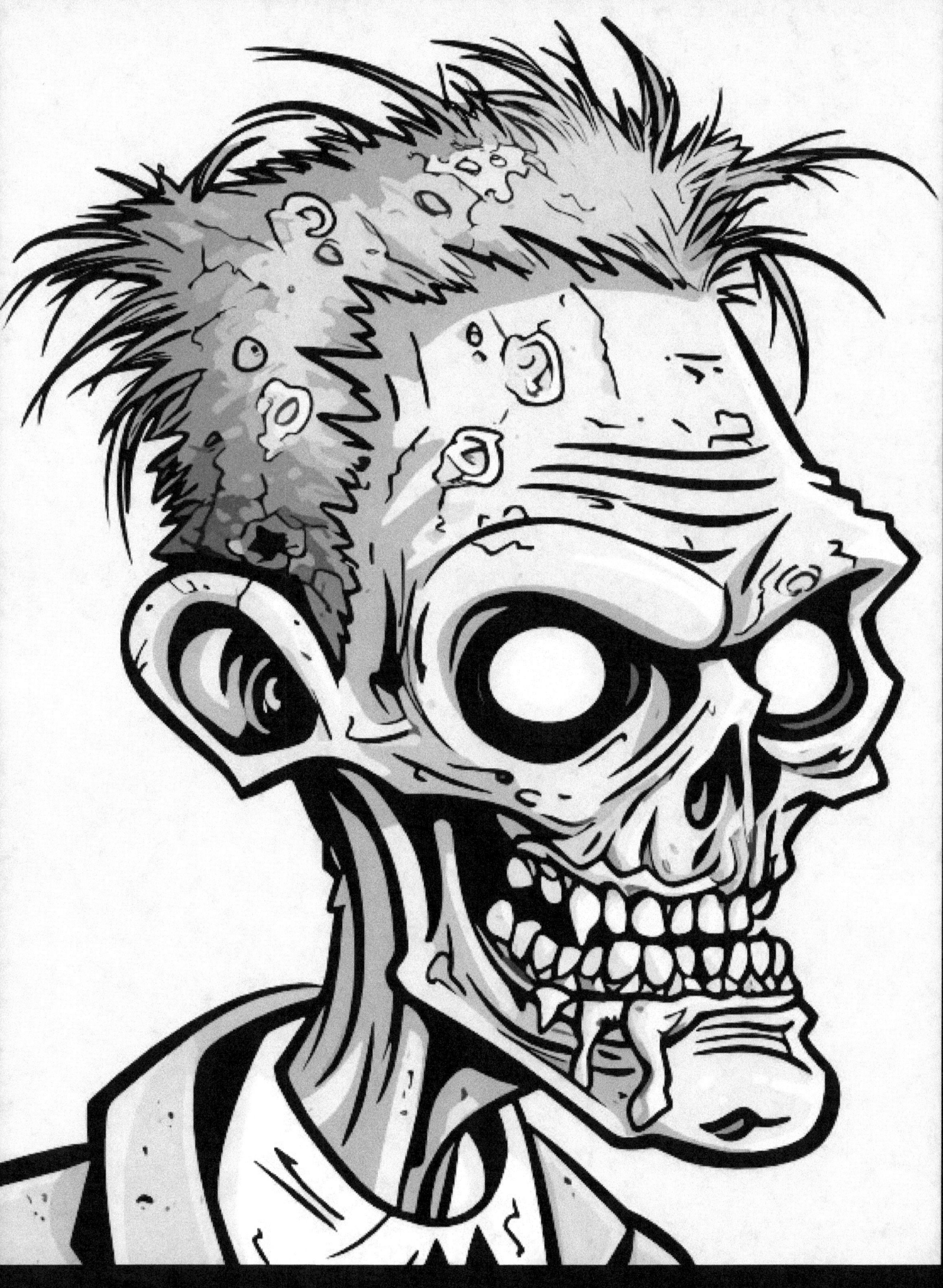

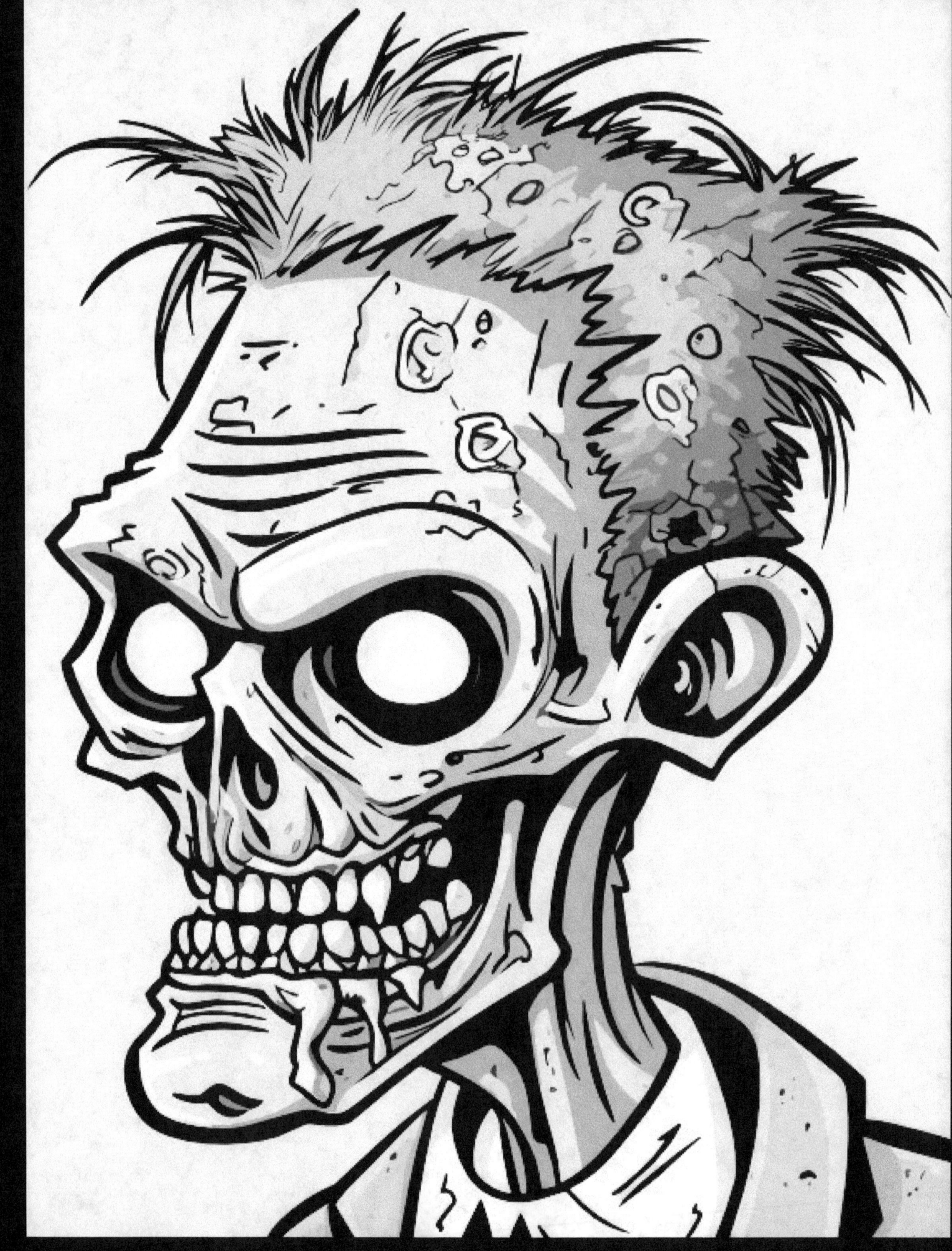

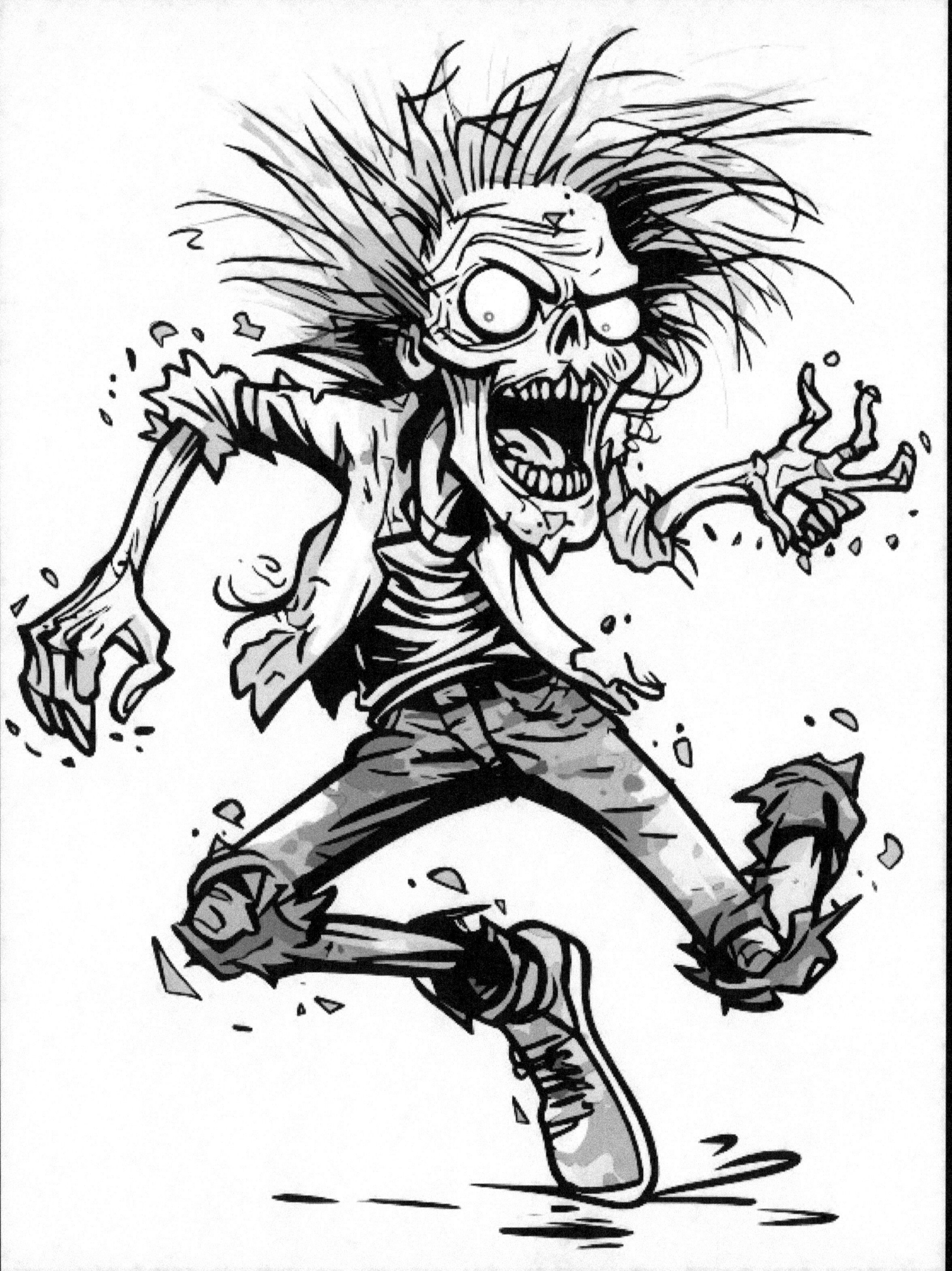

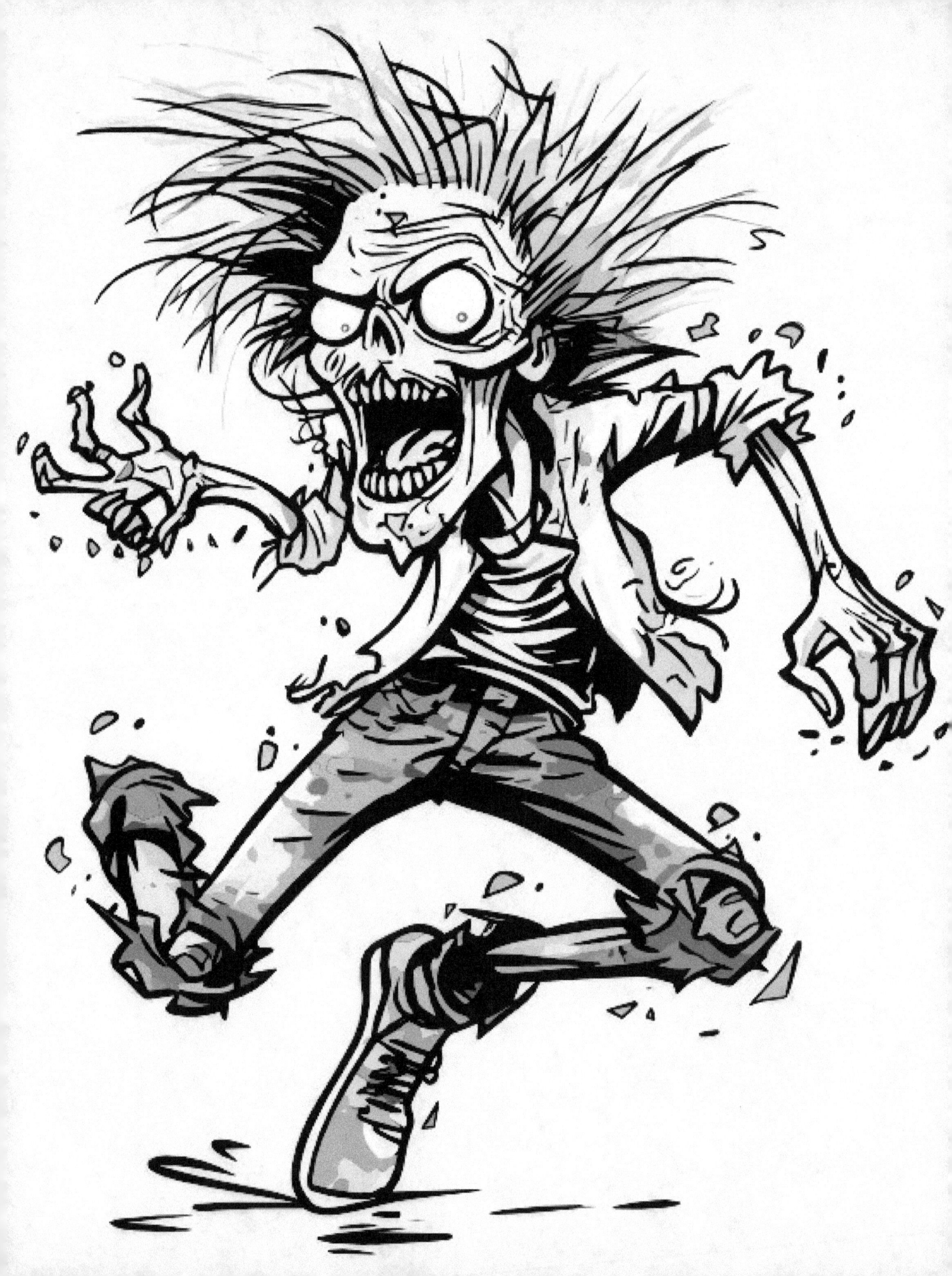

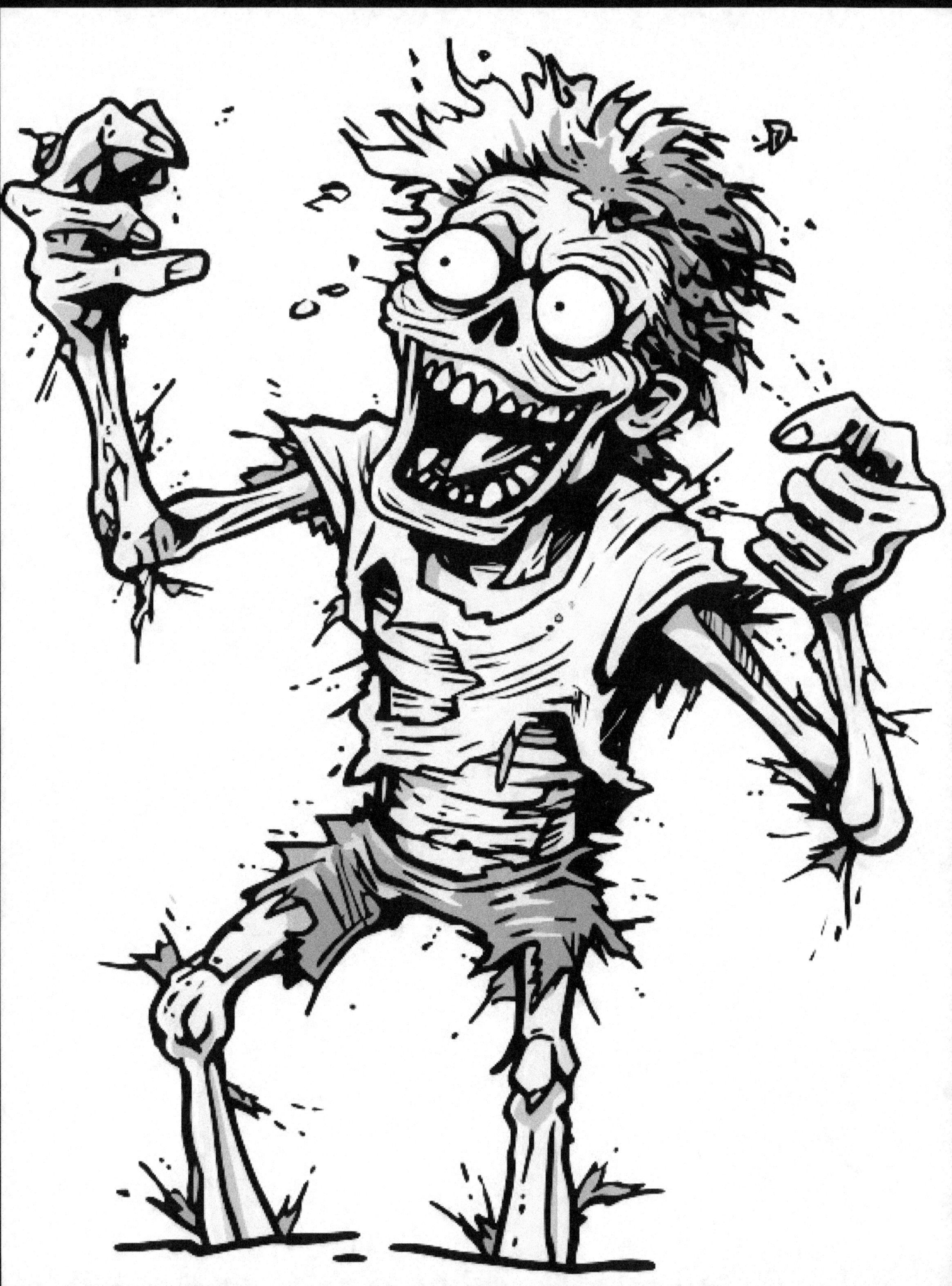

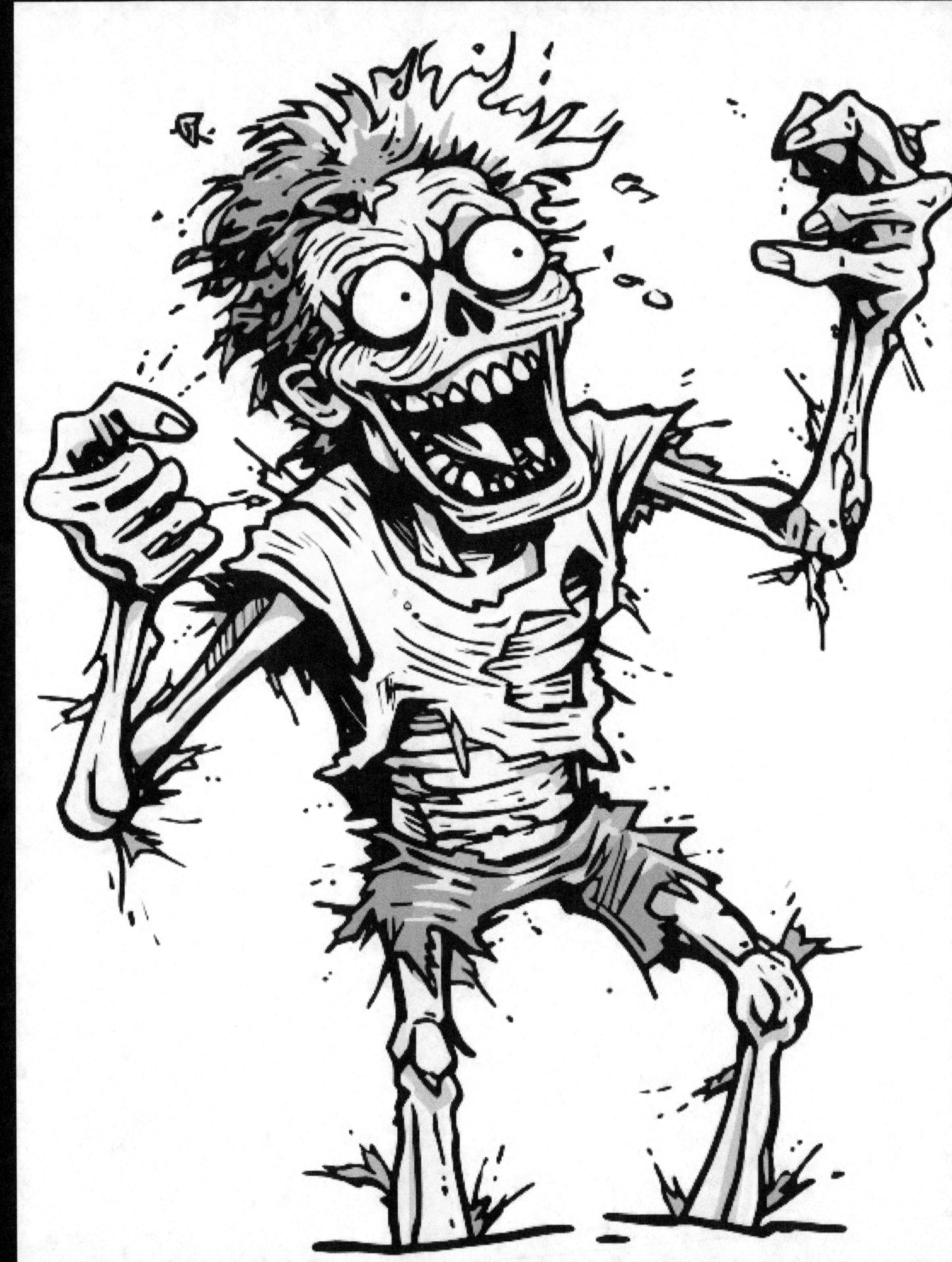

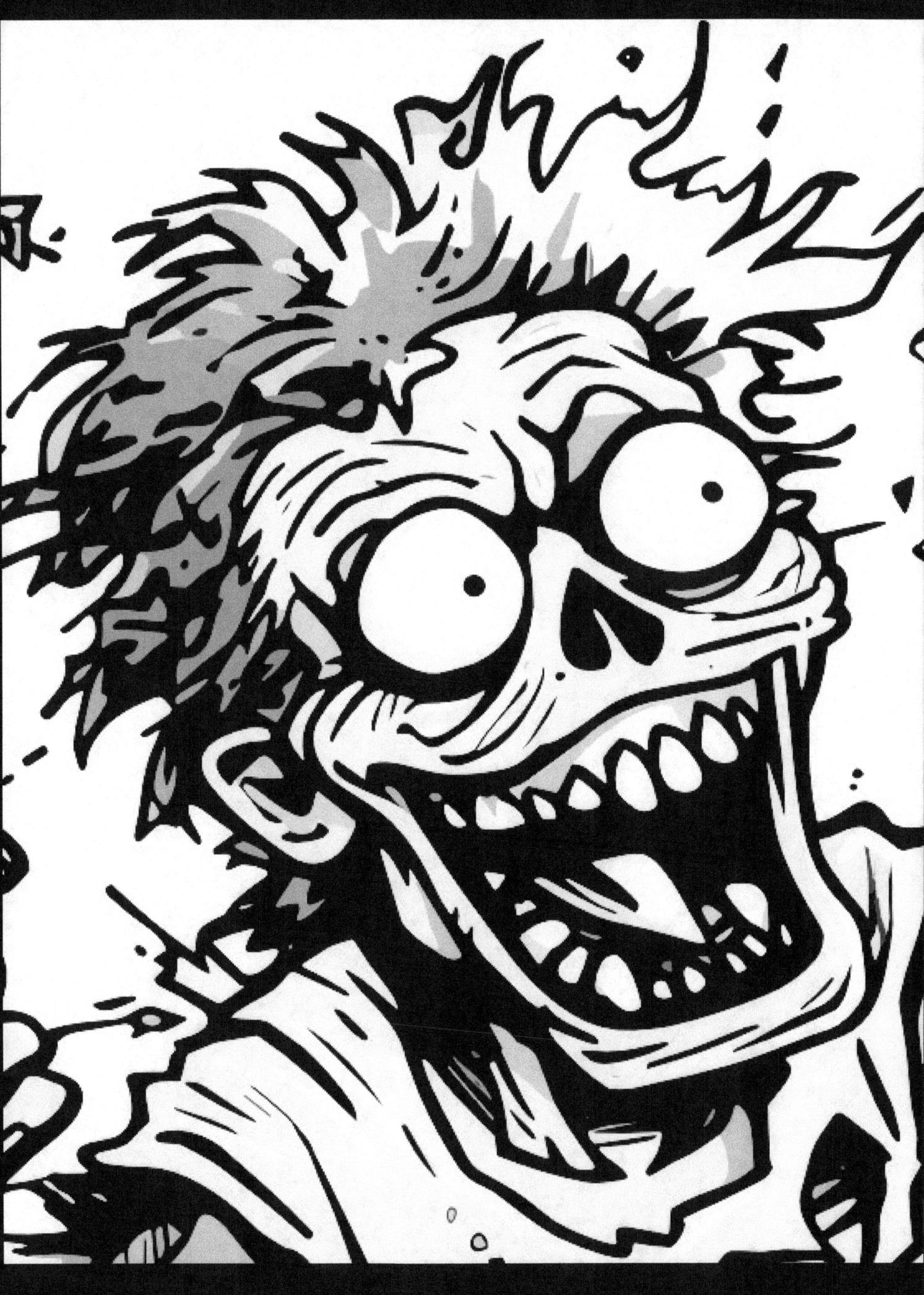

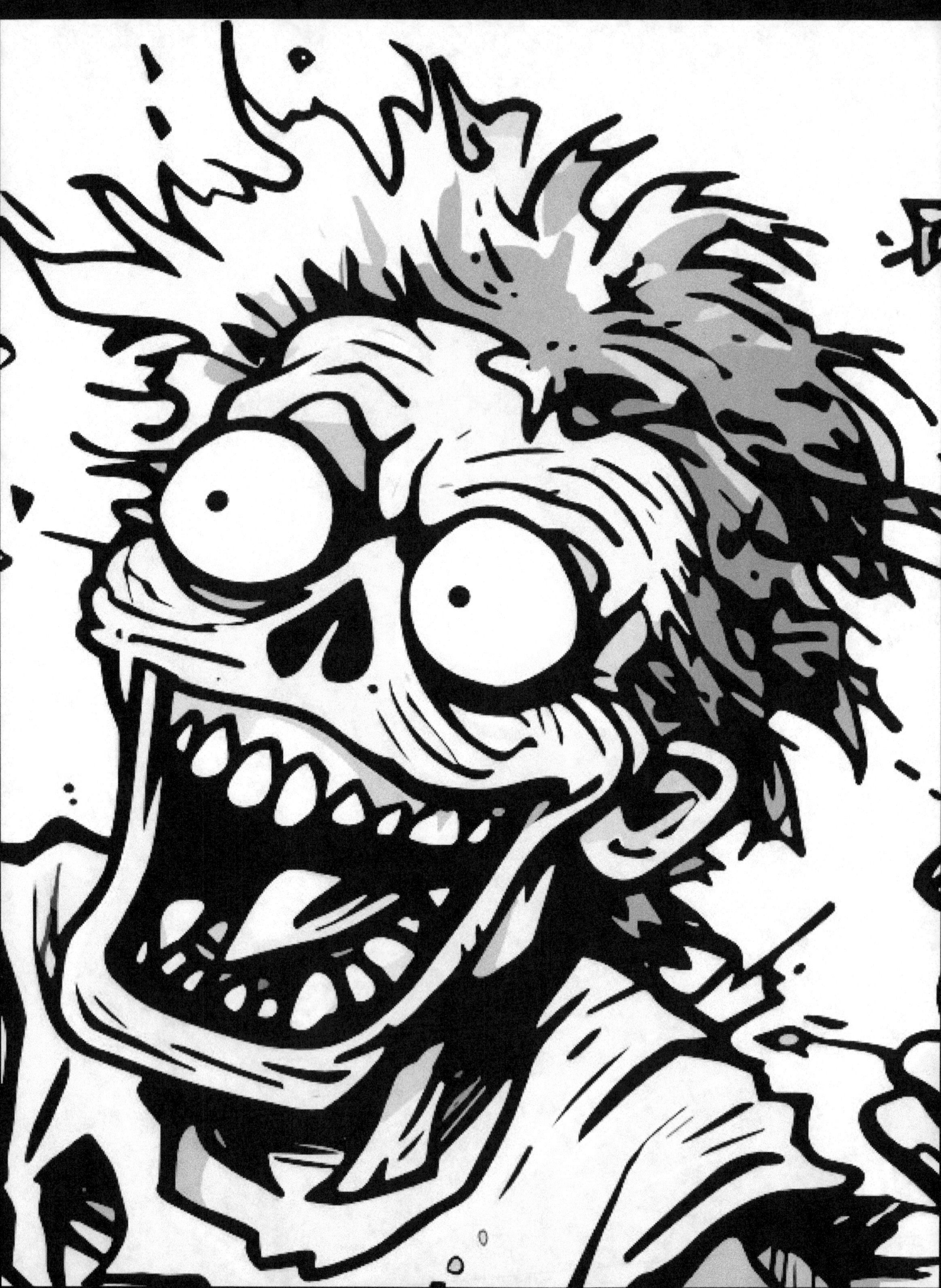

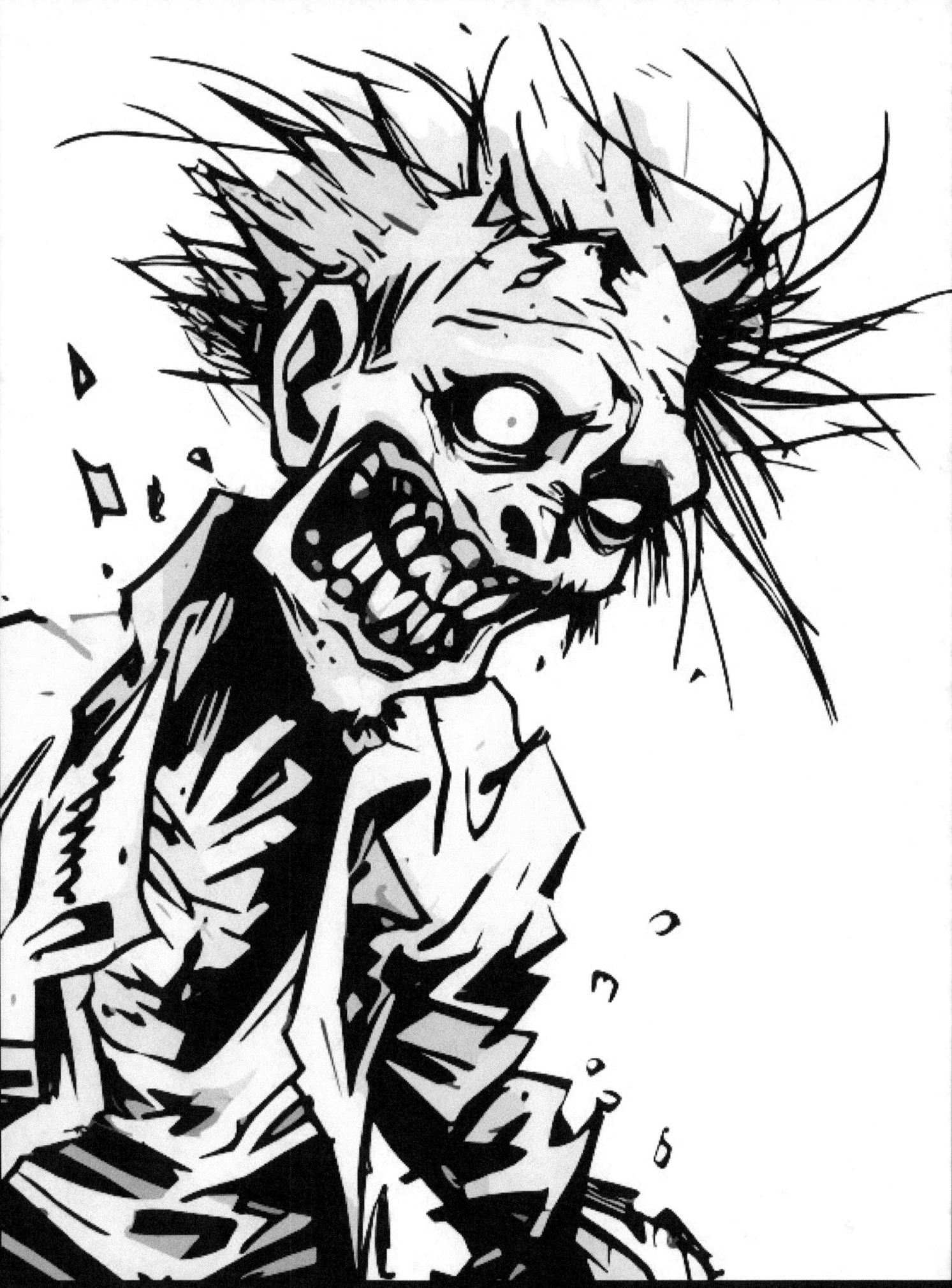

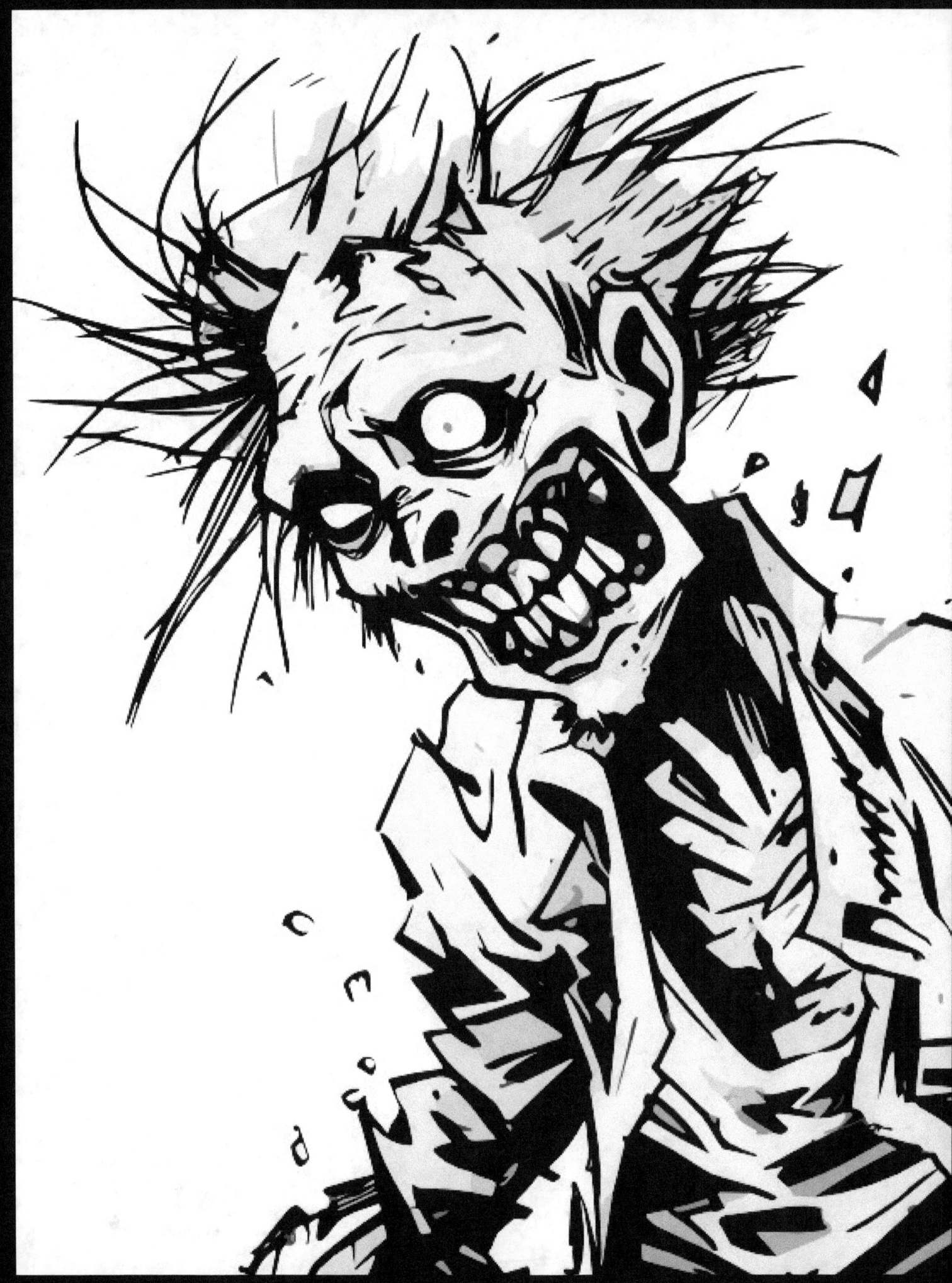

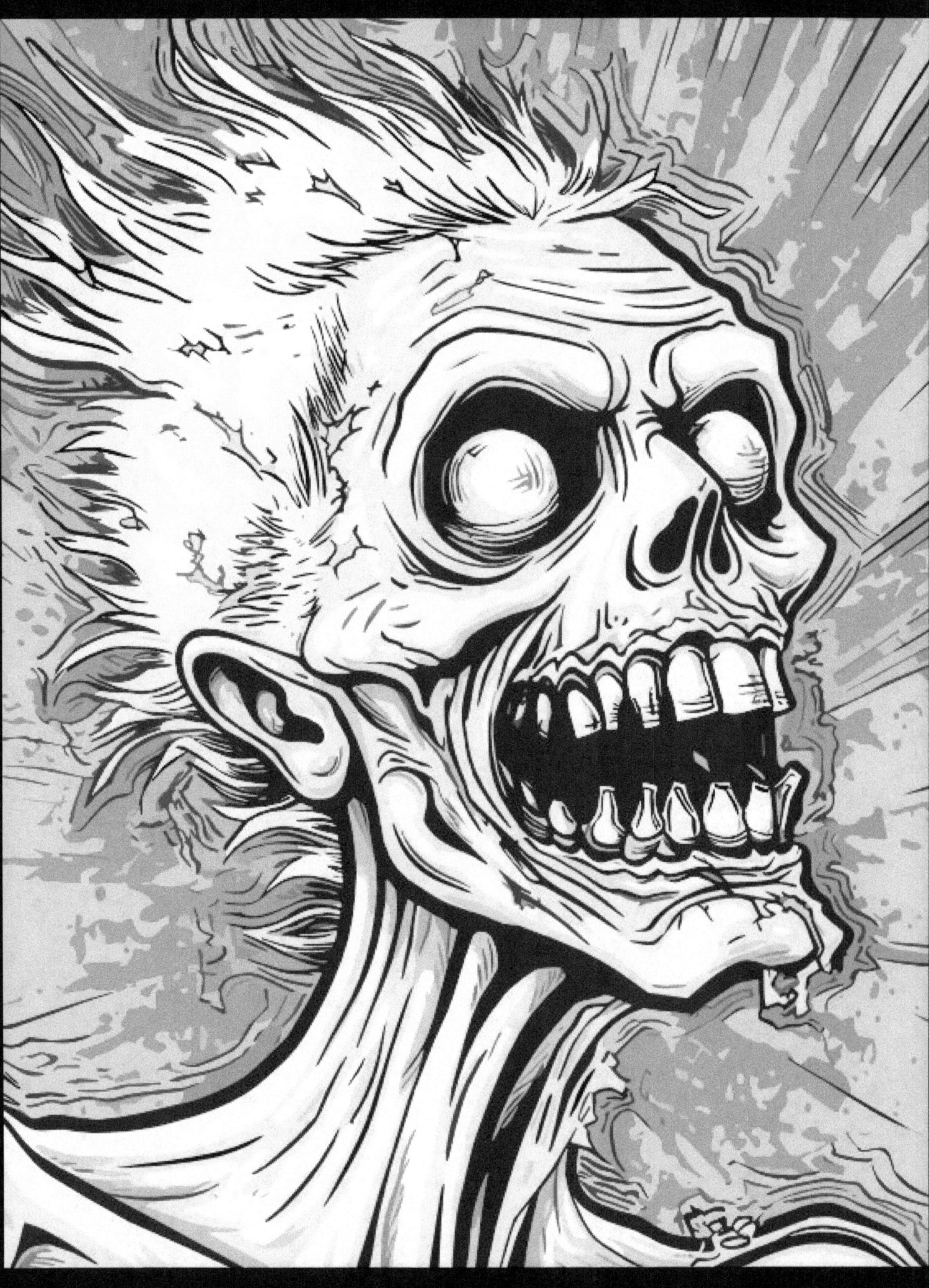

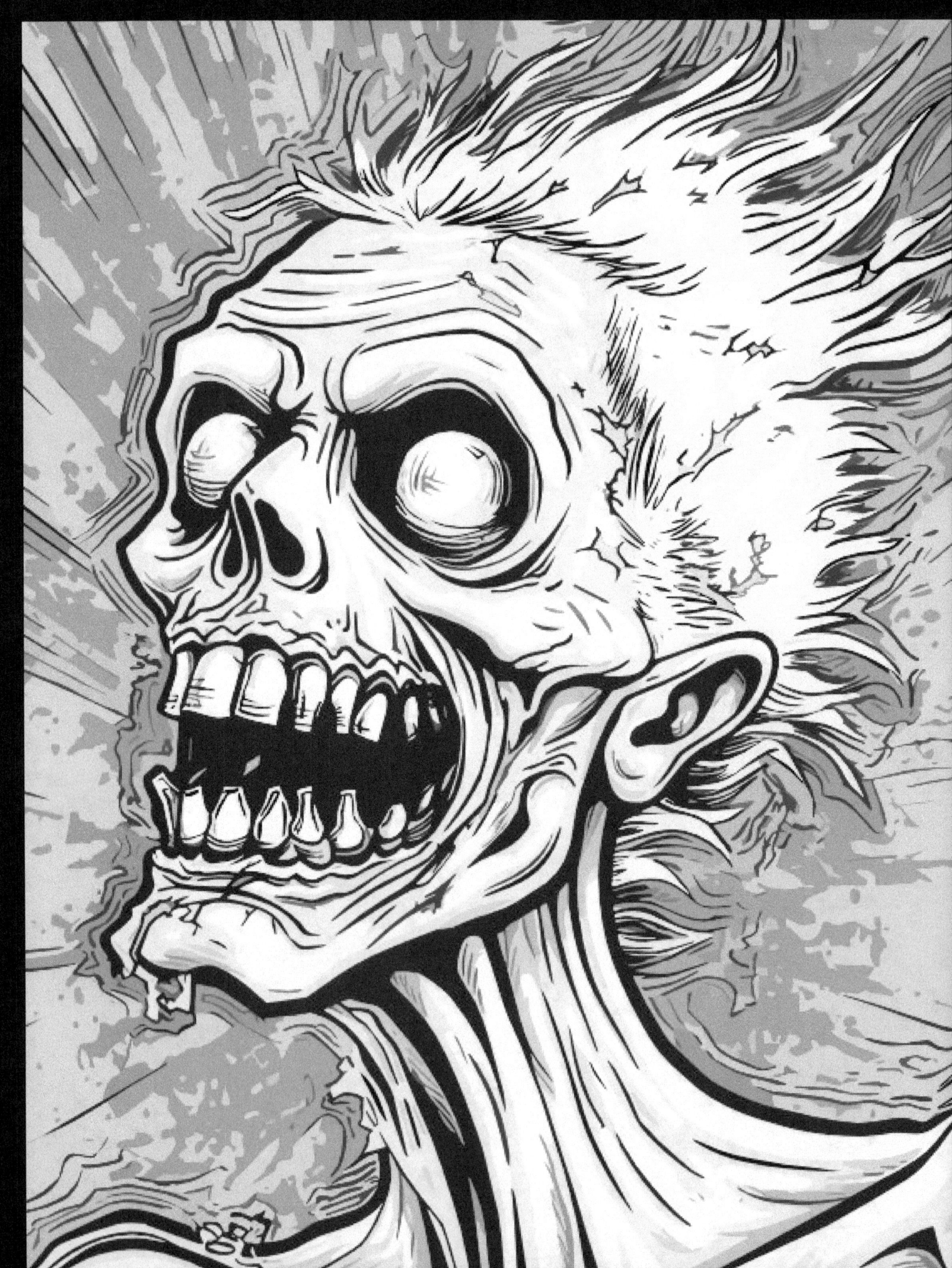